IMAGES
of America

ELMIRA

ON THE COVER: Pictured in front of the pond, below Cowles Hall, are "letter women." The 1937 Elmira College yearbook, *Iris,* noted, "Cream of athletes, stand forward and take your bows. Admiring glances and heart-felt sighs follow you as you pass, the symbol of your mightiness emblazoned on your breast. Every year you scan the college roster to see what new names you may favor to swell your honored ranks. Thus more girls become the proud possessors of a commanding 'E.' " (Courtesy of Elmira College.)

IMAGES
of America

ELMIRA

James E. Hare and James Arthur Kieffer

ARCADIA
PUBLISHING

ISBN 978-0-7385-9778-2

Published by Arcadia Publishing
Charleston, South Carolina

Printed in the United States of America

Library of Congress Control Number: 2012943563

For all general information, please contact Arcadia Publishing:
Telephone 843-853-2070
Fax 843-853-0044
E-mail sales@arcadiapublishing.com
For customer service and orders:
Toll-Free 1-888-313-2665

Visit us on the Internet at www.arcadiapublishing.com

We dedicate this book to our wives and children: Alicia and Aaron Kyle Hare; Sophie, James Arthur Jr., and Susanne Marie Kieffer.

Contents

ACKNOWLEDGMENTS

The creation of this book has been a joy in so many ways. Learning about our community is a reward in itself. What has been particularly enriching is meeting so many people who appreciate the history of our city and are eager to share their knowledge and information to help tell that story. We extend our gratitude to all of those who have made this volume possible.

Special thanks go to Andrew Patros, archivist Rachel Dworkin at the Chemung County Historical Society, Beverly Buckbee, and Alicia Hare for technological support and layout. Archival assistance from the Chemung County Historical Society (CCHS) and the support of the museum's staff and director Bruce Whitmarsh have been appreciated. All of the authors' royalties from the sale of this book go to the Chemung County Historical Society.

The chapter on Elmira College and Mark Twain was made possible because of the generous assistance of Mark Woodhouse, Elmira College archivist. Sister Marie Michael, Sister of St. Joseph; and Linda MacAuslan, System Director of Education/School of Nursing at the Arnot Ogden Medical Center, provided background and pictures for the chapter on the hospitals. Managing editor and general manager Lois Wilson of the *Elmira Star Gazette* offered support by making the paper's archives accessible for this project.

We would like to offer thanks to a number of other individuals who have been unselfishly helpful to us in this endeavor: Marsha Brown, Barbara Ramsdell, Superintendent Paul Chappius and Deputy Superintendent John Mizgala at Elmira Correctional Facility, Don Blide, Marge MacPherson, Irene Langdon, John Distefano, Marty Chalk, Greg Dunn, Chief Patrick Bermingham of the Elmira Fire Department, Chief Michael Robertson and Capt. Anthony Alvernaz of the Elmira Police Department, general manager Mark LaDouce at the Elmira Water Board, Holy Family Schools development director Joseph Kosmicki, Anne Bremer, and Diane L. Janowski and Allen C. Smith (authors of *The Chemung Valley*, also part of Arcadia Publishing's Images of America series).

INTRODUCTION

Michael Horigan, in his book *Elmira: Death Camp of the North*, quotes a journalist who, in 1857, referred to Elmira as a village that had "surpassed all its competitors in the race for improvements. . . . Its streets are handsomely laid out, churches and schools are numerous; it possesses enterprising business men, an energetic press, banks that pay specie on the strength of their promises and hotels kept by clever landlords, and stocked with the substantial things of life." No wonder that, seven years later, on April 7, 1864, the village was incorporated as the City of Elmira. This booming community, with a population of 13,000 people, was destined to become the "Queen City" of the Southern Tier.

Elmira can trace its origin to 1779, when, after the Battle of Newtown, Gen. John Sullivan established Fort Reid at the junction of Newtown Creek and the Chemung River. The fort was on the site of Canaweola, a Seneca Indian village of about 20 houses that had been burned. The hamlets of Newtown, Wisnerburg, and Dewittsburg were established in the 1790s. Collectively known as Newtown, they were incorporated as the Village of Newtown in 1815 and, on April 21, 1828, the name was changed to Elmira.

According to Ausburn Towner's *Our County and Its People*, the name Elmira "is of Moorish origin, and properly written was originally El Mira, or 'The Mira' meaning a 'fair outlook,' either something apparent to the senses or to the mind. A beautiful landscape could be so called as well as the promising future of some young person. . . . It came into the English language when Wellington was fighting in Spain, a novelist . . . attracted by its sound . . . named one of his female characters Elmira. Thence it came easily to be the name of a real person, as it is a common thing for mothers to select names for their children from those of characters in fiction who have struck their fancy." Nathan Teall and his wife, Polly, named their youngest daughter Elmira. She was "fair to look upon, a great favorite."

Towner continues: "In such a place as Nathan Teall's tavern in Newtown the Hon. Emanuel Coryell, member of the Assembly, was the surest to meet the most of his constituents. He heard them discuss the name of their town and express desire for some change. Often at such times Phoebe Elmira Teall, a bright, black eyed, dark-haired child of five or six years of age, would run in and out of the room, followed as frequently by the voice of her mother calling her name 'Elmira! Elmira!' In one of her appearances she clambered into the lap of Judge Coryell, 'snuggled' down, and fell asleep. He could not fail to be attracted by her beauty and her brightness so promising of her future. She was born and bred right there, her life being almost co-existent with the township itself. At his suggestion the name became its name, and there was no dissentient voice in the throng."

In 1864, Elmira had a bright future. The Civil War had had a significant impact on the city. Its selection as a rendezvous and depot for many New Yorkers going to or returning from the war stimulated the economy. Elmira's designation as the site of a prison for Confederate soldiers brought additional challenges to the community. The creation of the Elmira Female College in 1855 had focused the attention of many prominent Elmirans. It would be the first college to confer upon women a degree equal to that received by men. Building Cowles Hall, overlooking the city, established the college as an important part of the community.

Elmira's most famous future resident arrived in 1868. Sam Clemens (Mark Twain) came to the city to visit the girl he had fallen in love with when he first saw her picture. Traveling to the Middle East on the ship *Quaker City*, Sam had met Charles Langdon, a young man from Elmira. Langdon showed him a locket containing his sister Olivia's picture. Clemens was smitten. He came to visit Olivia and her family and within two years was married. The Clemens family would return regularly to Elmira, where Sam would write and relax and, indeed, where he would finally be buried.

The city's faith community was active. The mother church in Elmira was the First Presbyterian Church. From that church would spring others, formed because of disagreements over slavery, or established as a mission. Methodists, Episcopalians, and Baptists would experience the same challenges. Indeed, the issues of slavery and abolition, by their very nature, impacted all faiths. Elmira would become an important link on the Underground Railroad. That involvement stimulated the growth of the African American community. In the latter 19th and early 20th centuries, religious leaders played an important role in the community.

As the city grew, demands increased for improved public safety, a better water supply, and other basic enhancements in the quality of life. Professionalization of police and fire, to more adequately protect the residents, took place. Improved management of the water system was approved, and the school system was reorganized.

Elmira's excellent location and development as a transportation hub made it a center of economic activity. At one point in the late 19th century, as many as 67 passenger trains a day came through town. The burgeoning downtown and the creation of Eldridge Park made the city a popular destination. Eldridge Park was so popular that it had its own station until 1910. Professional baseball came to the city in 1888, and the Elmira team would become a springboard for many future major league ballplayers.

The quality of life was enhanced by the generosity of Marianna Arnot Ogden, who founded the Arnot Ogden Memorial Hospital in 1889. The town was further improved when the Sisters of St. Joseph opened St. Joseph's Hospital in 1908. Over the years, Elmira has benefitted from the philanthropy of many. Dr. Eldridge created a park, Esther Baker Steele founded a library, Edward J. Dunn bought land for baseball to be played on, and the Arnot family founded an art museum. The city has been built by the hard work, generosity, and vision of many people over the years.

This book will provide images of the history of our city from 1864 to 1964. We hope you find it interesting. It is far short of a complete picture, but we think it offers a sense of our community.

One

Elmira College and Mark Twain

Elmira College and Mark Twain have a special connection to the story of Elmira. The Mark Twain Study was relocated from East Hill to the college campus in 1952, and in 1982 Quarry Farm was donated by Jervis Langdon to the college to become the Center for Mark Twain Studies.

The origin of Elmira College can be traced to a meeting held at the Second Dutch Reformed Church in Albany, New York, on April 11, 1851. The men in attendance called themselves Friends of Education. They adopted resolutions calling for the education of females equal to that of men. Elmira emerged as the designated site. "By May, 1853 . . . the tree studded estate of Thomas Noyes, which crowned Prospect Hill on Main St." was chosen for a new building, and an architect was selected. In November of that year, Simeon Benjamin was elected president of the trustees, and bylaws were adopted with the stipulation that "while it is our aim to make it [Elmira Collegiate Seminary] highly evangelical in its character, it shall never assume a sectarian cast."

The seminary became the Elmira Female College and, in 1890, Elmira College. When the college opened in 1855, 242 young women were enrolled. According to the first catalog, "it will be required of the boarding pupils that each shall furnish her own napkins and towels, a pair of sheets and pillow cases, a coverlet and blankets, for her own use. . . . [E]ach pupil should also bring a spoon, for use in her own room. An umbrella and overshoes should form a part of the outfit. Also a copy of the Bible,—one with references would be found convenient." The cost was $120 per year, including room, light, and fuel—payable semiannually in advance.

Twain found Elmira to be the scene of some of his happiest and saddest moments. He courted, married, and buried his beloved Livy (Olivia Langdon) here. His first-born child and only boy, the two daughters who preceded him in death, and the only daughter to survive him, are buried here. He spent nearly 20 summers writing some of his best works at his octagonal study on East Hill at Quarry Farm. Authors Bob Jerome and Herb Wisbey Jr. note that "from his first visit in 1868 until his burial in Woodlawn Cemetery in 1910, Elmira played a central role in Mark Twain's private and professional life."

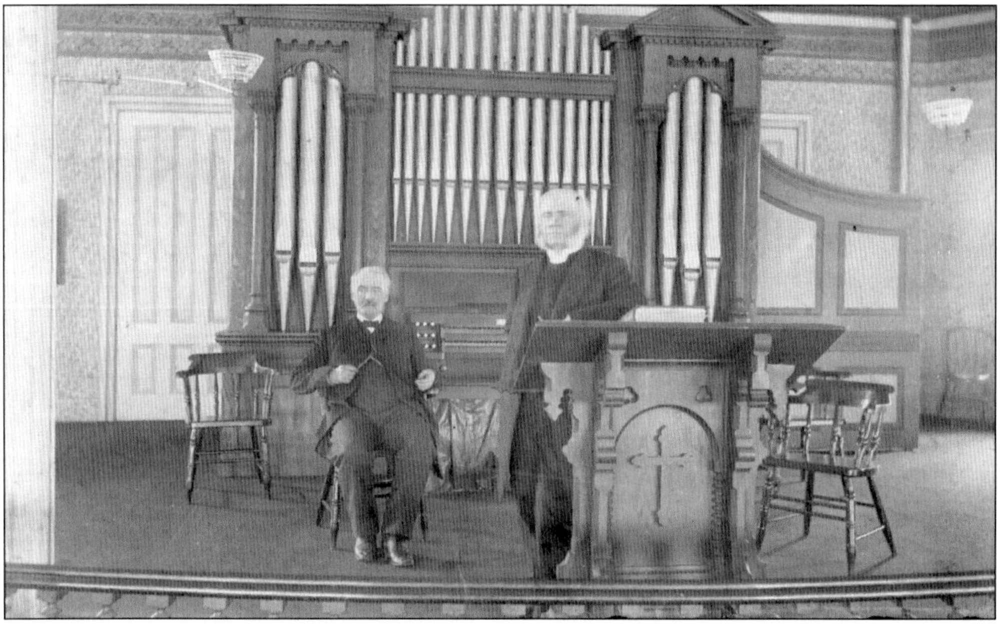

Dr. Augustus Cowles (right), the first president of Elmira College, was described by Hank Walshak as "a Renaissance man of multiple vocations—an educator, a teacher, a great preacher, an accomplished painter, a flautist and a violinist. An overriding trait was his undaunted persistence . . . for the funds the college badly needed each year." He and Dr. Darius Ford share the stage in Cowles Hall for services. (Courtesy of Elmira College.)

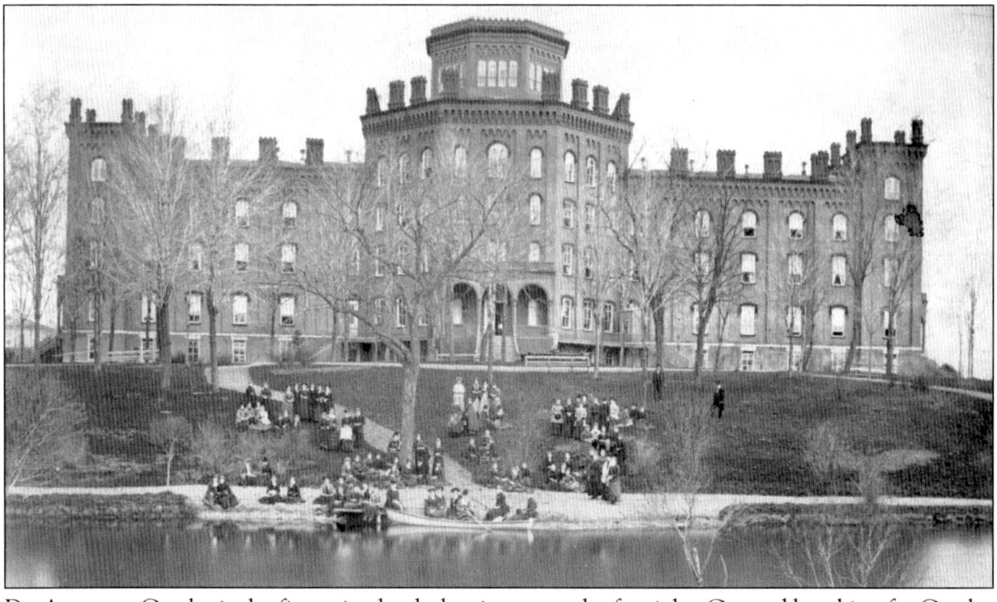

Dr. Augustus Cowles is the figure in the dark suit coat at the far right. Ground breaking for Cowles Hall was in 1854. As described by Charles Barber in his book *Elmira College*, after visiting the campus during construction, the Auburn *Christian Advocate* editor wrote, "when completed this will be one of the most imposing structures in the country. Elmira will have no other building that can compare with it. . . . [T]he course of study is designed to be thoroughly collegiate—equal to our best colleges." (Courtesy of Elmira College.)

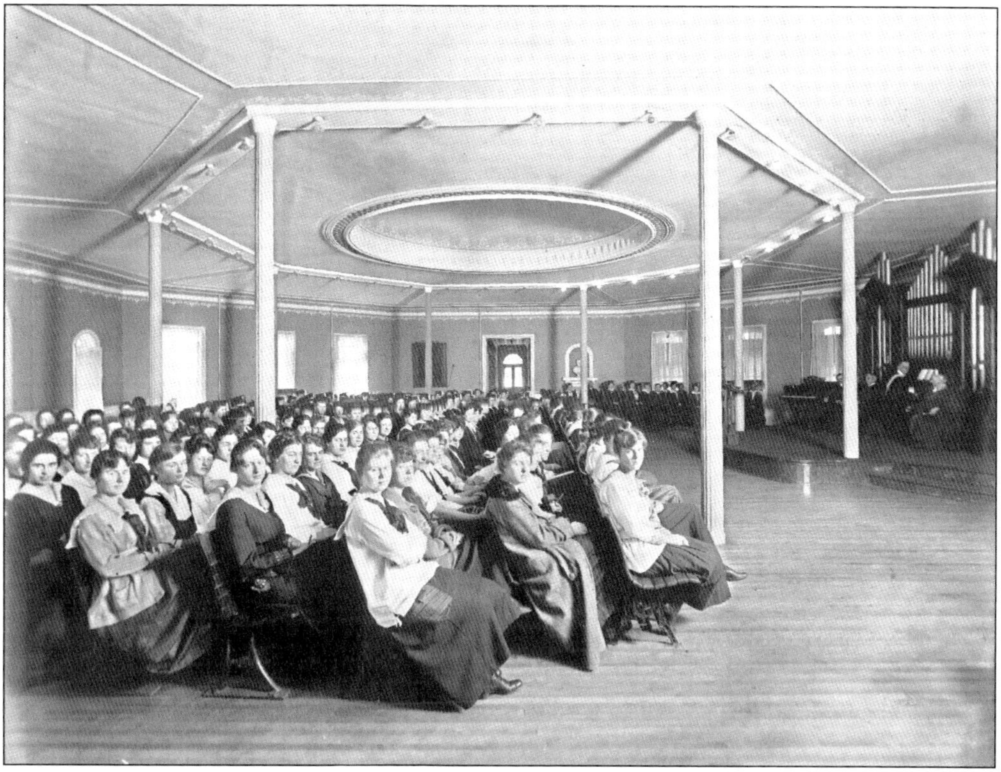

Attendance at services in Cowles Hall was required until the 1930s. Barber writes that, according to Dr. Cowles, "Females are worthy of the best and highest education which their time and means will permit. . . . [T]he mission of this college is a holy one, it is a child of prayers . . . religious plans and purposes lie at its foundations." (Courtesy of Elmira College.)

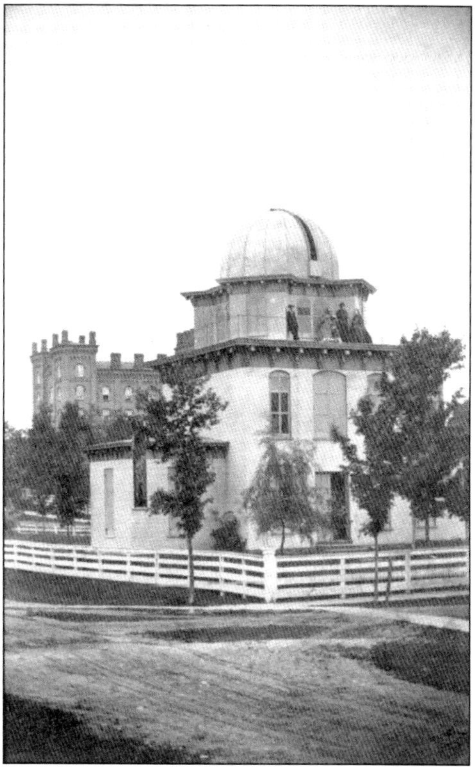

The Elmira College Observatory (1858–1939) was located south of Cowles Hall. Charles Barber recounts the words of Mary C. Davis (class of 1869): "On November 14, 1868, our class in astronomy took our positions about the dome of the Observatory. . . . [A]bout eleven P.M. a perfect Kappa Sigma appeared in the northwest . . . meteors came thick and fast . . . over five thousand. . . . Dr. Ford . . . furnished us with 'eats' and blankets, for it certainly was frosty that November night." (Courtesy of Elmira College.)

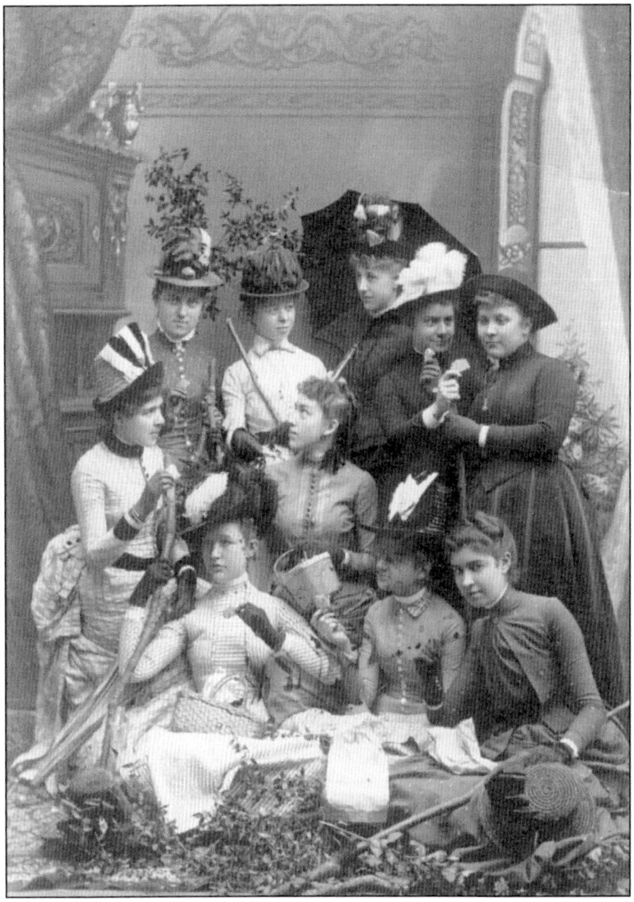

Even picnic clothes had "class" in the 1880s. This 1887 photograph was taken indoors. Mary Gray Peck (third row, center) became involved in the suffrage movement, working with Carrie Chapman Catt and writing her biography. (Courtesy of Elmira College.)

Athletics were important to the educators at Elmira College. Dr. Frederick Lent became president in 1918 and expanded the athletic activities. He built a wooden gymnasium in 1924 that was intended to be a temporary structure, but the Depression derailed plans for a permanent facility until 1954. These girls are learning the finer points of archery in the 1930s. (Courtesy of CCHS.)

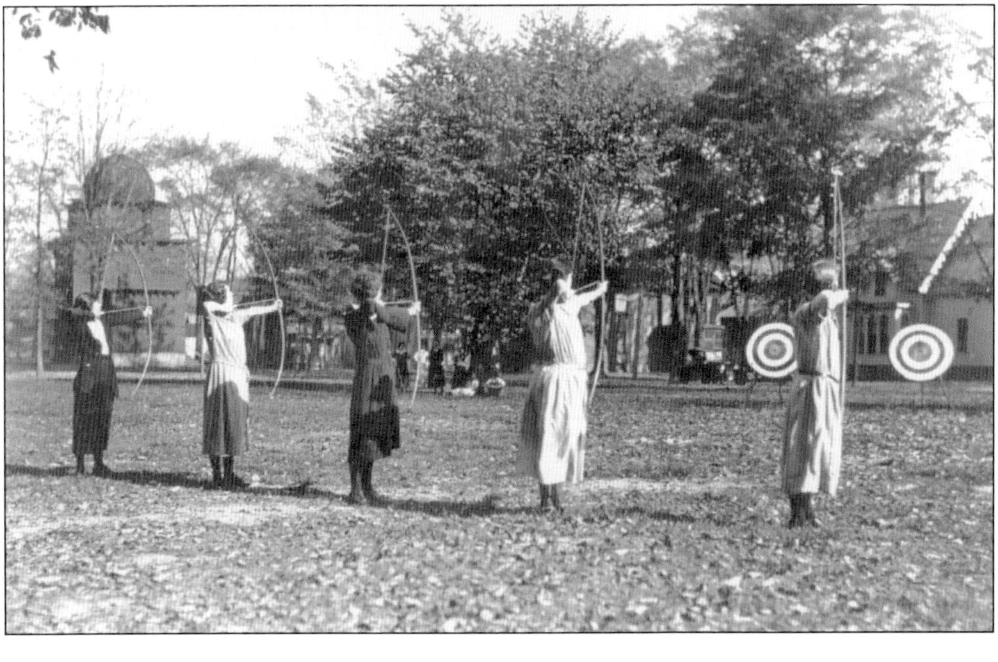

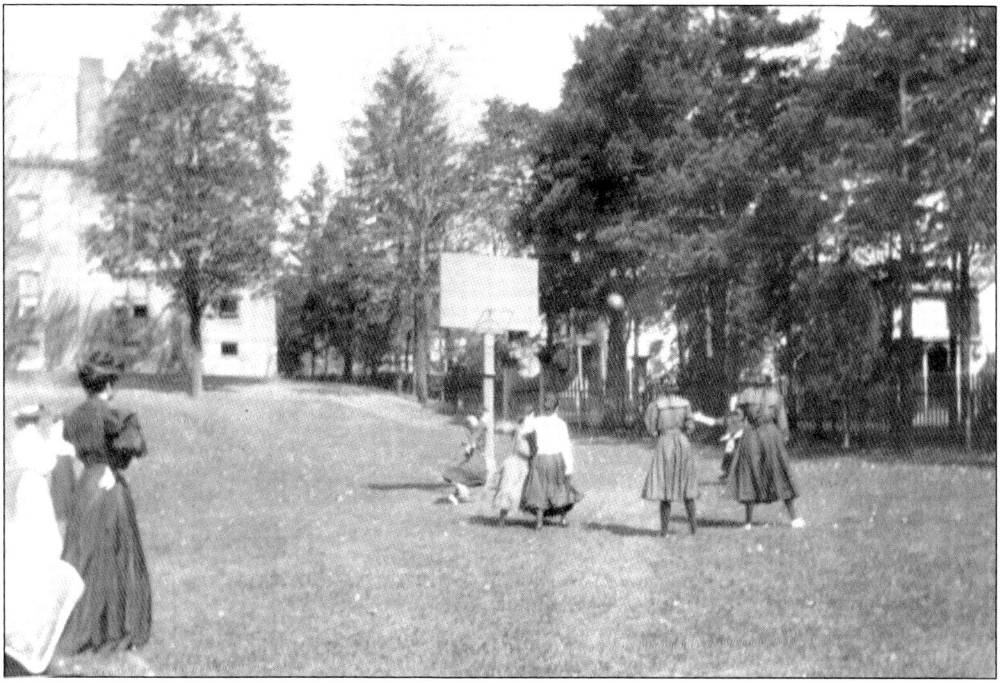

Basketball was a favorite recreation at the college, as it was throughout the city. Many churches in Elmira had their own girls' teams. In the above photograph, college students enjoy the sport on campus. As seen in the 1920s photograph below, one of the interscholastic sports enjoyed by Elmira College girls was field hockey, played on the Carnegie Lawn below Cowles Hall. (Courtesy of CCHS.)

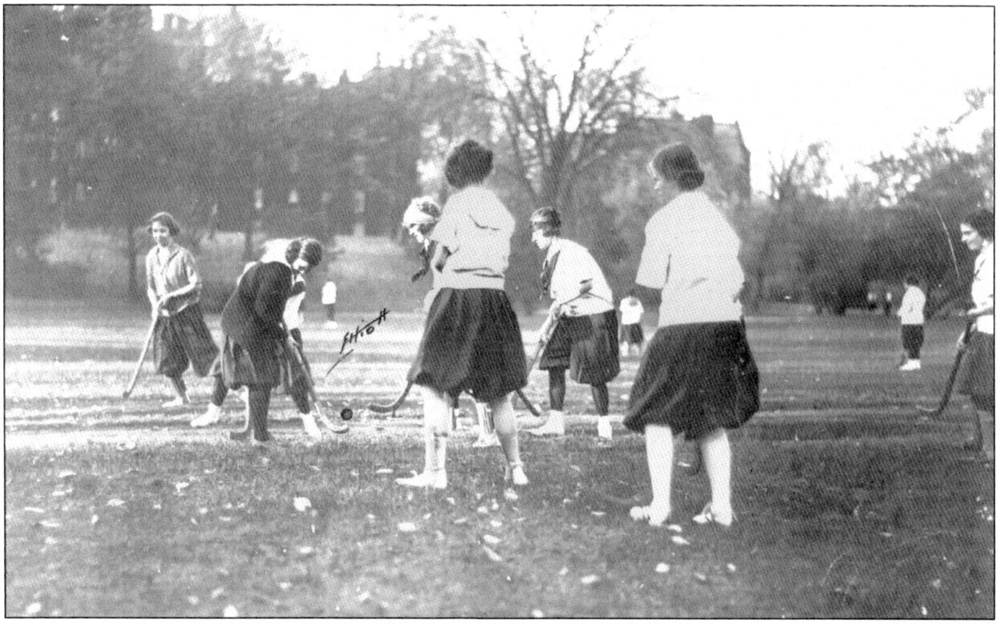

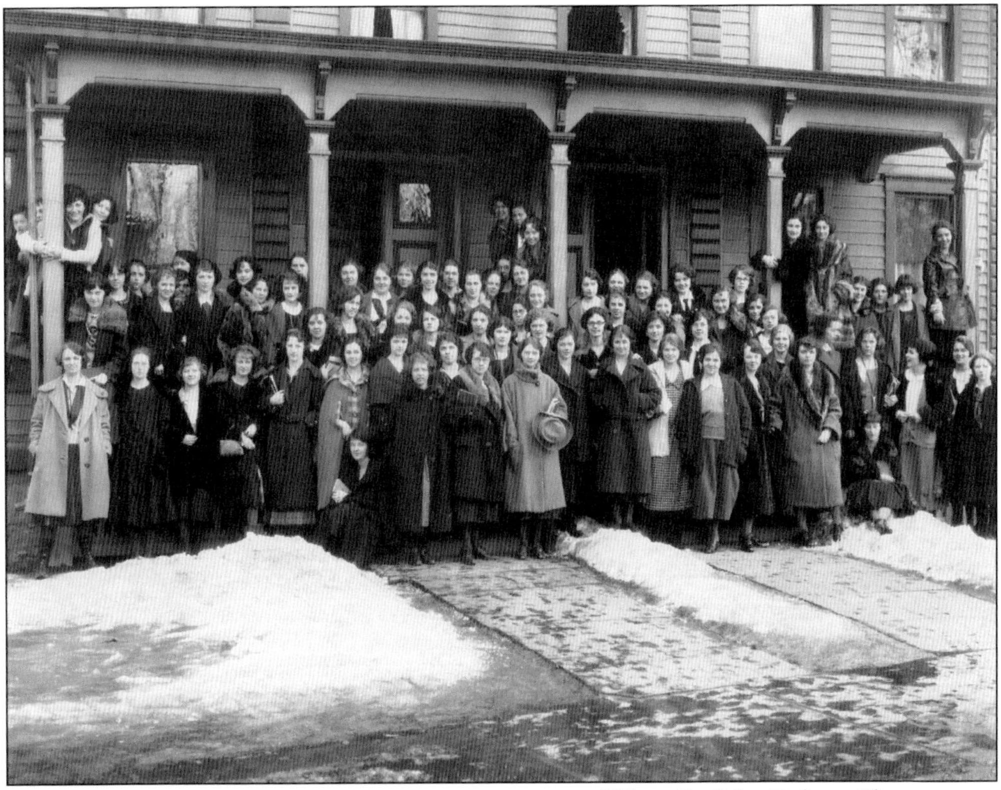

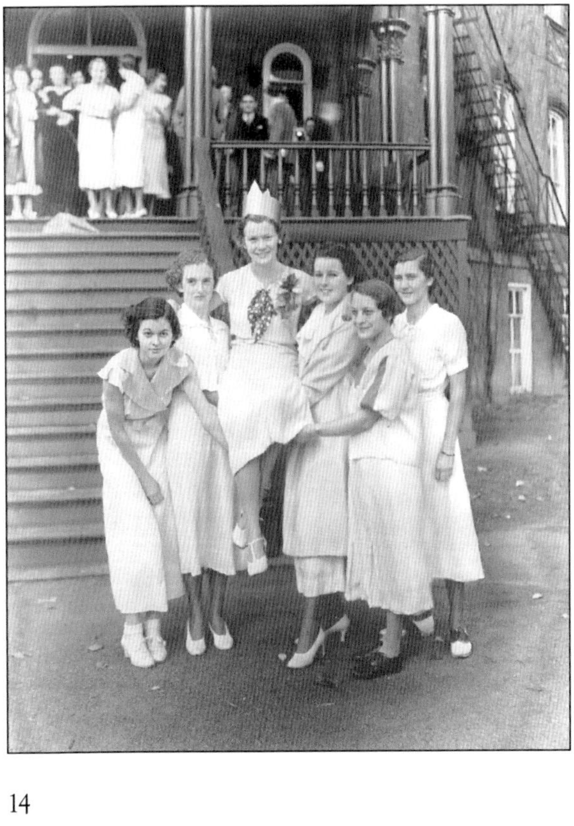

When Dr. John Balcom Shaw became president of the college in 1915, the student body had nearly tripled from the 110 students enrolled in 1910. According to Hank Walshak, the college building program began with Shaw's administration. This 1923 photograph shows freshmen students who were obliged to live off campus because of a lack of dormitory space. (Courtesy of Elmira College.)

Elmira College has had major observances in the spring and fall. May Day was celebrated with Greek dancers and maypole winders and May Day royalty. On Mountain Day, students and professors hiked to the hills. Shown here is the celebration for a new freshman president during the 1934–1935 school year. (Courtesy of Elmira College.)

President Lent (left) invited former US president William Howard Taft to be the commencement speaker in 1919. Correspondence indicates that Dr. Lent believed the honorarium was a little steep. As Charles Barber tells it, "Taft held to the Biblical tenet that the laborer is worthy of his hire and Lent held to the belief . . . that it is more blessed to give than receive." The issue was resolved, and Taft spoke on the League of Nations. (Courtesy of Elmira College.)

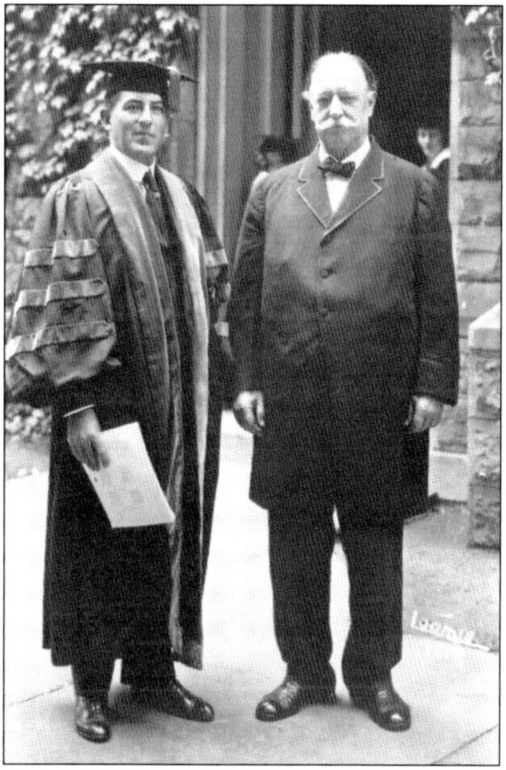

In 1930, Mrs. Lou Henry Hoover, first lady of the United States, was given an honorary doctor of laws degree. Here, she plants a tree on campus, assisted by Elmira College president Dr. Lent. (Courtesy of Elmira College.)

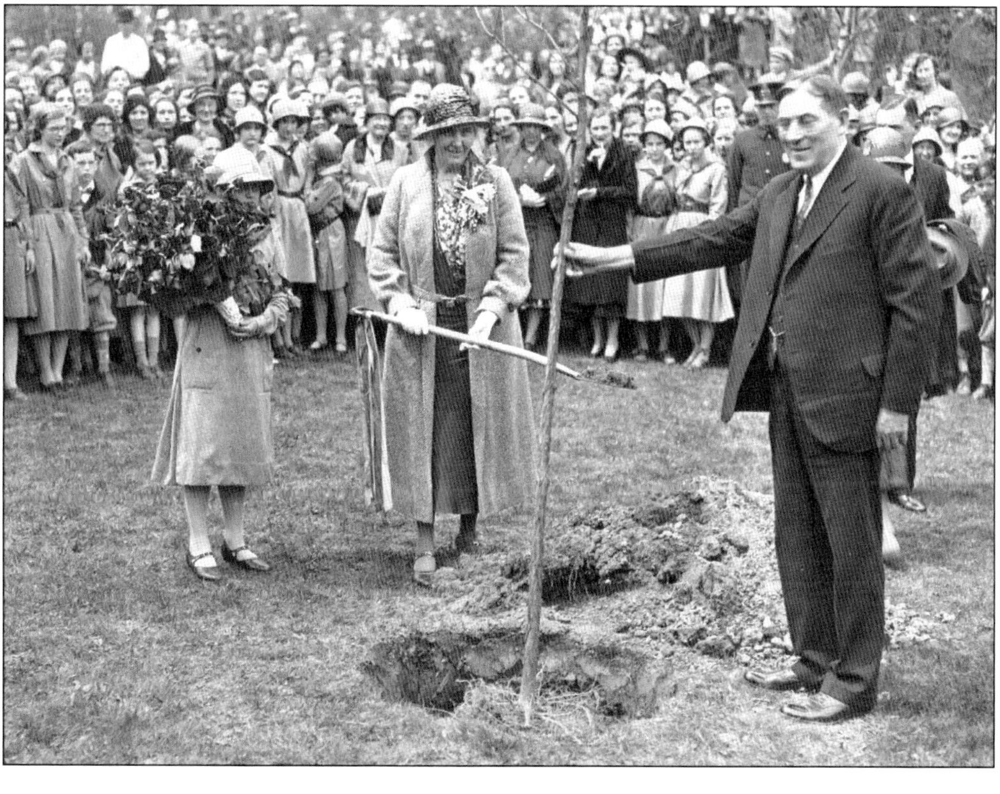

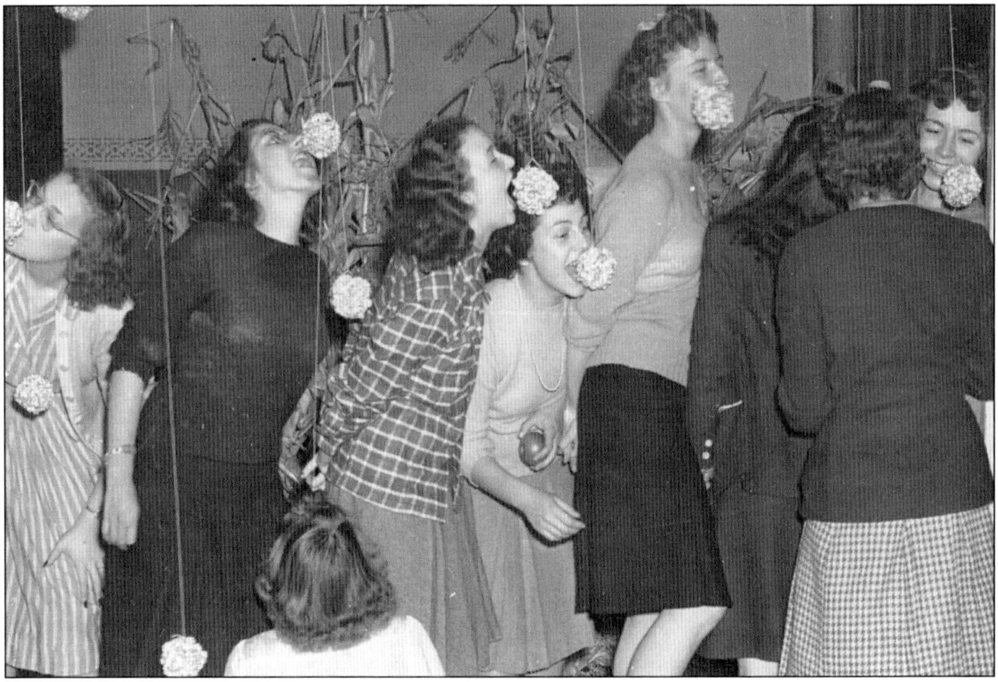

Dr. William Sumner Appleton Pott served as the eighth president of Elmira College, from 1935 to 1948. According to Hank Walshak, Pott's "ideal of Freedom and Responsibility pervaded life at the college." Classes were informal, women came and went essentially at will, knowing the rules of the college and giving them their due allegiance. Above, the girls search for relief from the pressures of studying in 1944. The below photograph relates to the smoking ban on campus; when you can't blow smoke rings, you blow soap bubbles. (Courtesy of Elmira College.)

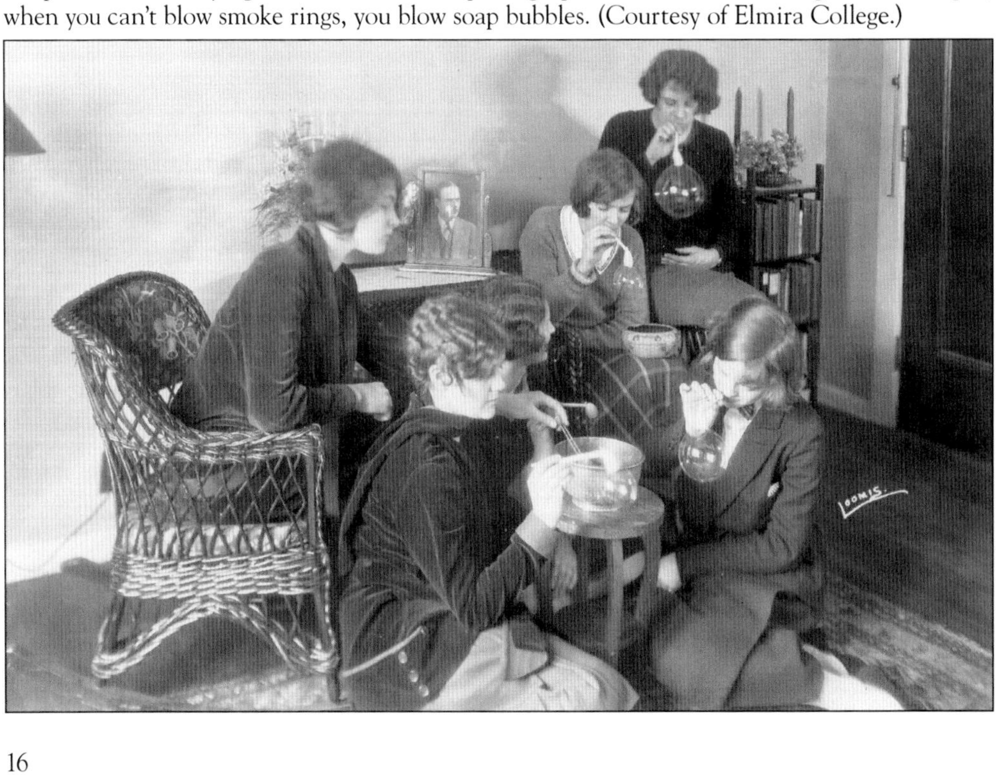

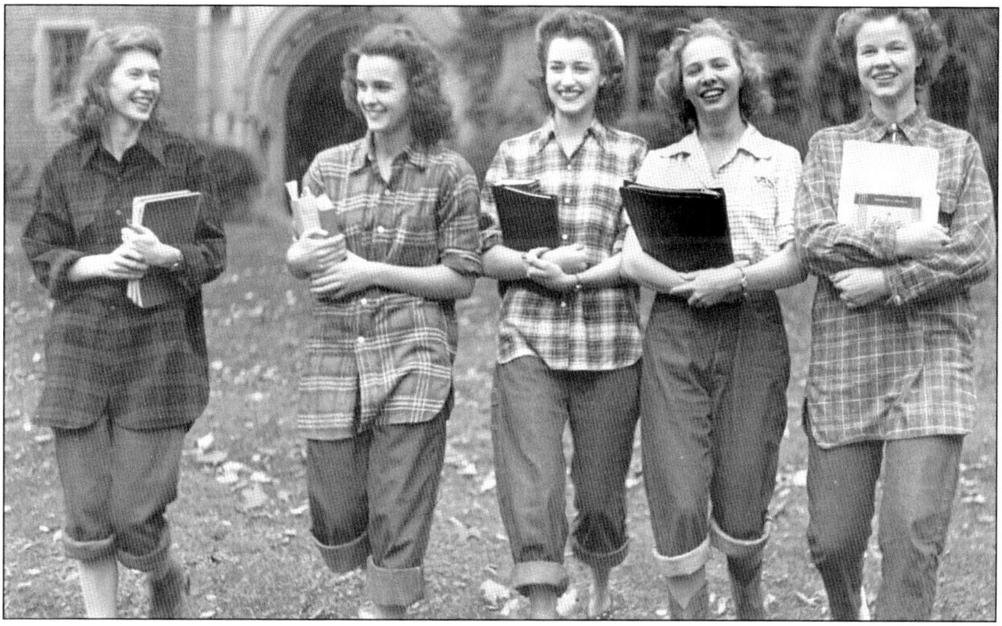

Dr. Pott worked to relax the rigidity of campus life. According to Walshak, he replaced the traditional, daily chapel services with Sunday afternoon vesper services at which attendance was voluntary. These girls reflect the changed atmosphere. They are, from left to right, Joyce Kink (class of 1944), Jesse Bushell (class of 1945), Nancy Sanford (class of 1944), Barbara Schermerhorn (class of 1945), and Marjorie Mallory (class of 1945). (Courtesy of Elmira College.)

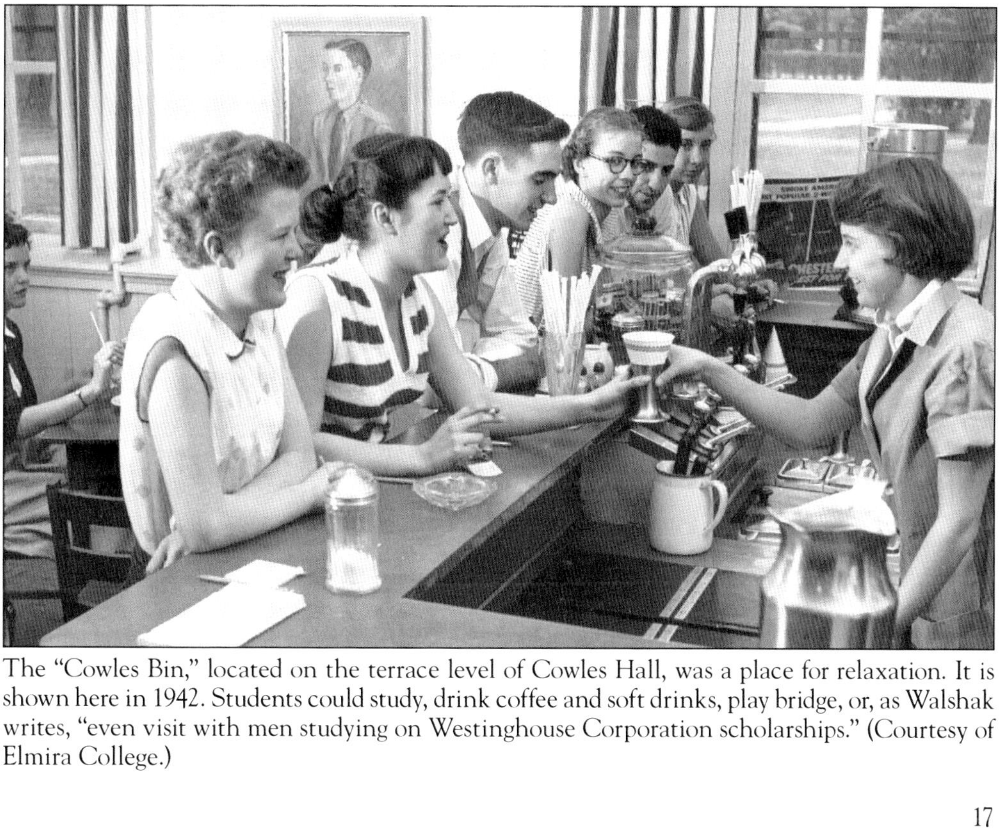

The "Cowles Bin," located on the terrace level of Cowles Hall, was a place for relaxation. It is shown here in 1942. Students could study, drink coffee and soft drinks, play bridge, or, as Walshak writes, "even visit with men studying on Westinghouse Corporation scholarships." (Courtesy of Elmira College.)

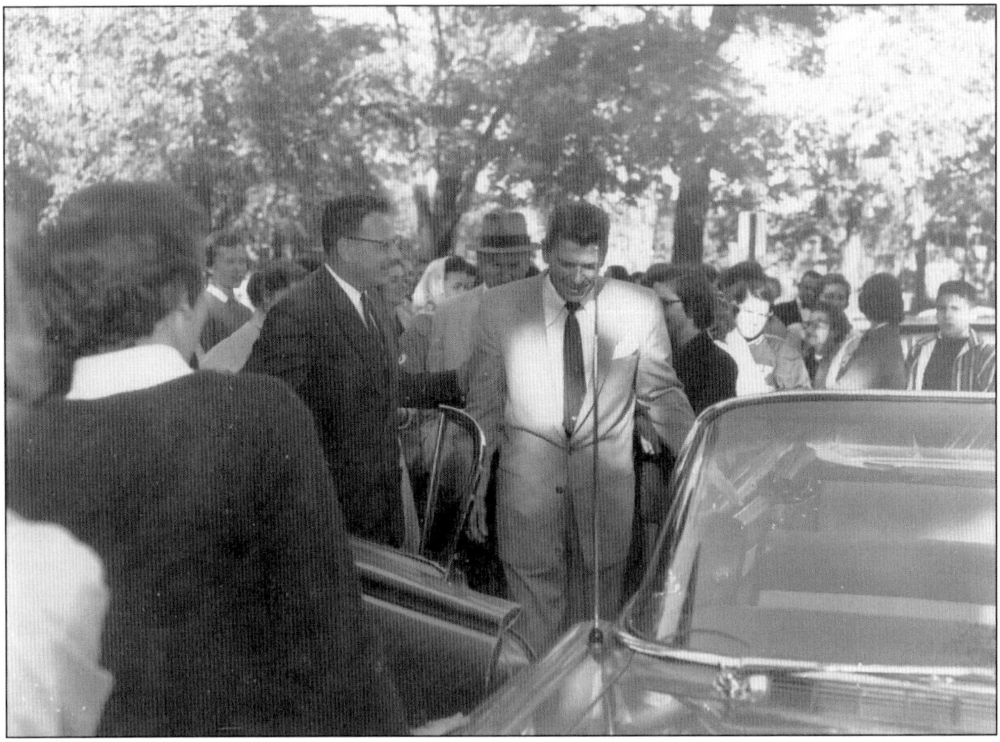

Ronald Reagan, on a speaking tour for General Electric, visited Elmira College in the late 1950s. Above, he is accompanied at the car by Dr. J. Ralph Murray. Below, Dr. Murray (right) joins Reagan on stage. (Courtesy of Elmira College.)

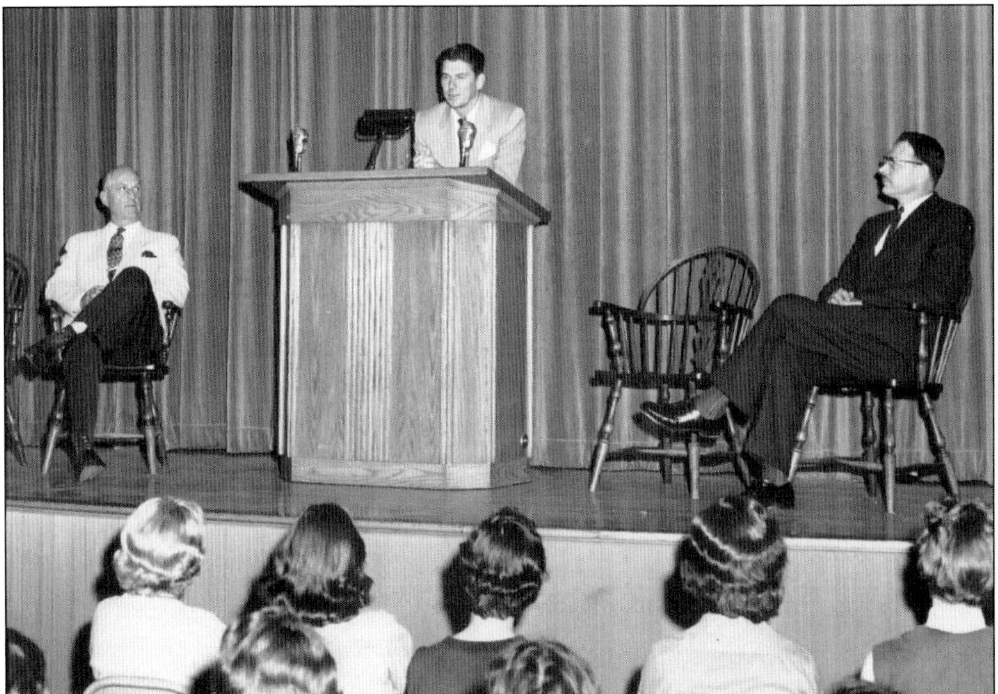

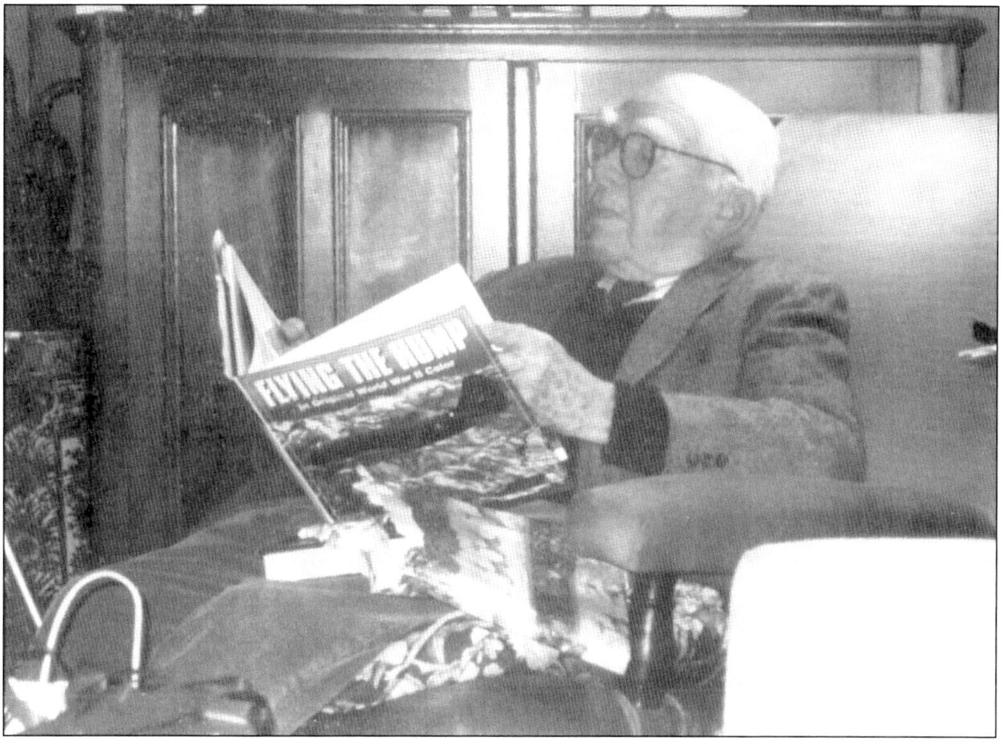

Jervis Langdon Jr. (1905–2004), great-nephew of Mark Twain, met his famous uncle when he was very young. Langdon, shown here around 2000, served as president of Penn Central and B&O, among others during a four-decade-long career. He was very proud of his service during World War II as a colonel in the Army Air Corps, "flying the hump" over the Himalayas. In 1982, he donated Quarry Farm to Elmira College for use as the Center for Mark Twain Studies. (Courtesy of Irene Langdon.)

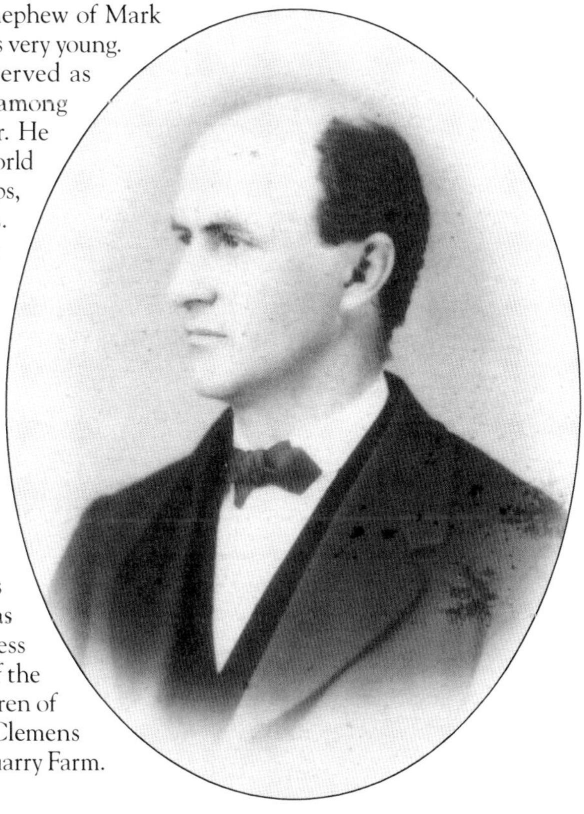

Theodore W. Crane was the husband of Olivia Clemens's older sister Susan. The Clemens family lived with the Cranes at their home, Quarry Farm, in Elmira, New York, for many summers during the 1870's and 1880's. Crane was the financial manager of the coal business J. Langdon and Company, and a leader of the Park Church. The Cranes had no children of their own. They were devoted to their Clemens nieces, all three of whom were born at Quarry Farm. (Courtesy of Elmira College.)

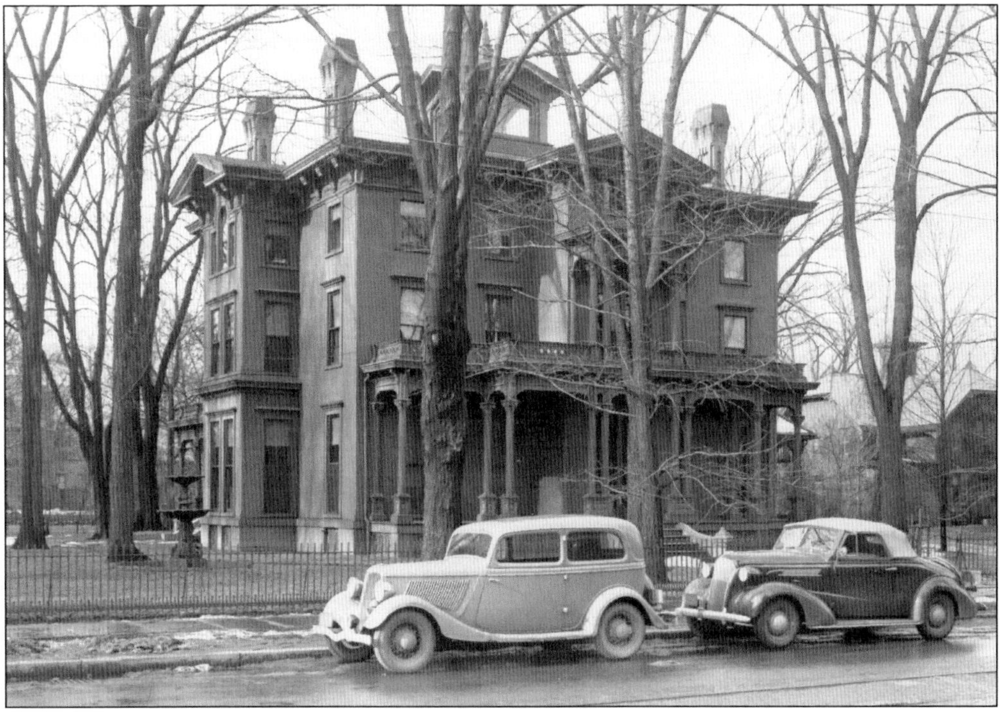

In the presence of nearly 100 people, Sam Clemens and Olivia Langdon were married in the Langdon home, at the corner of Main and Church Streets, on Wednesday evening, February 2, 1870. In 1939, Jervis Langdon offered to turn the home over to the city. Thomas Byrne recounts the process in his book, *Chemung County: 1890–1975*. The *Star Gazette* polled taxpayers about acquiring the property at a cost of approximately $57,000, thus increasing the tax rate of about $1 per $1,000 for one year. The vote was 150 in favor and 276 opposed. The city declined the offer, and the property was sold to a commercial developer and became Langdon Plaza. The building is shown here in the 1930s. (Courtesy of *The Star Gazette*.)

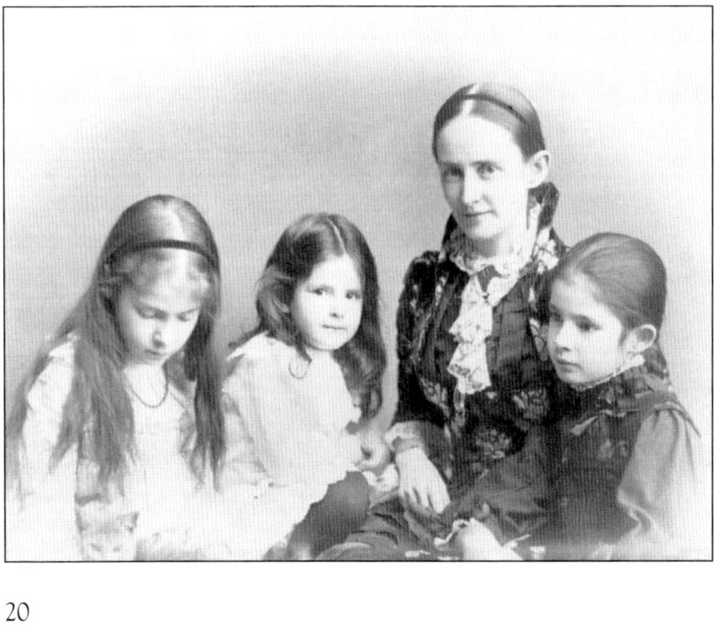

Sam and Livy had four children. Livy is pictured here with, from left to right, Susie, Jean, and Clara. The couple's son, Langdon, would die at 22 months. Clemens would outlive Susie, Jean, and Livy. According to Resa Willis, Clemens wrote in "Eve's Diary" a tribute to Livy through the mouth of Adam: "Wheresoever she was *there* was Eden." (Courtesy of Elmira College.)

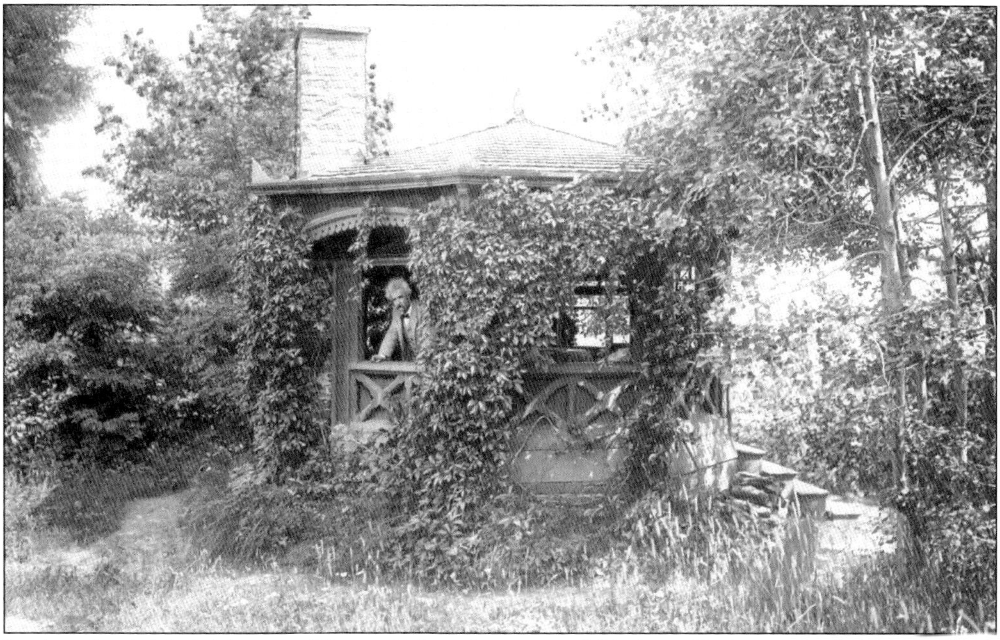

In their book *Mark Twain in Elmira,* Robert Jerome and Herbert Wisbey describe a special gift given to Twain. In 1874, Mark Twain's sister-in-law, Susan Crane, and her husband surprised him with an octagon-shaped study, a place of uninvaded quiet where he could write. Twain wrote, "It is a cozy nest . . . when the storms sweep down the remote valley and the lightning flashes, behind the hills beyond, and the rain beats upon the roof over my head, imagine the luxury. . . . On hot days I spread the study wide open, anchor my papers down with brickbats and write in the midst of hurricanes, clothed in the same linen we make shirts of." Working on *The Adventures of Huckleberry Finn* in July 1883, Twain reported, "I wrote 4000 words to-day and I touch 3000 and upwards pretty often. . . . And when I get fagged out, I lie abed a couple of days and read and smoke, and then go at it again for 6 or 7 days." (Courtesy of Elmira College.)

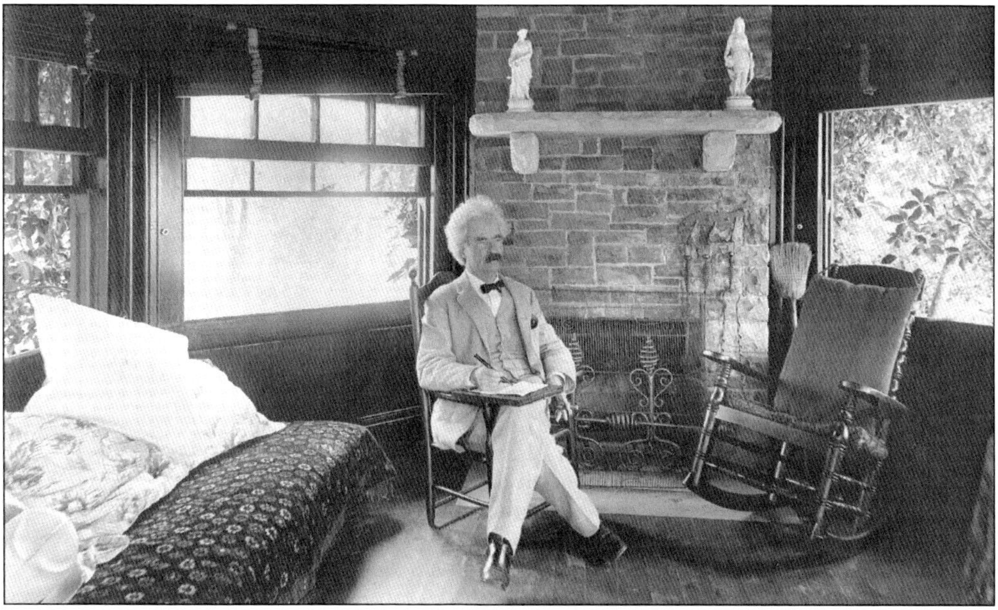

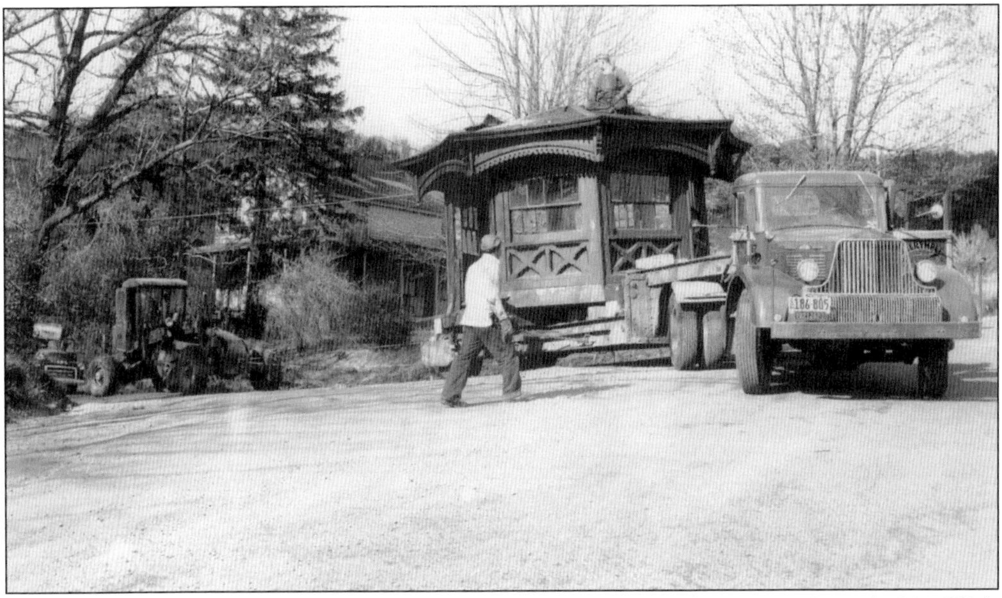

Mark Twain visited Elmira during the summer for nearly 20 years, between 1874 and 1894. With his passing, the study was not used and was exposed to vandalism. In 1952, it was moved (above) to the Elmira College campus, where it has become a focal point for those interested in Mark Twain. Dr. Ida Langdon, Twain's niece by marriage, spoke at the dedication of the study at its new location (below). Also in attendance were Elmira College president Lewis Eldred (second from left) and Charles Perry, chairman of the board of trustees (far right). (Courtesy of Elmira College.)

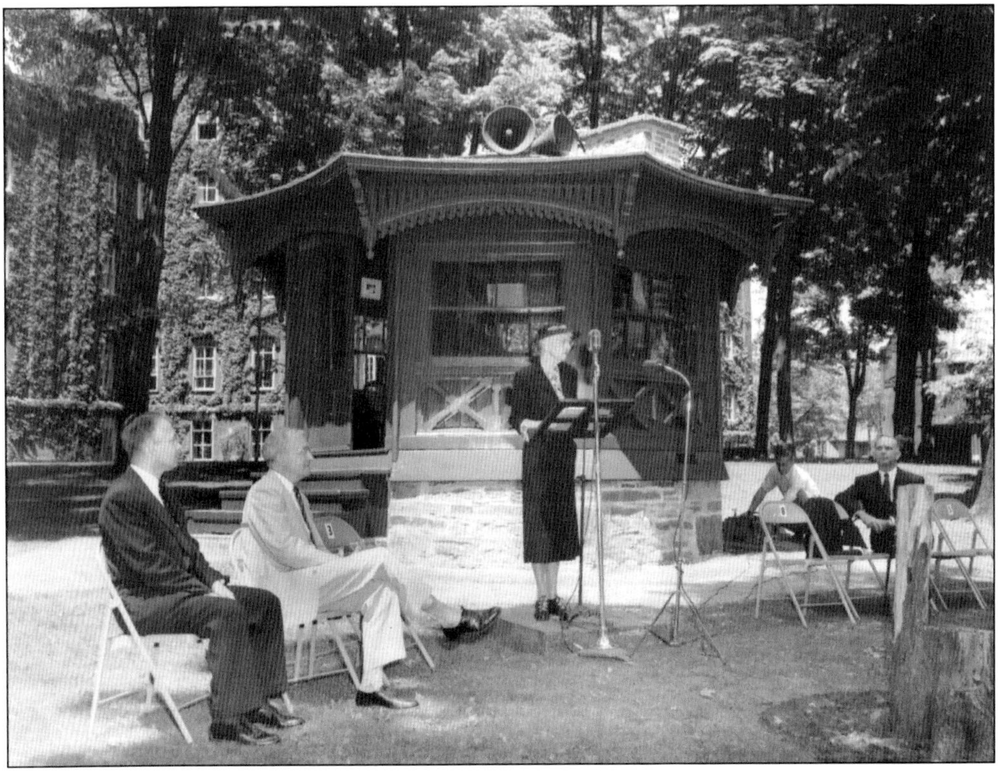

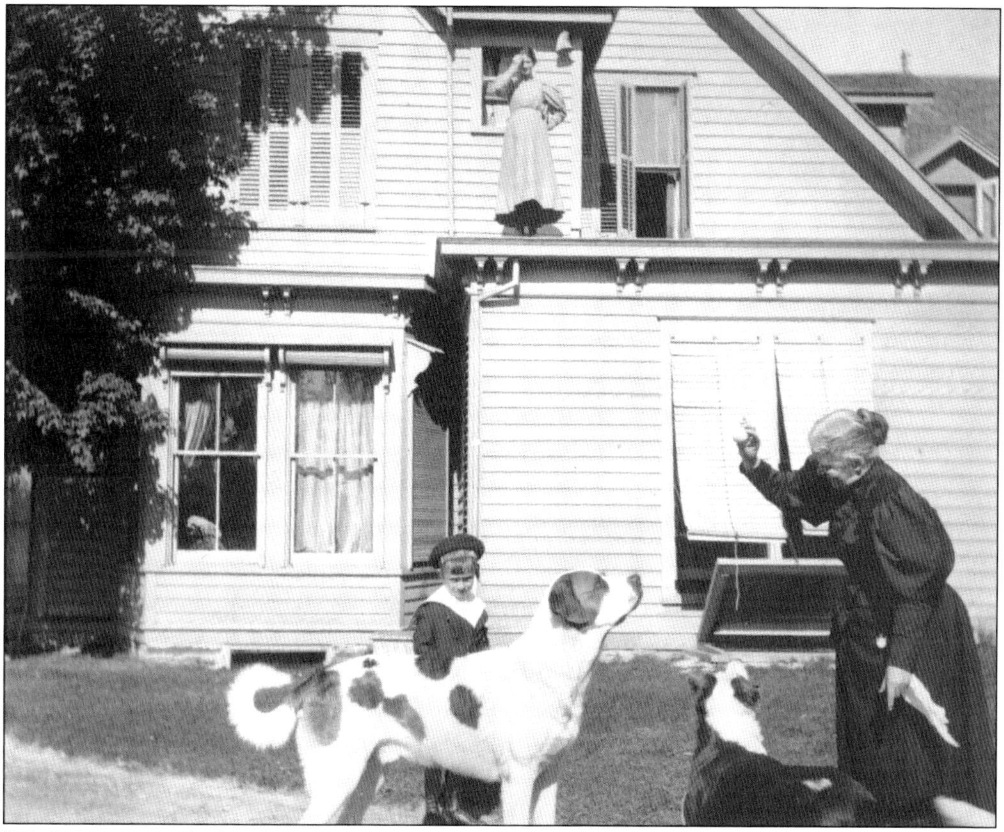

While Twain worked in his study, others were enjoying themselves. In this Quarry Farm scene from around 1895, Susan Crane (Twain's sister-in-law) is addressing the dog and Bim Pond. In the background, on the roof, is 15-year-old Jean Clemens. (Courtesy of Elmira College.)

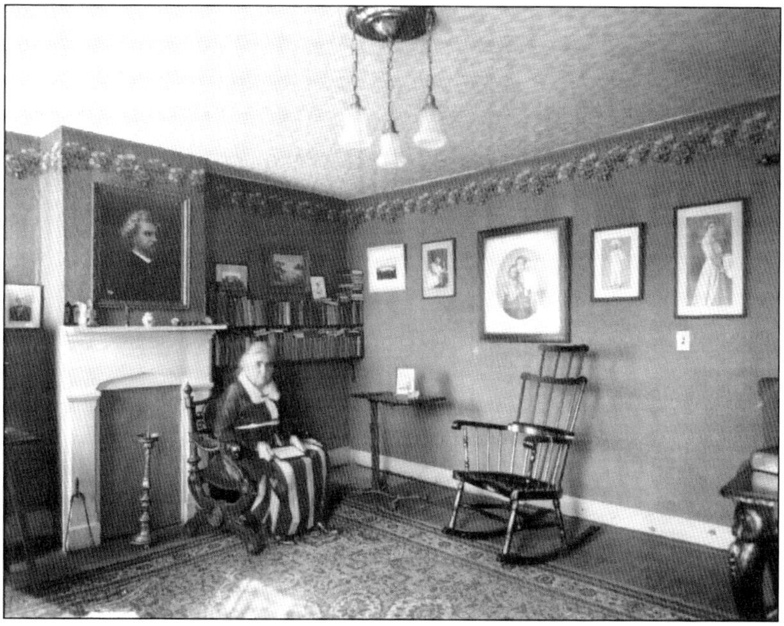

Katy Leary, whose home is now the site of Katy Leary Park on Elmira's south side, was as much a friend as a servant. She went to work for the Clemens family in Hartford in 1880, and stayed with the family until after Mark Twain's death in 1910. She is shown here around 1930. (Courtesy of Elmira College.)

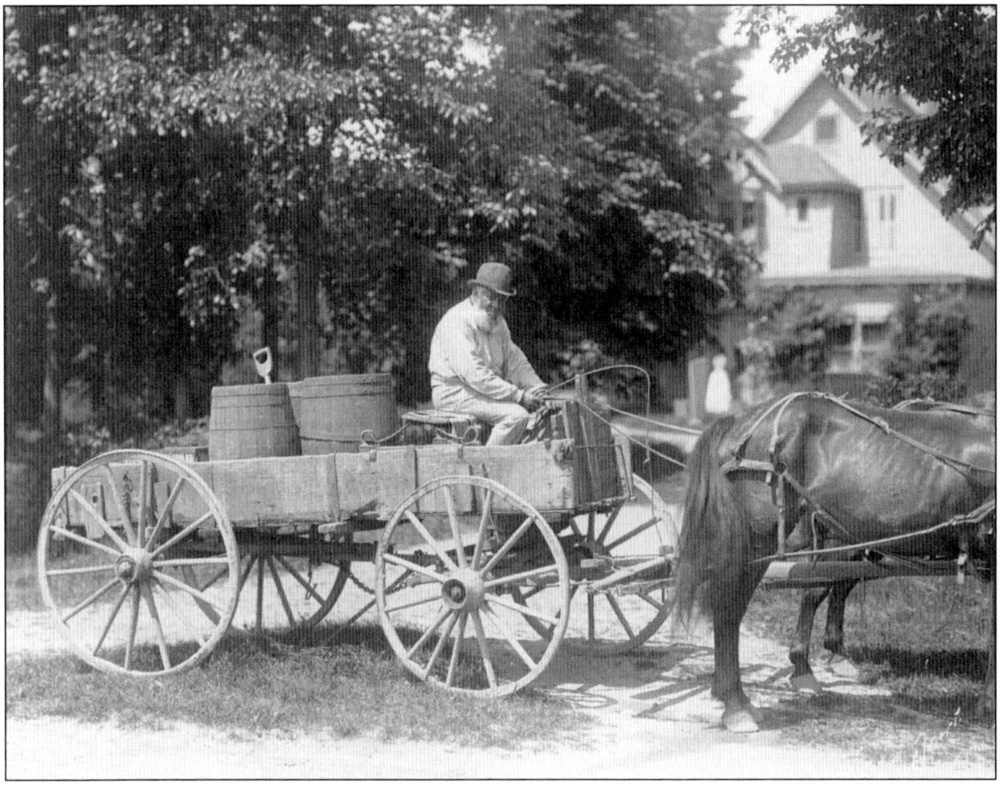

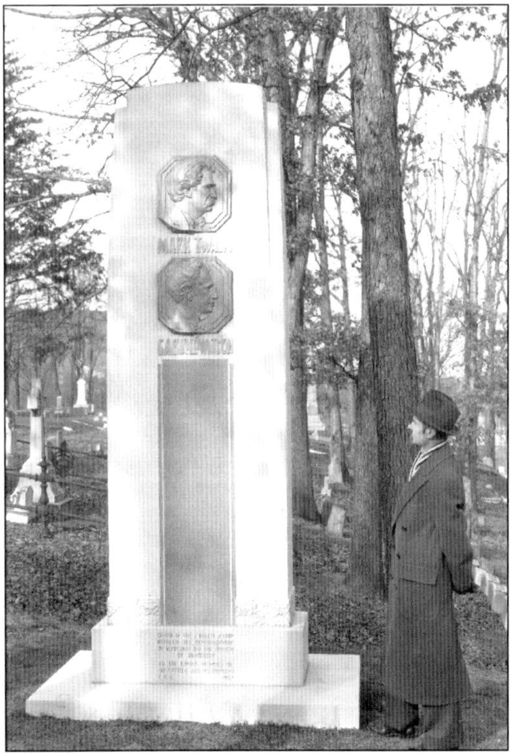

Jerome and Wisbey wrote about John T. Lewis, an ex-slave who worked for the Crane family. According to Ida Langdon, he and "Auntie Cord" furnished Samuel Clemens with endless interest and pleasure because often they were not in "complete harmony." Lewis heroically stopped a runaway horse and buggy. Twain reported that Auntie Cord proclaimed, "Lewis the Lord sent you there to stop that horse." Says Lewis, "Then who sent the horse there in sich a shape?" (Courtesy of Elmira College.)

When Clara Clemens Gabrilowitsch discussed a memorial to her husband, who died in 1936, with sculptor Ernfred Anderson, he suggested a monument that would honor both her father and her husband, and she agreed. Anderson stands next to the marble shaft with portrait medallions located at the Langdon plot in Woodlawn Cemetery. (Courtesy of CCHS.)

Two

FAITH COMMUNITY

On the eve of Elmira becoming a city, the *Village Directory* (1863–1864) listed 10 churches. By 1925, there were 46 churches, representing all of the leading denominations. According to that directory, "Elmira could properly be called a City of Churches." For the community, the "noble edifices" added to the attractiveness and charm of the city; the "full and adequate supply of churches" was a "factor for progress."

Churches date to the frontier days. In *First Presbyterian Church of Elmira, The First 200 Years*, author Edward B. Hoffman describes the scene: "The settlers, like the frontier, were rough; drunkenness, gambling, wife beating and later horse racing were said to be the chief recreation. In the tiny village [Newtown] were six taverns. Bloody noses were more common than Bibles." The Reverend Simeon Jones recorded in 1805 that "The Sabbath was desecrated by sports, labor and business . . . intemperance was almost universal."

Baptists arrived first in Chemung County, worshipping in Wellsburg in 1789. The Presbyterians came a year later and were the first group to settle in what would become Elmira. They worshipped in a log frame dwelling that also served as the jail and courthouse. Methodist circuit riders and itinerant preachers visited the area. By 1812, Newtown was a full-fledged circuit station. Episcopalians organized their first parish in 1833. The number of Catholics increased after 1825, a result of the building of the Chemung Canal. Elmira became a stop on the mission circuit after 1834. In 1849, the Bishop of Buffalo designated Father Sheridan to take up residence and begin construction of a church.

According to Thomas Byrne, "By 1862 . . . Elmira included about one hundred Jewish families and there had been enough contact with Jewish itinerant peddlers to have brought about the 'legend' that Jerusalem Hill had been named because of a Jewish cemetery." The "German" church was founded in 1874 as the German Evangelical Society to serve the immigrant population. The German community had also been active in establishing St. John the Baptist Catholic Church in 1866. Two Lutheran churches emerged in the 1890s: Bethany on the south side and Trinity on the north side. African Americans were also busy building congregations as their numbers increased in the 1850s. The Salvation Army has been a part of Elmira since 1892. Originating from the tradition of tent revivals, the Pentecostal Tabernacle was founded in 1944. It began with four persons, all members of the founder's family.

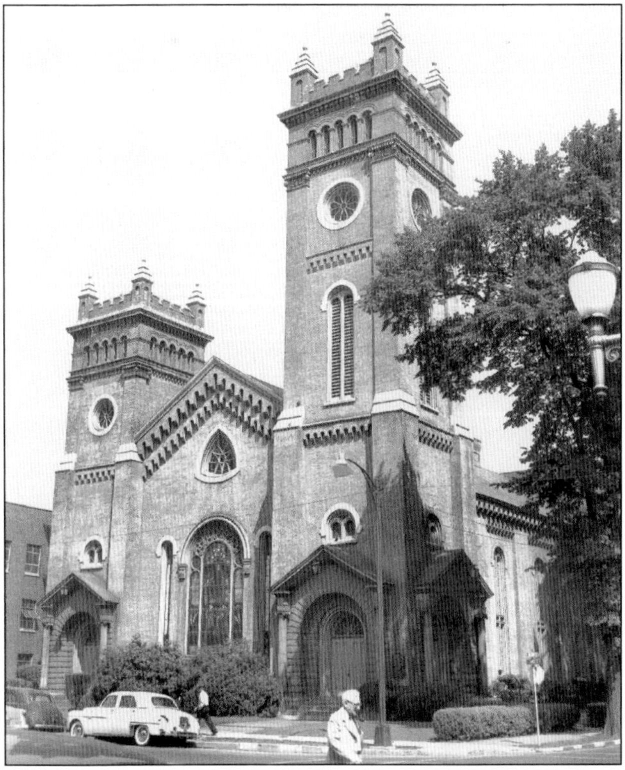

First Presbyterian Church was organized in 1795, in the village of Newtown. The church met either outdoors or in the homes of its members. Its first meetinghouse was built in 1820 on the corner of Church and Baldwin Streets. Two buildings followed, in 1835 and 1865. In 1881, the building was damaged by a tornado and eventually redesigned and, in 1896, renovated as shown in the photograph. First Presbyterian moved to its West Clinton Street location in 1967, and the old site became part of Elm Chevrolet. (Courtesy of CCHS.)

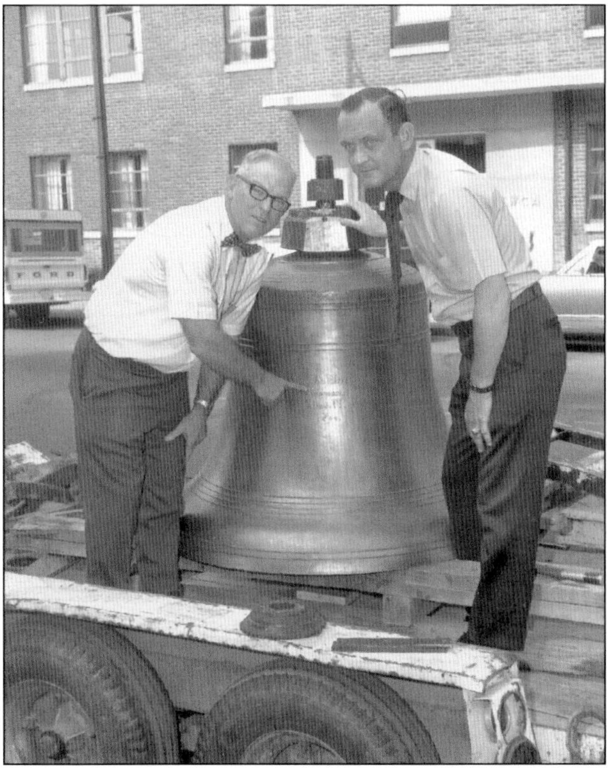

S. Edward Rose wrote, "Ours is the sweetest toned bell in the Valley." After the downtown building was demolished, the First Presbyterian Church bell was stashed away in a warehouse. While restoring the courthouse, Chemung County building superintendent, and coauthor of this book, J. Arthur Kieffer, persuaded the church to make a permanent loan of the bell to the county. Archie (left) and Ed Flannery moved the 1857 bell to its new location in 1975. (Courtesy of CCHS.)

Sarah C. Smith became a member of the First Presbyterian Church in 1867. In 1880, she heeded a call to embark upon missionary work in Japan and became a recognized figure in Japanese education. In 1923, Emperor Taisho conferred upon her the Imperial Decoration of the Sacred Treasure, an honor rarely bestowed upon foreign women. (Courtesy of the First Presbyterian Church.)

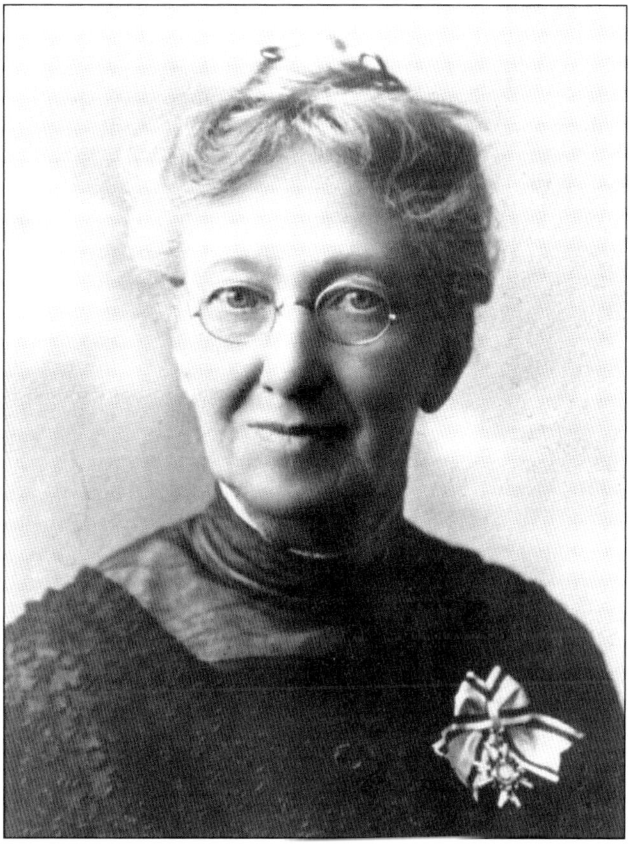

When First Presbyterian Church was renovated in 1896, the organ was moved from the rear of the sanctuary to the front. That organ was replaced in 1928 with a new W.S. Stevens organ, which had more than 1,300 pipes. (Courtesy of CCHS.)

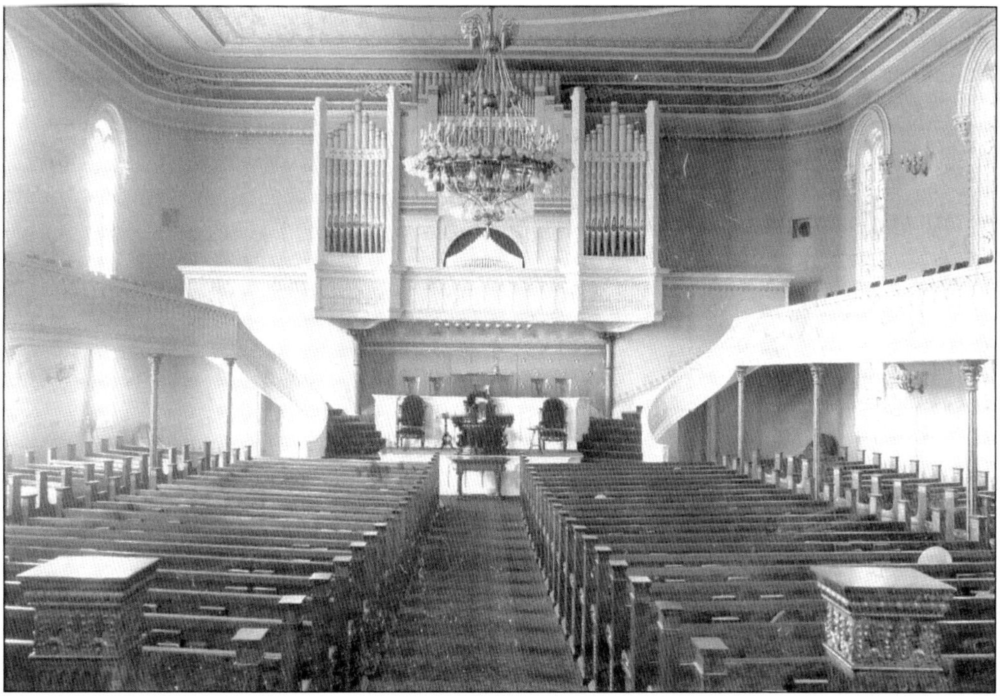

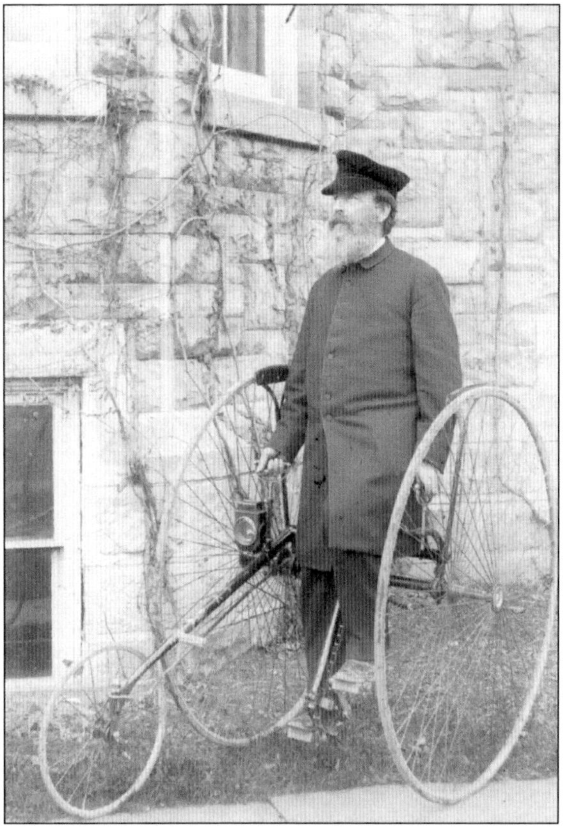

The Reverend Thomas K. Beecher (1824–1900) was pastor of The Park Church from 1854 to 1900. A brother to Harriet Beecher Stowe and Henry Ward Beecher, he preached when and where he wanted, and such great crowds gathered to hear him that the church building was quickly overwhelmed. He preached in the opera house and at Eldridge Park. (Courtesy of The Park Church.)

In 1846, a group of 40 ardent abolitionist members of the First Presbyterian Church formed The Independent Congregational Church of Elmira. In 1871, they became The Park Church. This building was constructed between 1874 and 1876, replacing the previous, wooden structure. Under the leadership of The Reverend Thomas K. Beecher, the new building had a stage and a place where young people could dance and play billiards. It had the town's first public library and special quarters for homeless people. (Courtesy of The Park Church.)

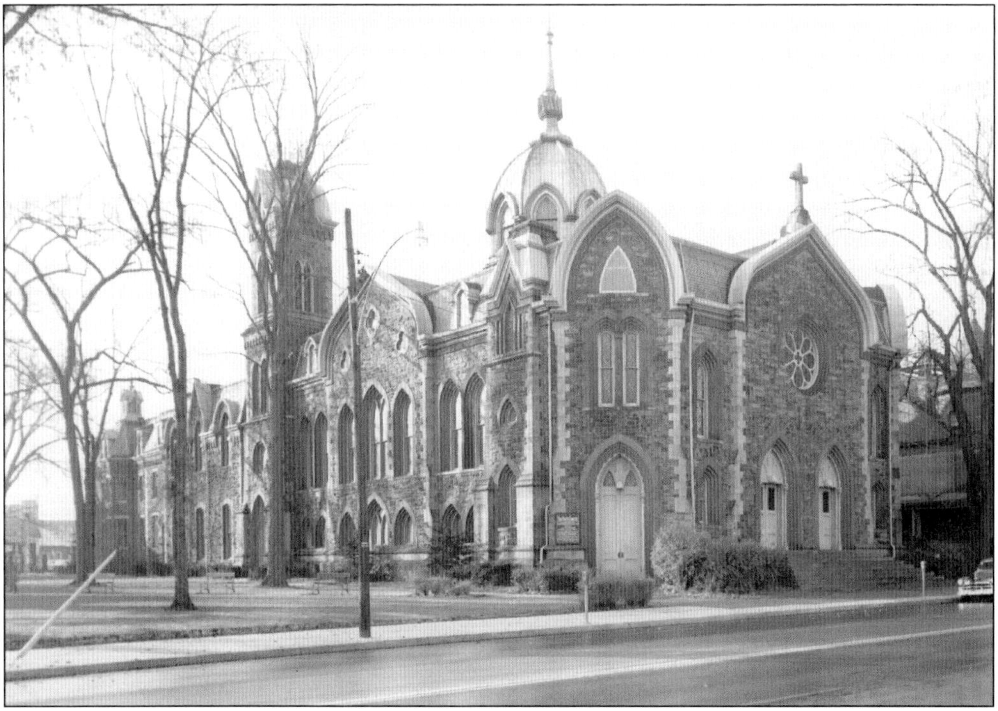

Julia Jones Beecher was the second wife of Thomas. Her Missionary Ragbaby, or Beecher Baby, was originally made for her niece. They became very popular and Julia, with the aid of The Park Church sewing circle, made the dolls from 1893 to 1910. The dolls were made of donated pink silk or cotton underwear, and the features were needle-sculpted. Looped yellow yarn formed the hair. The dolls came in sizes ranging from 16 to 23 inches. The sale of "Beecher dolls" raised $1,111.89 for the church. (Courtesy of CCHS.)

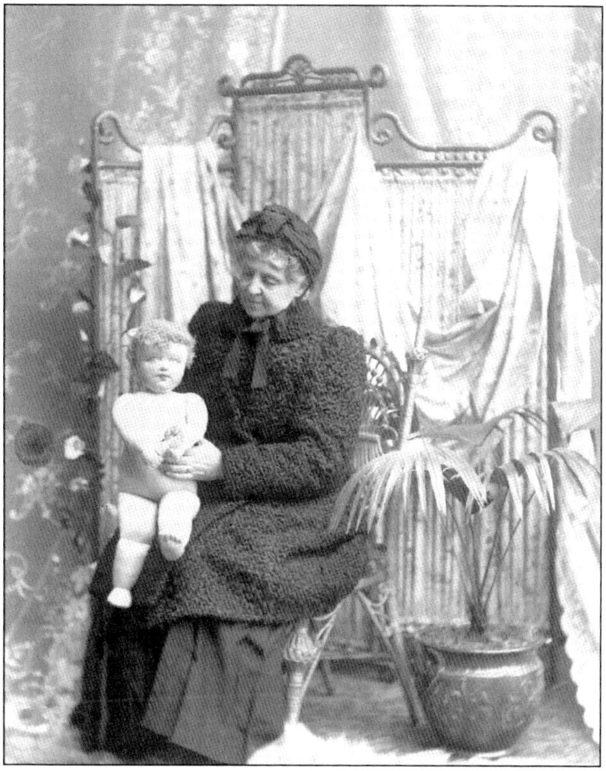

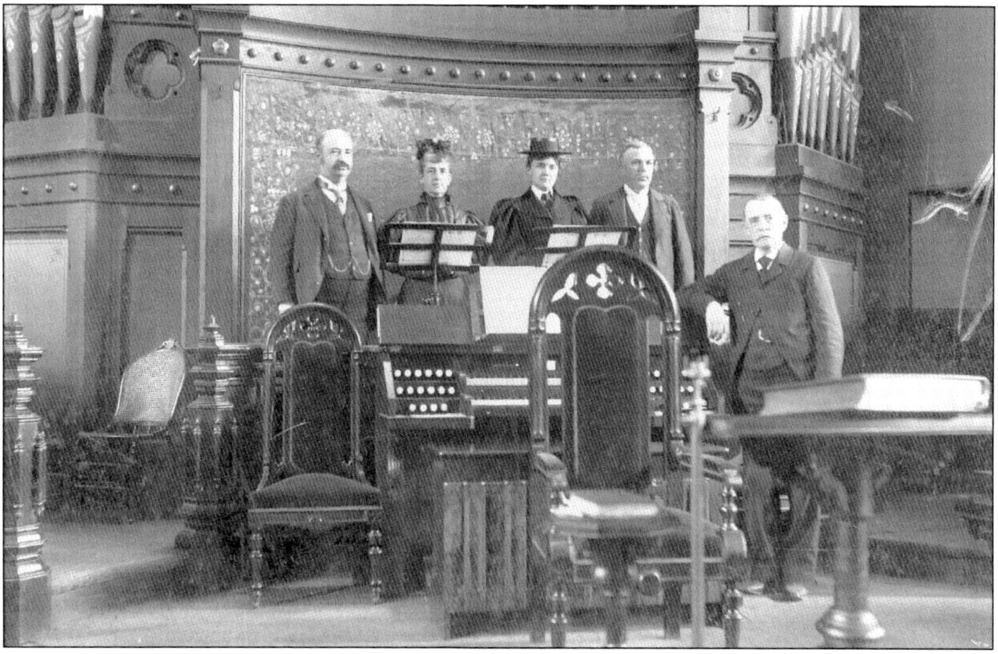

Park Church provided many performance opportunities for its members. It might be a scene from Dickens or a piece for quartet. Shown in this c. 1893 photograph are, from left to right, David Codwise Robinson (bass), Mrs. D.C. Robinson (contralto), Elizabeth Glee (soprano), Robert Parmenter (tenor), and John B. Marsh (leader and organist). (Courtesy of CCHS.)

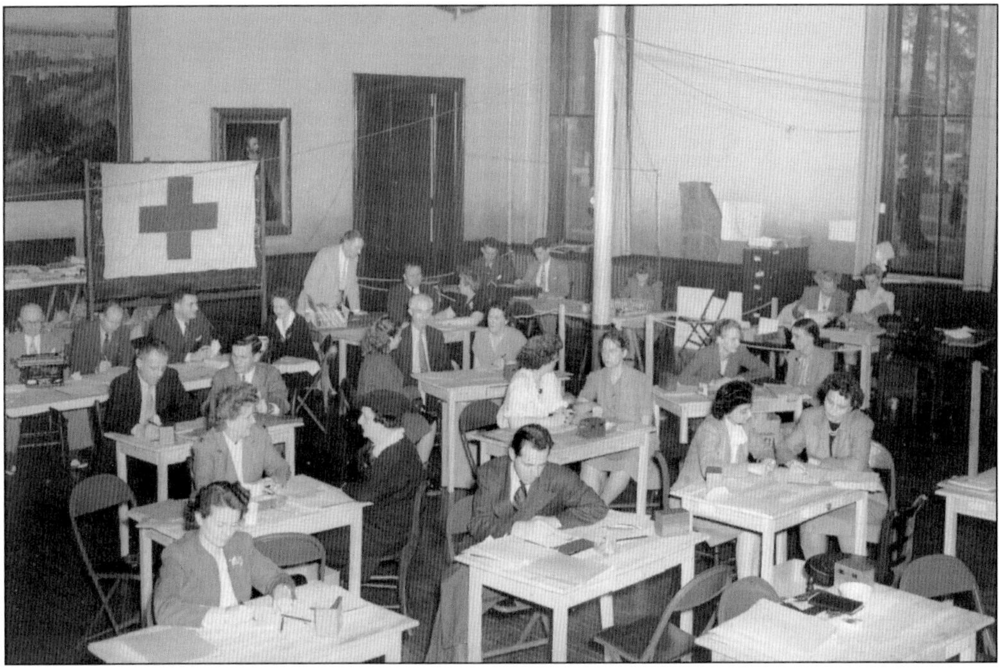

Beecher Hall at The Park Church is located just south of the sanctuary. It is truly a multipurpose room, used for entertainment, church dinners, and, as seen in this 1946 photograph, a place where the Red Cross might set up operation. (Courtesy of The Park Church.)

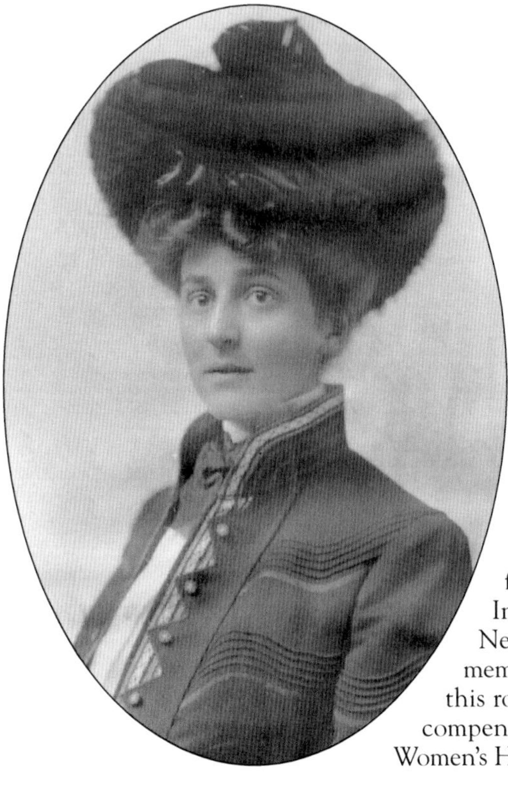

Crystal Eastman (1881–1929), whose father succeeded Thomas K. Beecher as pastor of The Park Church, was a suffragette, a pacifist, and a founder of the American Civil Liberties Union. In June 1909, Charles E. Hughes, governor of New York, appointed Eastman the first woman member of the Employer's Liability Commission. In this role, she drafted New York State's first worker's compensation law. She is a member of the National Women's Hall of Fame. (Courtesy of CCHS.)

In 1860, Dr. David Murdoch resigned after nine years as pastor of the First Presbyterian Church. He and his followers became known as the Second Presbyterian Society and formally organized on February 8, 1861. That congregation became the Lake St. Presbyterian Church. This is an 1890 view of the church. (Courtesy of The Lake St. Presbyterian Church.)

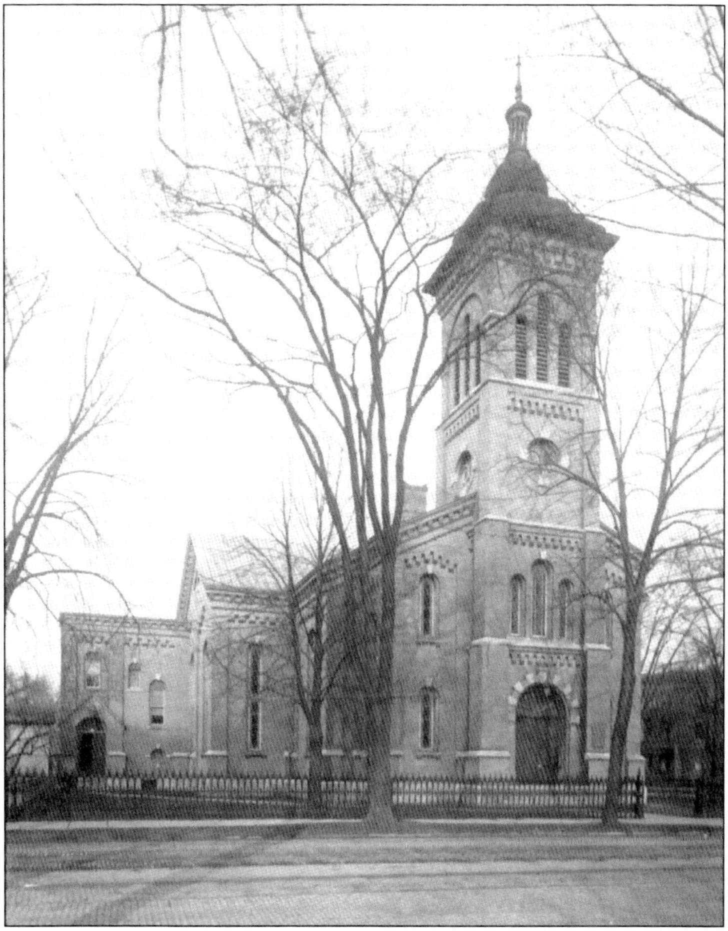

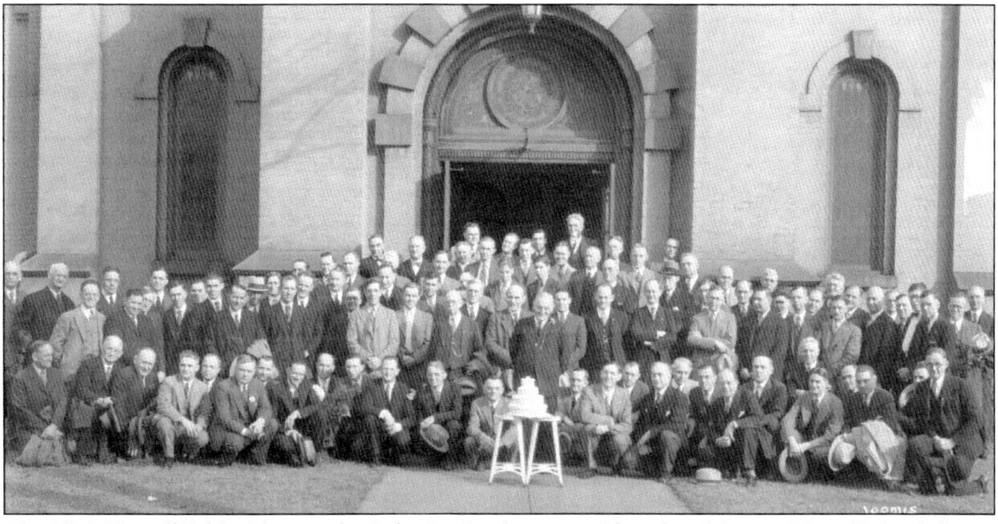

The F.M. Howell Bible Class at the Lake St. Presbyterian Church celebrates Howell's birthday in 1931. Howell is standing behind the cake. He founded F.M. Howell & Co. in 1883, and was its president until his death in 1934. (Courtesy of The Lake St. Presbyterian Church.)

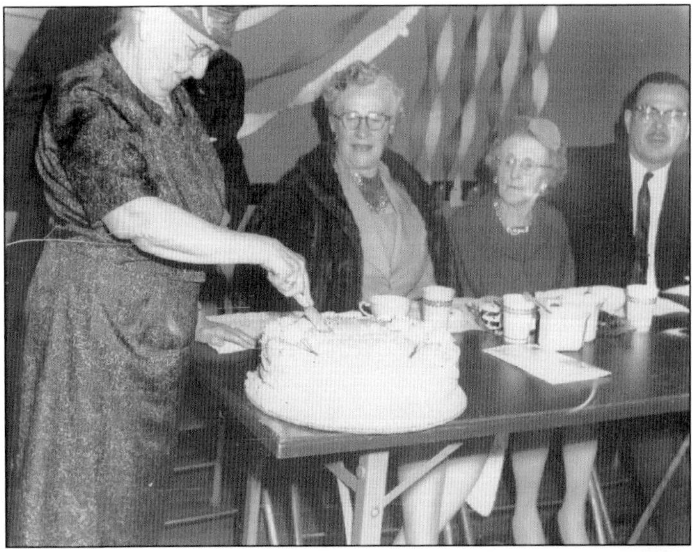

Lake St. Presbyterian Church celebrated its 100th anniversary on December 26, 1961. Clara Roy cuts the cake. Looking on are, from left to right, Mrs. Elwin Bracon, Mrs. Dewitt A. Brown, and Dr. J. Ralph Murray, president of Elmira College. (Courtesy of The Lake St. Presbyterian Church.)

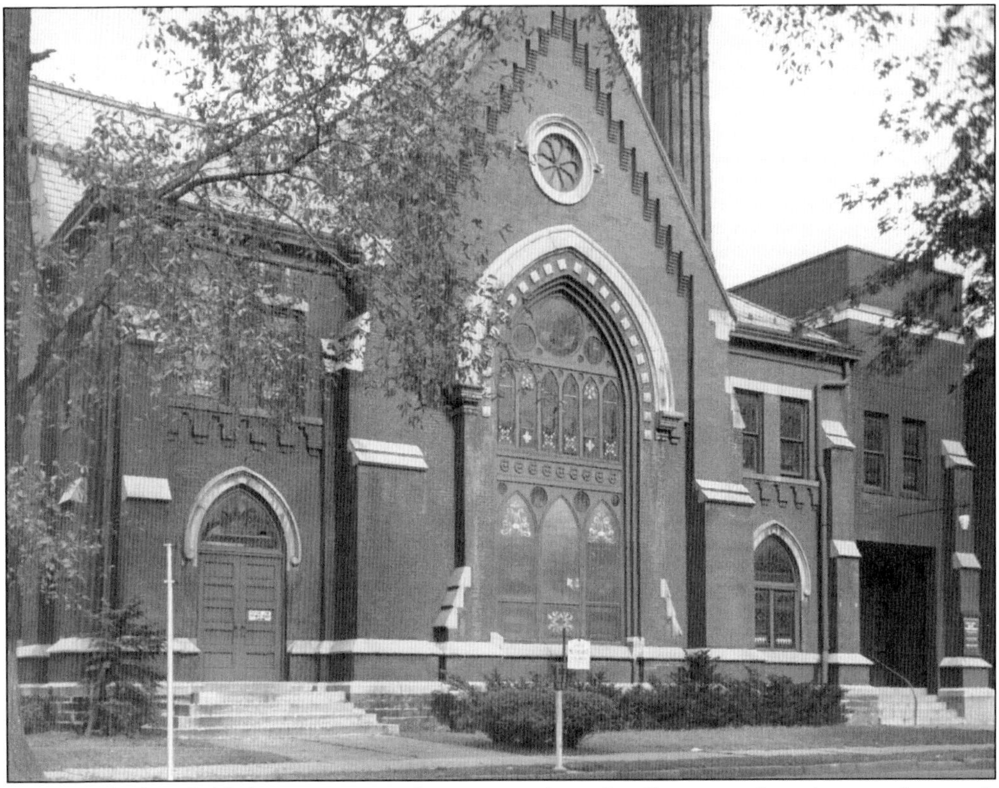

Early Methodists held their services in homes, in a log schoolhouse, and in the courthouse. A deputy sheriff's wife objected to the lusty "amens and hallelujahs," and so they began a subscription to fund their own building, which was constructed in 1830–1831 at 322 Baldwin Street. A larger structure was built in 1873, but was destroyed by fire in 1886. The building shown here was dedicated in 1887. In 1968, First Methodist Church merged with Hedding Methodist Church. The congregation relocated, and the building was sold for commercial development. (Courtesy of New Beginnings United Methodist Church.)

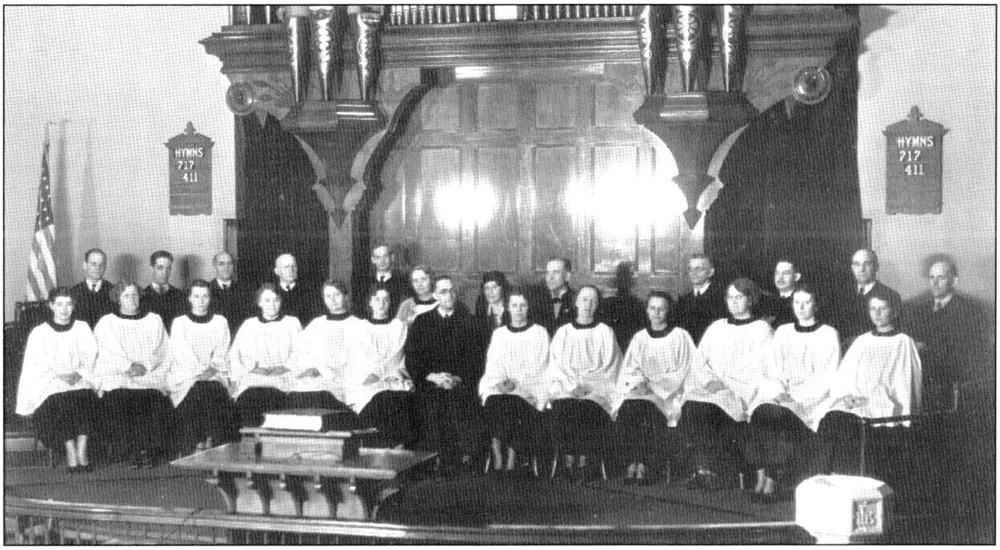

In 1968, the First Methodist Church, Hedding Methodist Church, and St. John's Methodist Church merged to form Christ United Methodist Church, located on the corner of Columbia and Church Streets. Pictured here is the choir at First Methodist Church sometime before 1968. (Courtesy of New Beginnings United Methodist Church.)

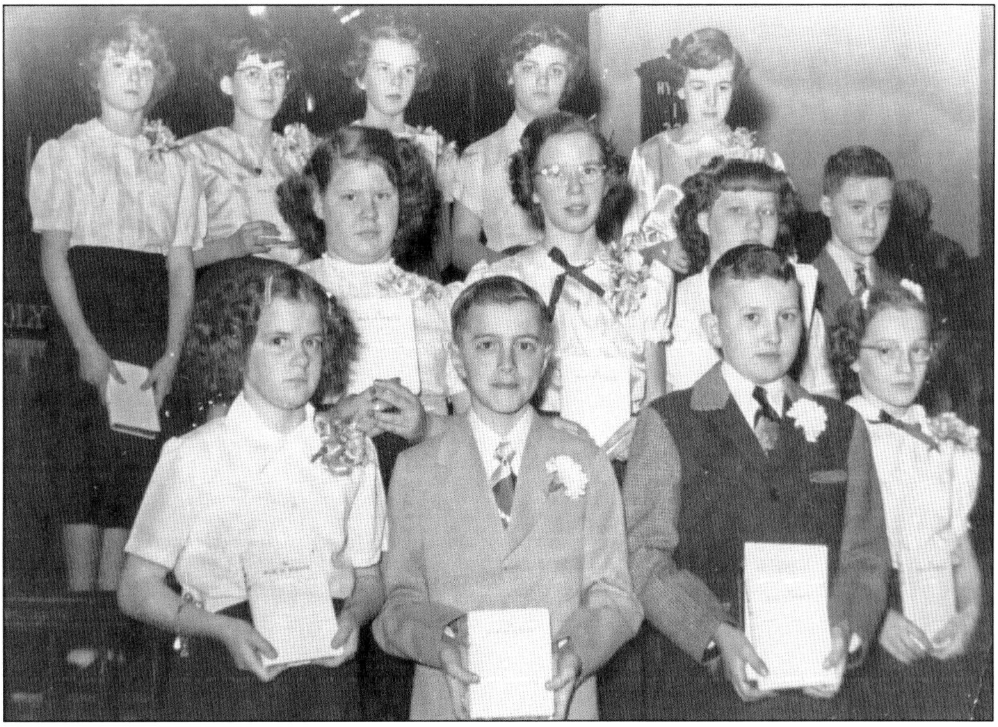

Pictured here are members of the First Methodist Church confirmation class of 1951. From left to right are (first row) Mary Vincent, Robert McConnell, Charles Woodard, and Sandra Phillips; (second row) Darlene Baker, Mary Personius, unidentified, and Paul Hawley; (third row) unidentified, Beverly Kline, Martha Personius, Joyce Nagy, and Constance Torrence. (Courtesy of Robert McConnell.)

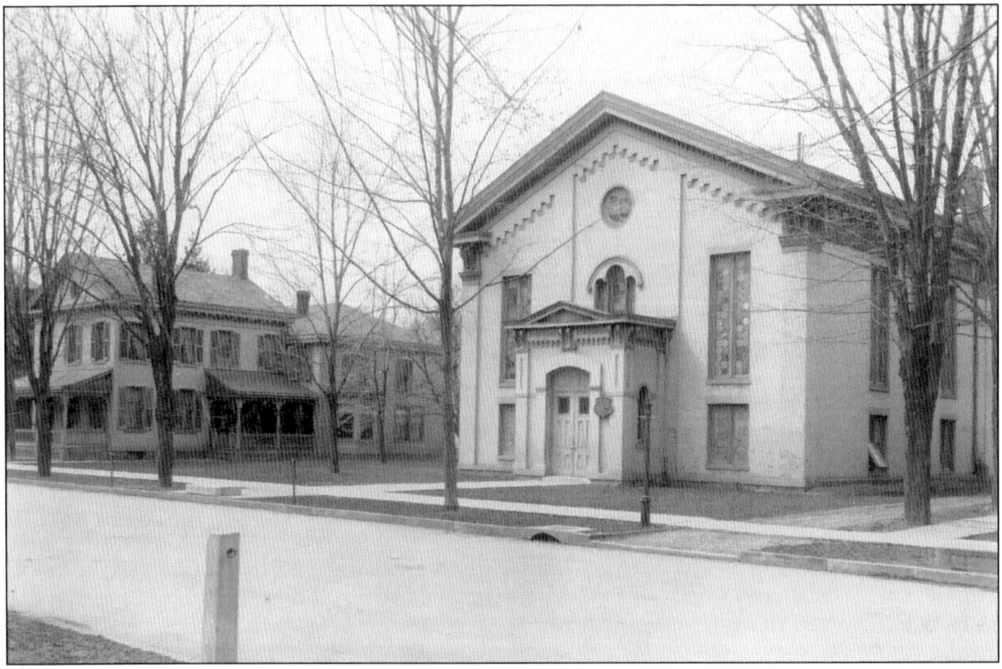

By 1851, the First Methodist Church was so overcrowded that a second building was needed. Built at a cost of $6,000, the Hedding Methodist Church was dedicated in 1852. It was named after Bishop Elijah Hedding. The spire of the original building was blown off and thrown to the ground by a tornado in 1881. (Courtesy of New Beginnings United Methodist Church.)

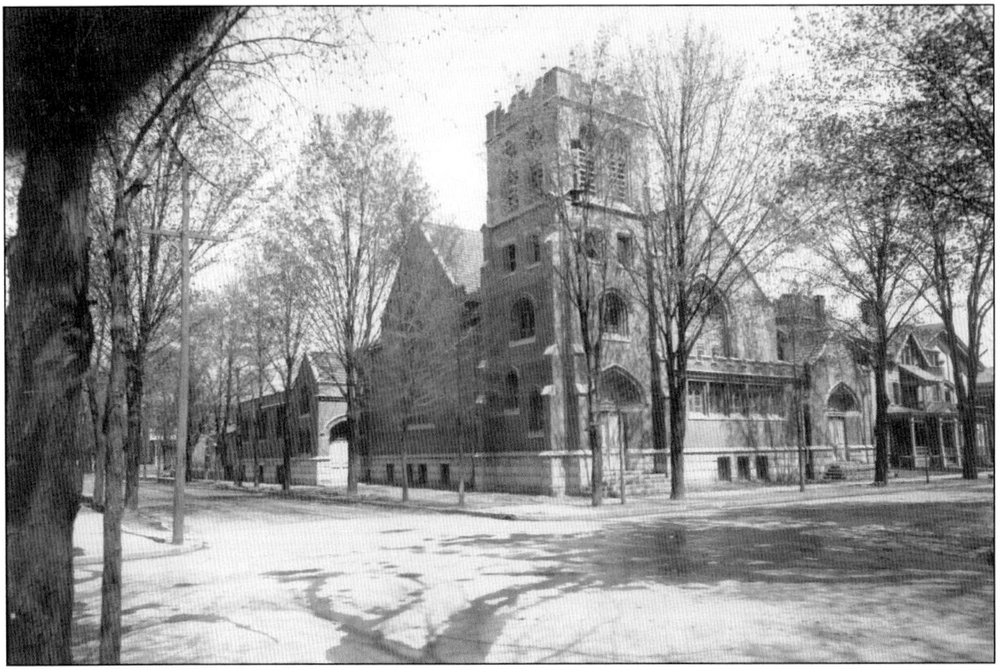

As Methodism grew in the late 19th century, more space was needed. In 1901, Hedding Methodist erected a new building on the corner of Church and Columbia Streets. (Courtesy of New Beginnings United Methodist.)

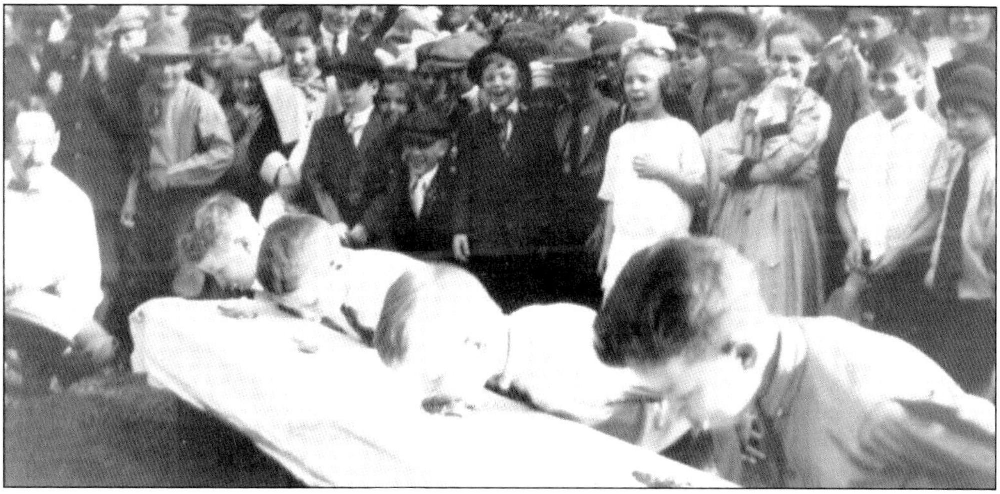

Over the years, a variety of activities kept the congregation at Hedding Methodist Church busy. Above, Hedding Methodist boys had fun in a pie-eating contest at a Sunday school picnic in 1915. Many years later, members of the congregation get a briefing prior to taking the church census on January 24, 1954 (below). (Courtesy of New Beginnings United Methodist Church.)

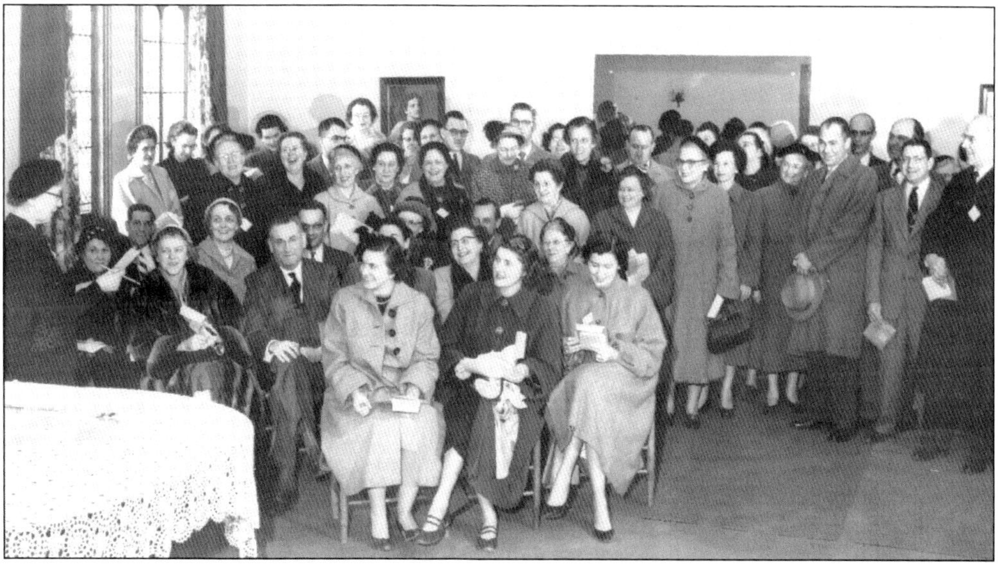

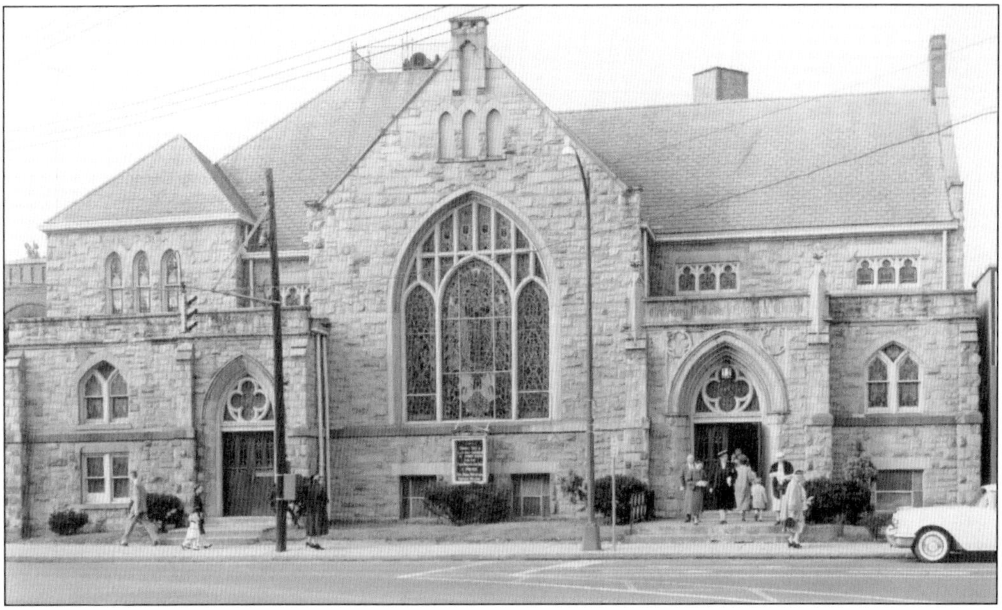

The South Main Street Methodist Episcopal Church was organized in 1871 on property purchased from Trinity Episcopal Church, located at the corner of South Main Street and Pennsylvania Avenue. In 1884, a new brick building was erected. Because Methodists were celebrating the 100th anniversary of their first general conference, the name was officially changed to Centenary Methodist Episcopal Church. In 1901, the cornerstone was laid for a new, beautiful bluestone church. A member coined the phrase, "a penny a day the mortgage will pay." (Courtesy of New Beginnings United Methodist Church.)

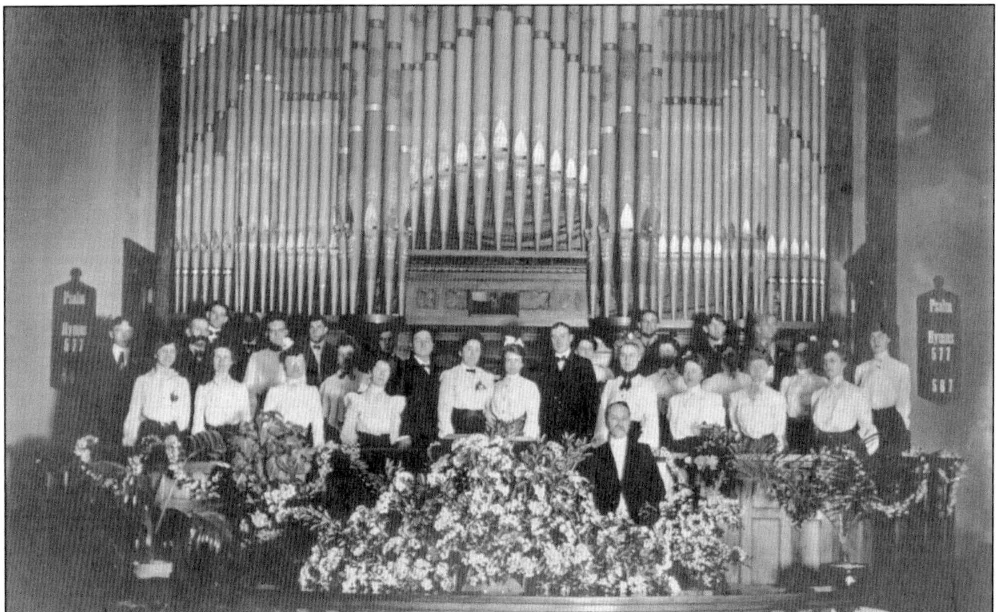

On September 21, 1902, a "Night of Church Dedication" was held at Centenary. Shown here is the church choir at that event. Dr. D.D. Campbell was the pastor, and George A. Palmer was the choir director. (Courtesy of New Beginnings United Methodist Church.)

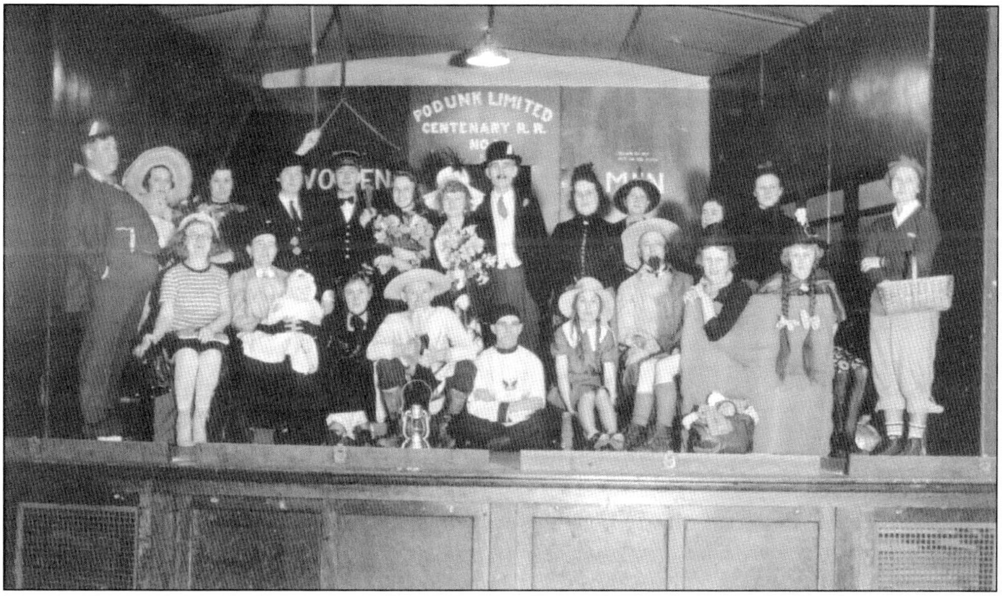

In 1929, an annex to Centenary Church was built, consisting of a stage, gymnasium, a new kitchen, and additional Sunday school rooms. The Thoburn Philathea Class put on many productions, such as this one in the 1940s. (Courtesy of New Beginnings United Methodist Church.)

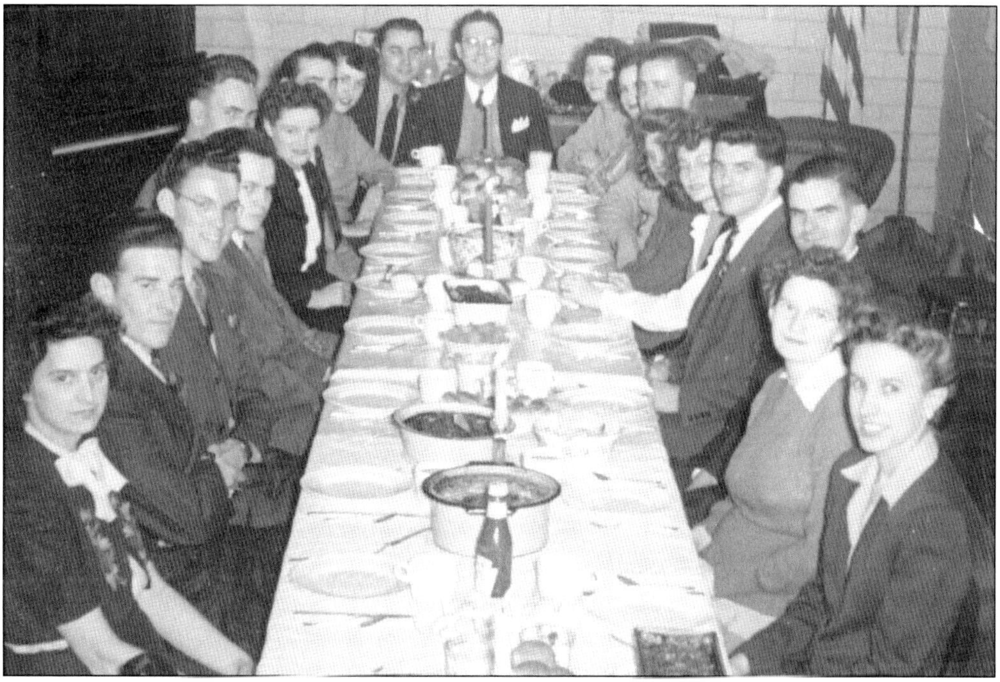

A night out for Centenary Church members might be joining friends in the Sunday school classroom for dinner. Shown here in the 1940s are, clockwise from lower left, Edna Dibble (teacher), Everett Hess, Sterling Reynolds, Bill Norton, Bill Parfitt, Ellie Parfitt, Walt Judge, Jean Judge, Don Judge, Bill Hewitt, Jean Sullivan, Shirley Harper Dunlap, Harry Dunlap, Jean Tobias, LaMae Warters, Albert Warters, Howard Escott, Gladys Escott, and Arleen Carter. (Courtesy of New Beginnings United Methodist Church.)

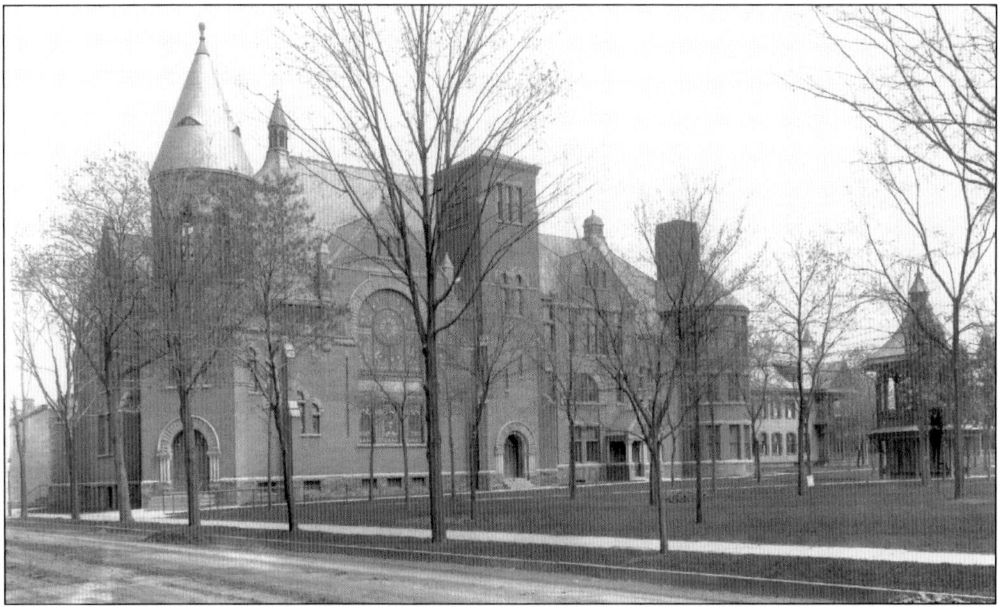

The First Baptist Church was organized in 1829. Land was purchased from Jeffrey and Elizabeth Wisner for $1.50, to be used for a church and cemetery. It was really a donation, as their daughter was married to the first pastor. Three buildings have occupied this site, the first erected in 1832, the second in 1848, and the present building in 1892. The first building (a barnlike structure) cost $954. The present Romanesque-style structure cost $70,000. The church opens on to Church Street. At the rear was the parsonage, where the Verizon building now stands. The First Baptist Church building was decommissioned on September 20, 2009. (Courtesy of CCHS.)

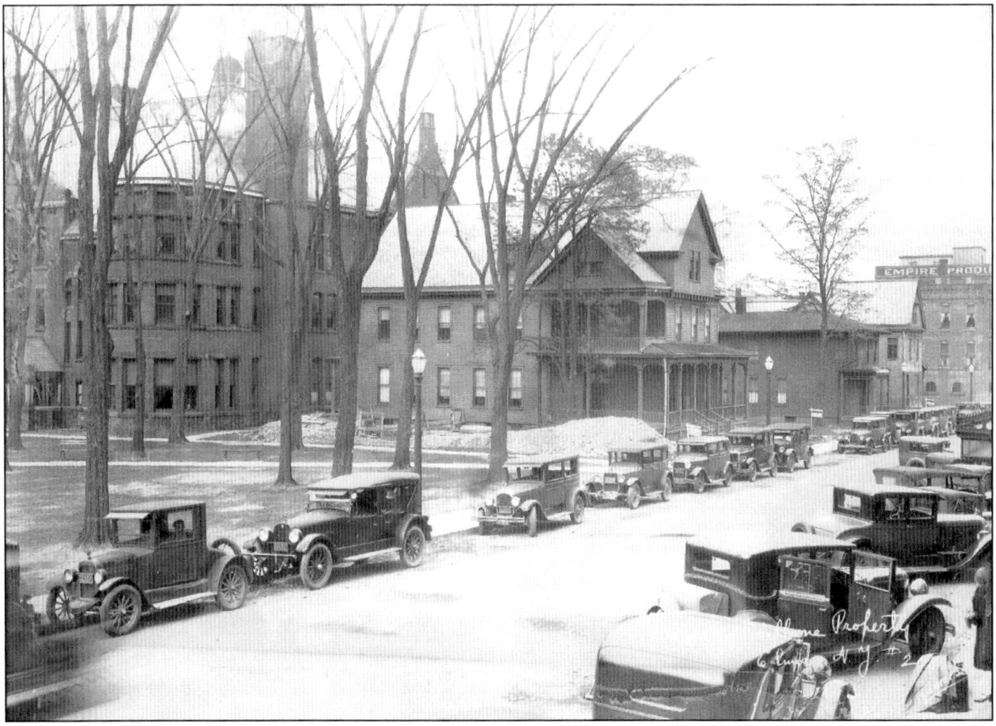

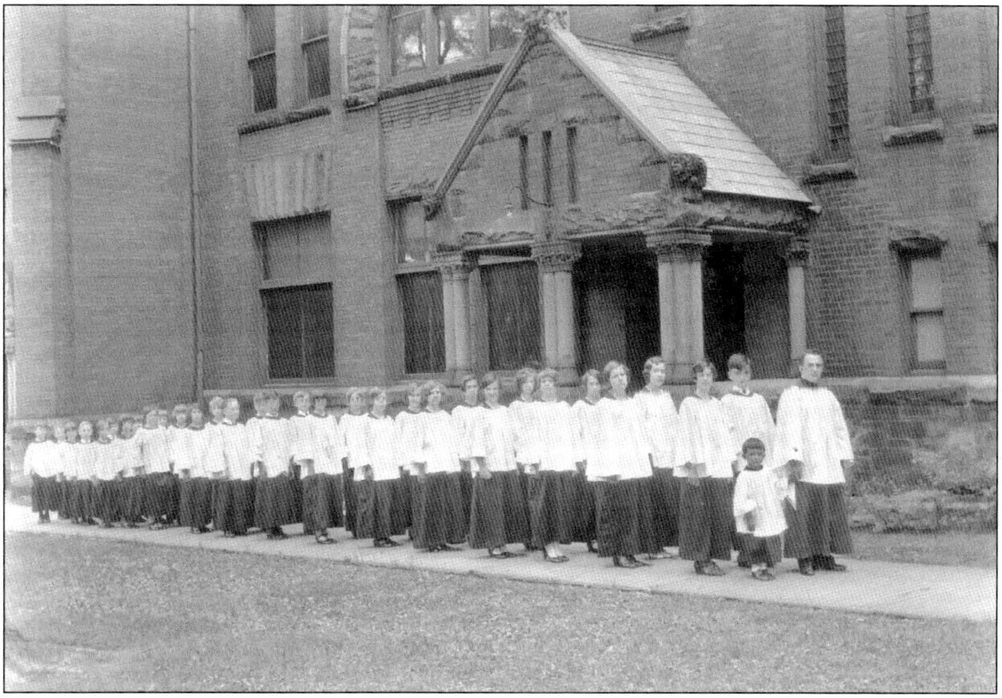

Dr. William T. Henry arrived as pastor of the First Baptist Church in 1877. At that time, there were 346 people on the rolls. When he retired in 1921, the congregation numbered over 1,000. Shown here is the First Baptist Church youth choir about 1929. (Courtesy of Barbara Ramsdell.)

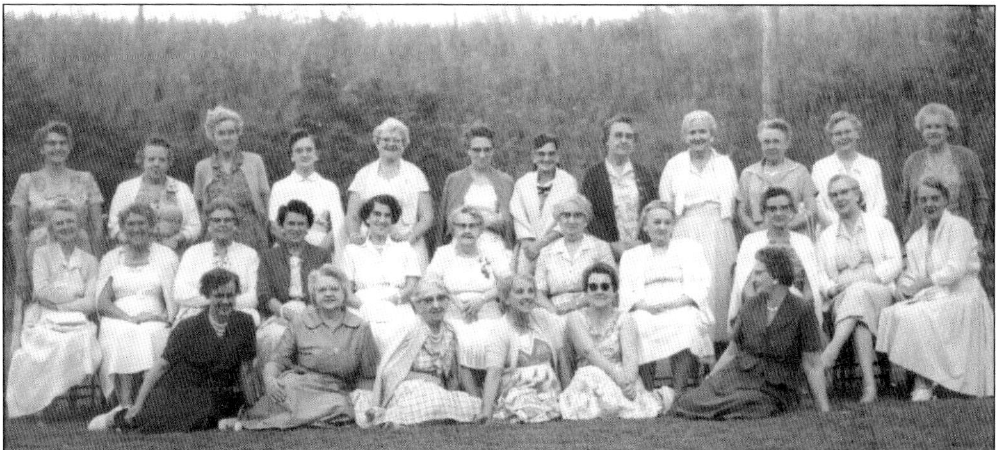

The Marytha Sunday school class of First Baptist Church celebrates the 90th birthday of teacher Nettie Davis (seated in the center of the first row) in July 1963. (Coauthor Archie Kieffer's mother is in the first row at far right.) (Courtesy of Barbara Ramsdell.)

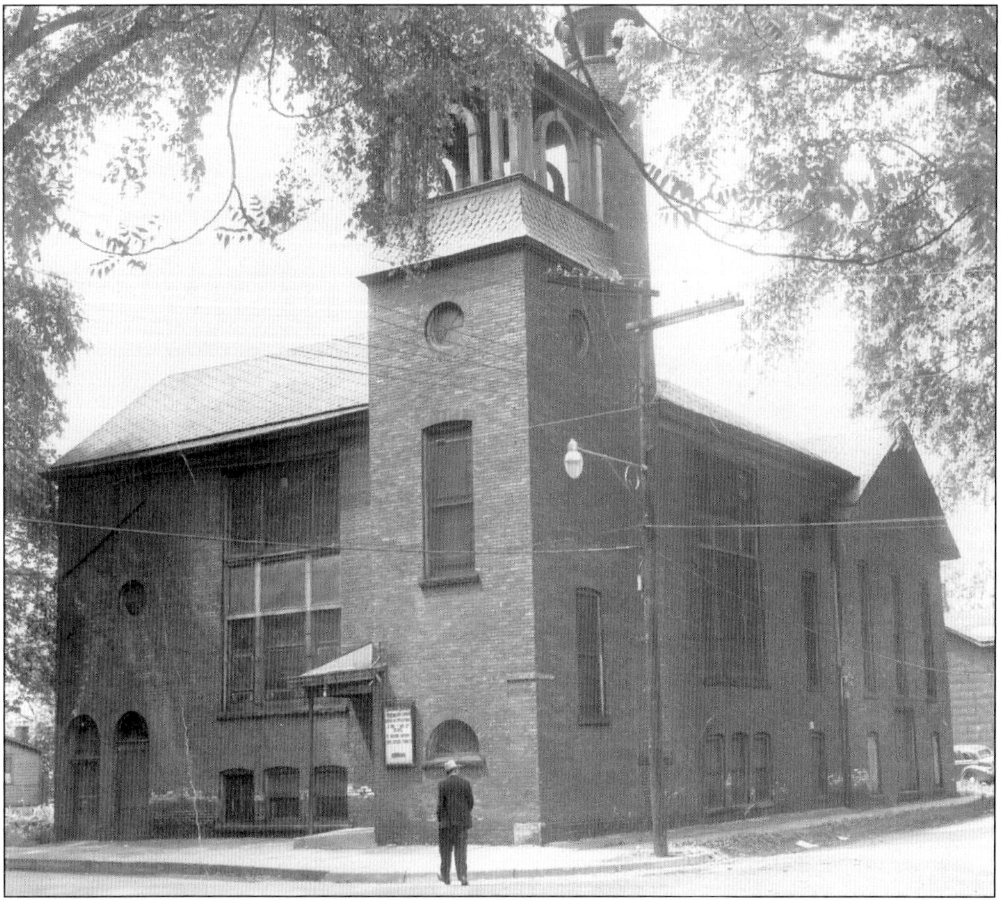

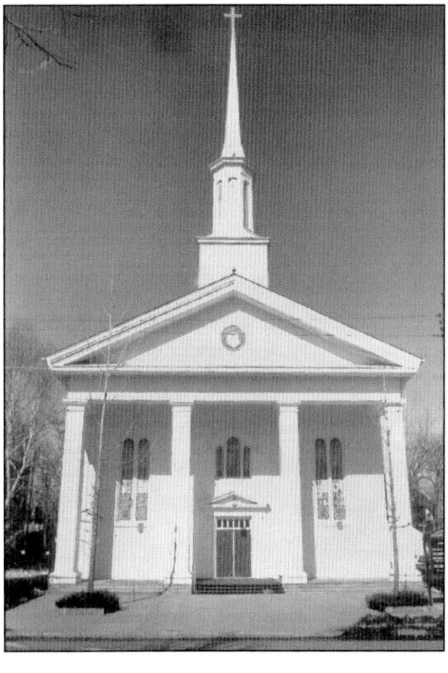

Cal Brewer wrote in the September 2008 *Chemung County Historical Journal* that the Frederick Douglass Memorial African Methodist Episcopal Zion Church was located where the former Jones Court Housing project now stands. The mission society named Zion began in 1840, when a meager community of "26 coloreds living in six households" began praying together in a house on Benjamin Street. As the population grew, so did the church. The site was acquired in 1951 by the Elmira Housing Authority. (Courtesy of CCHS.)

On September 17, 1899, the Evangelical Lutheran Church of the Holy Trinity was organized. The congregation purchased the former Hedding Church in 1903, and it was remodeled in 1969 to its present dimensions. The tip of the cross is 113 feet above the street. (Courtesy of CCHS.)

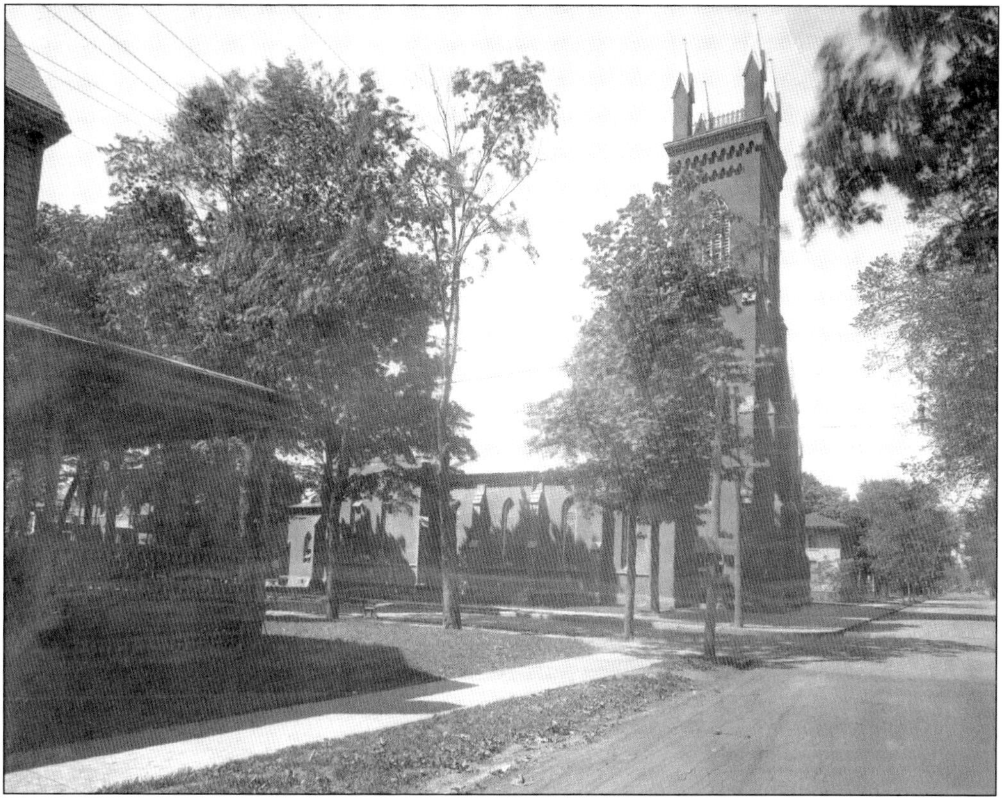

On October 11, 1845, Owen O'Hanlon sold a stretch of land on the corner of High and Market Streets to the Catholics of Elmira. Three years later, a small brick church, facing High Street, was erected and dedicated to Saint Peter and Saint Paul. Upon completion, the church was immediately too small. At a cost of $50,000, three years, and one life—that of Father John Boyle, who fell from the scaffolding and died in December 1856—the present building was finished. On July 19, 1857, Bishop John Timon came from Buffalo to consecrate and dedicate the church. (Courtesy of CCHS.)

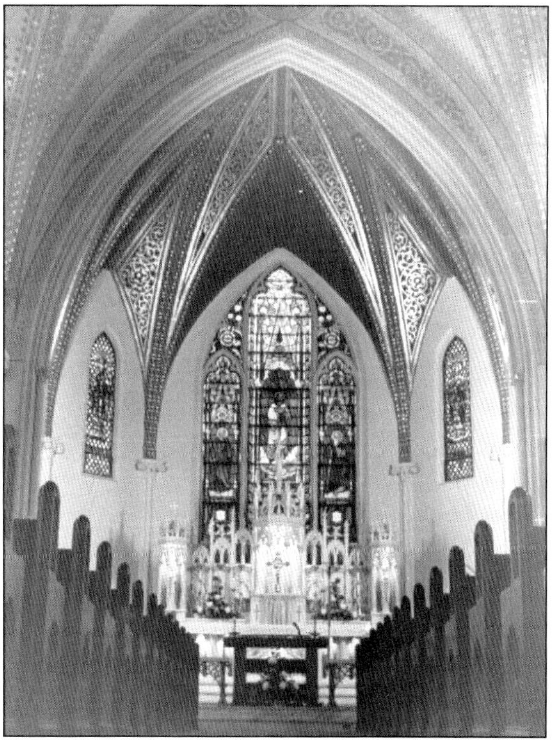

St. Peter and Paul's is the second-oldest Catholic church building in the Diocese of Rochester. It has survived a fire in 1900 and the floods of 1946 and 1972. Pictured here are the sanctuary windows at St. Peter and Paul's Catholic Church. (Courtesy of Parish Archives.)

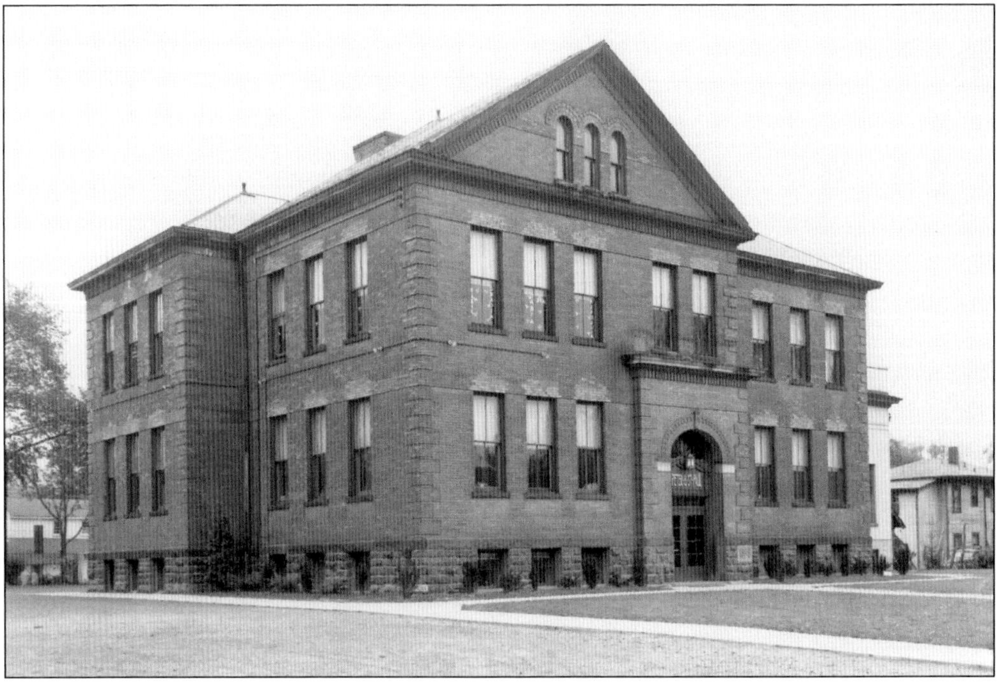

In his book on the history of Chemung County, Tom Byrne describes the origins of Catholic education in Elmira. St. Peter and Paul's parish school began in 1857. From 1867 to 1876, it operated on the so-called Poughkeepsie Plan. That meant it was incorporated into the public school system. The school board rented the building and paid the salaries of the teachers. It was here that the Catholic High School was inaugurated in 1930. It occupied the third floor. The school is shown here around 1957. (Courtesy of Parish Archives.)

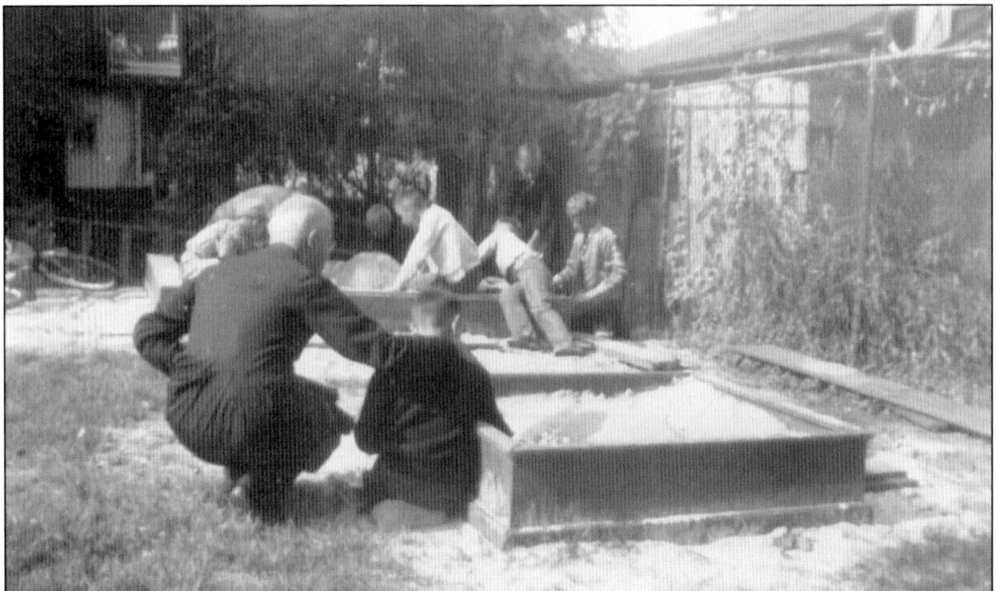

Father Merkel and Lawrence Sheahan play at the large and small sandboxes, which were a part of the playground at St. Peter and Paul's School, in August 1949. (Courtesy of Parish Archives.)

Elmira's original Polish Catholic residents worshipped in St. John the Baptist Church. As their numbers grew, they wished to have a national parish set up among them. Father John Pitasz, sent by Bishop Stephen Michael Vincent Ryan of Buffalo, purchased property on Davis Street, and St. Casimir's Church was erected there. This original building was replaced by the current structure in 1917. (Courtesy of St. Casimir's Church.)

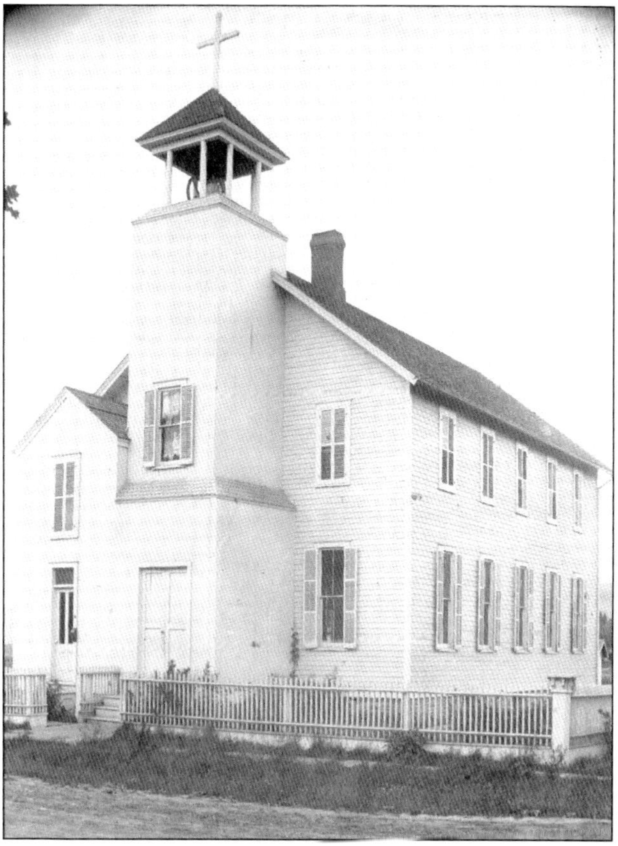

One way that patriotic Americans helped the war effort during World War I was raising money with Liberty Bond parades. St. Casimir's Parish sponsored this parade down Roe Avenue in 1918. Note Fire Station No. 3 and St. Casimir's Church in the background. (Courtesy of Ray Winieski.)

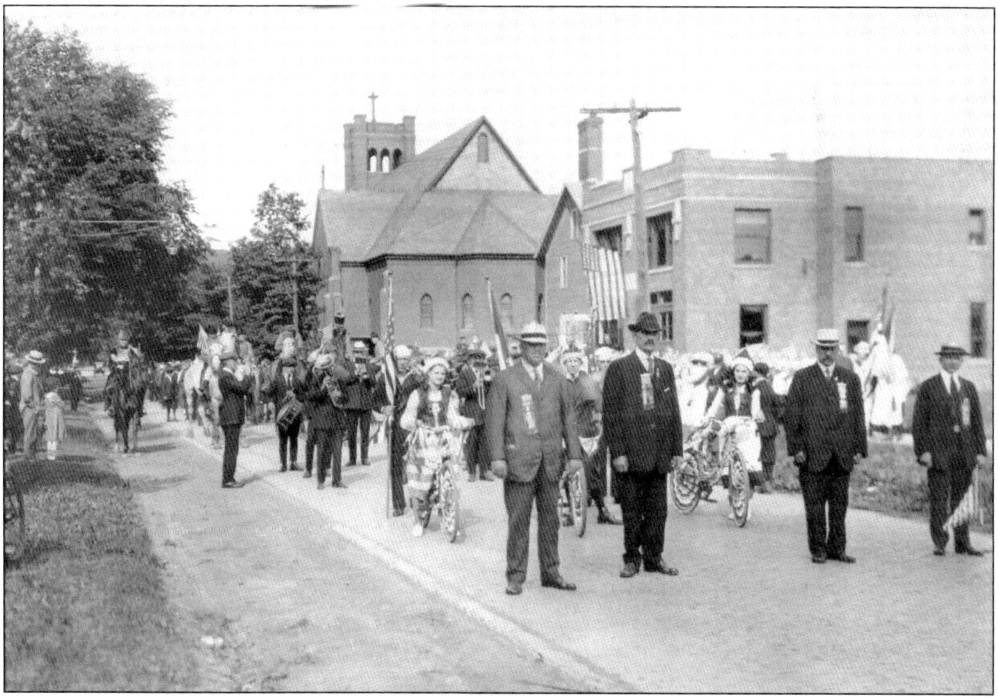

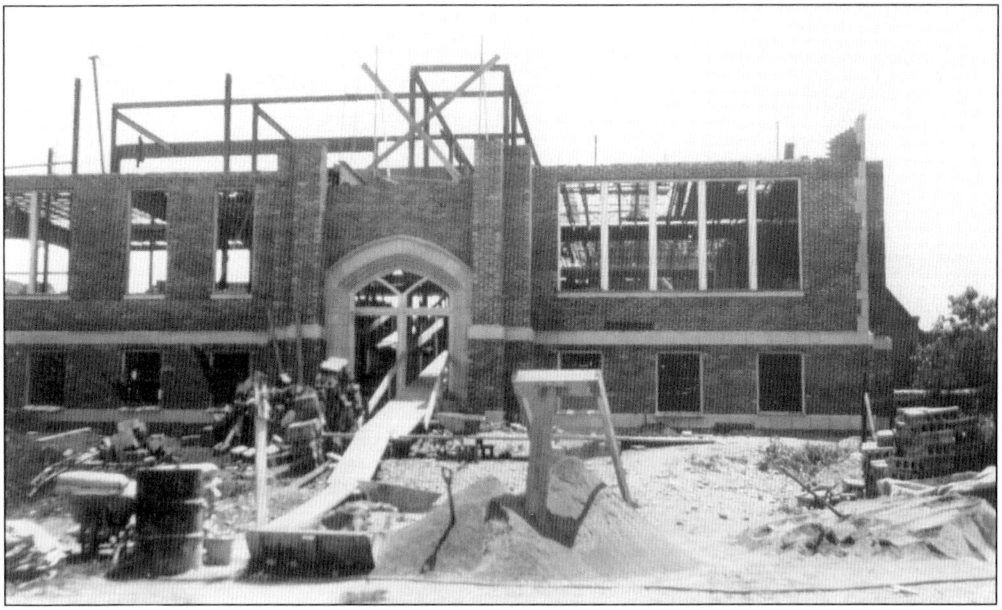

In 1921, the Reverend Joseph A. Balcerak, "Father Joe," purchased, under his own name and without diocesan permission, a half-block of land adjacent to the church property as a site for a new convent and school. He diplomatically informed the bishop of the diocese of his purchase and willingness to transfer the property. The new school was dedicated in 1930. It cost approximately $125,000 at the time of construction, and funds were raised almost exclusively by the Polish congregation. This photograph is from around 1929. (Courtesy of St. Casimir's Church.)

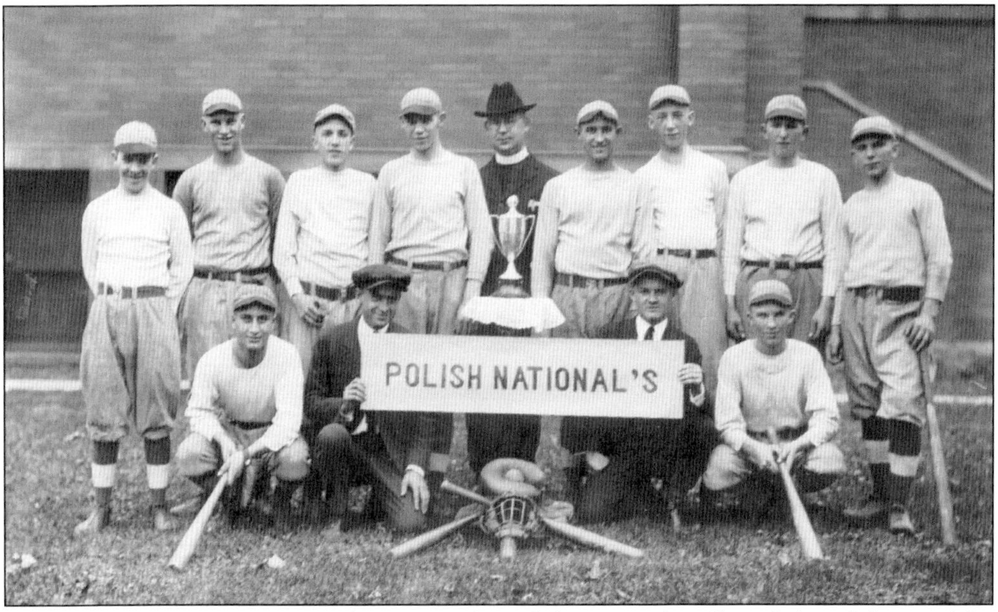

Baseball was a major pastime in the 1920s. The Polish National's reflected the solidarity of the Polish community. Pictured from left to right are (first row) Jimmy Frisk, Freddy Winiecki, "Jas" Christastie, and Thomas "Whitey" Malanoski; (second row) Danny Claire, "Rosy" Kozloski, Joseph Witucki, Michael Piekarski, Rev. Joseph A. Balcerak, Max Winieski, John Zuris, Joseph Stachowski, and John Kosmicki. (Courtesy of St. Casimir's Church.)

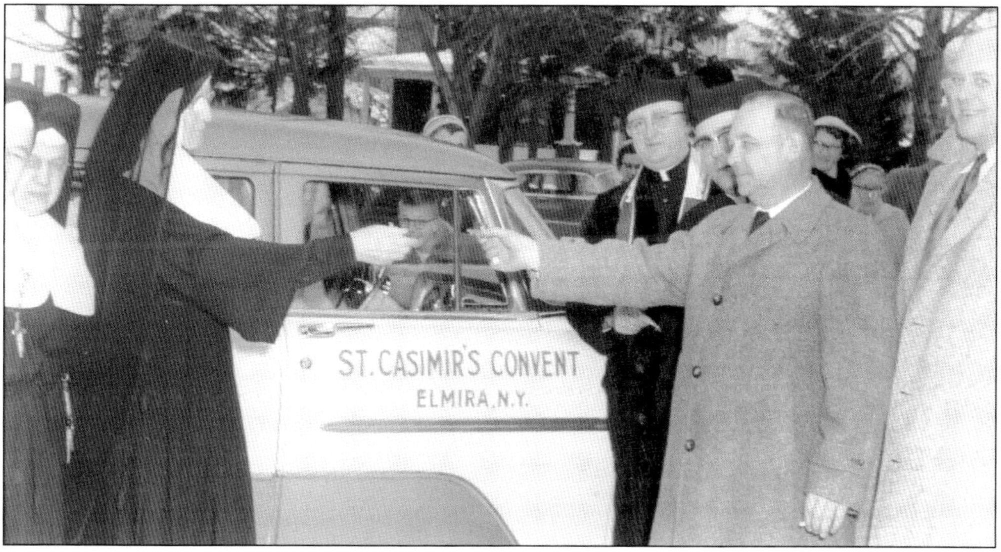

Edward Lepkowski, president of the St. Casimir's Recreation Club, presents to Sister Anne Catherine the keys to the first car for the Sisters of St. Casimir's Convent. Father Ladislaus "Walter" Szczepansiki, closest to the car, and Father Leonard Kujawski look on. (Courtesy of St. Casimir's Church.)

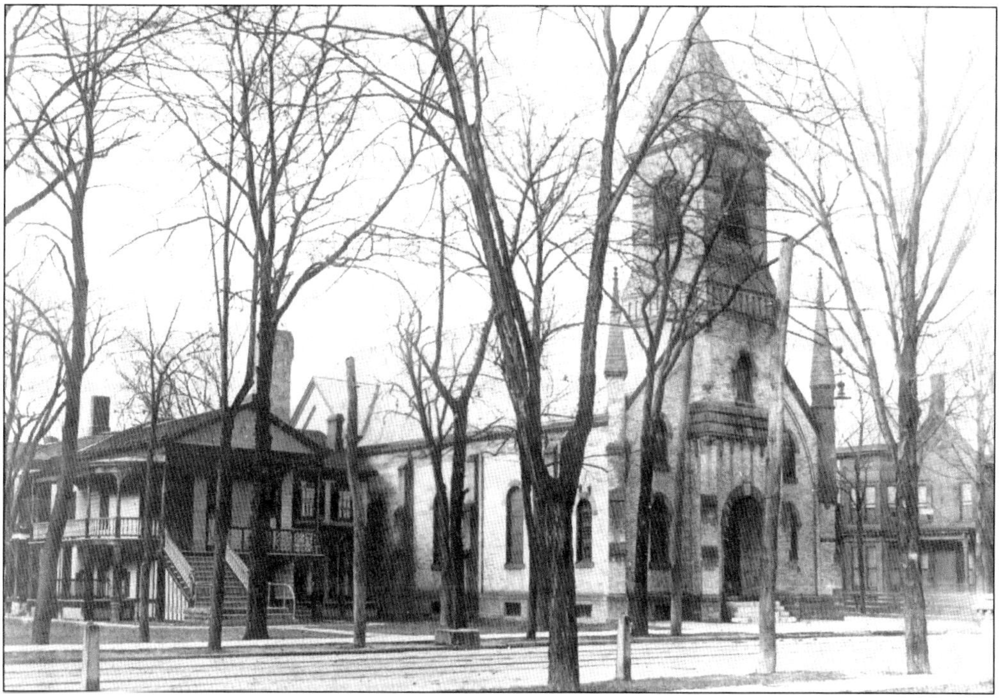

Germans were among the early settlers of Elmira. The Catholics among them attended mass at St. Peter and Paul's Church until 1866, when they formed a separate congregation. They had been encouraged as early as 1857 by a visiting German priest to form their own congregation. The cornerstone for St. John's Catholic Church's first building was laid in 1866. The site shown in this c. 1900 photograph is on the corner of Lake and Second Streets. It was purchased in 1890, the cornerstone was laid in 1891, and the church was dedicated in 1892. (Courtesy of the CCHS.)

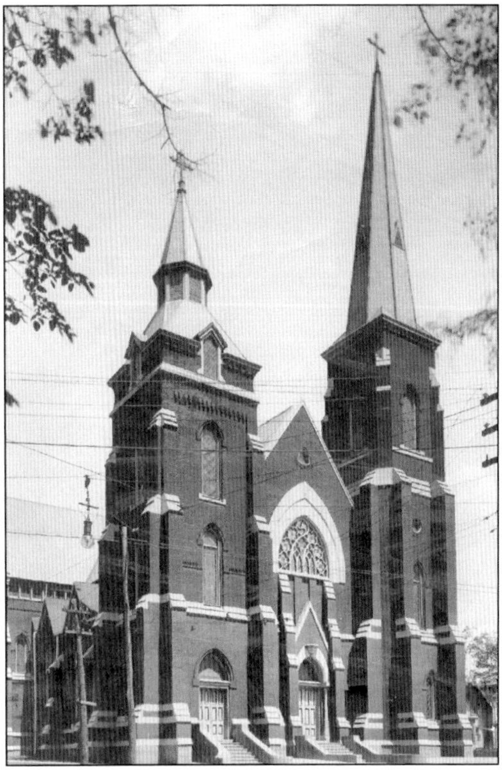

Located on Clinton Street between North Main Street and Park Place, St. Patrick's is the most conspicuous Catholic church in the city. It was built in 1871 and consecrated on December 13, 1875. The construction of this imposing church is due to the zeal and intelligence of the Reverend James J. Bloomer. Father Bloomer also purchased property diagonally across from the church for a house and a school. A three-story brownstone school was erected in 1893 and opened in 1894. St. Patrick's School was at one time the largest parochial school in Elmira. It is now the site of the St. Patrick's Apartments. (Courtesy of CCHS.)

The 25th anniversary dinner for the Right Reverend Monsignor William J. Brien was held at Notre Dame in 1957. Auxiliary Bishop Lawrence B. Casey attended. It was also the kickoff for a fund drive for St. Patrick's School. (Courtesy of Parish Archives.)

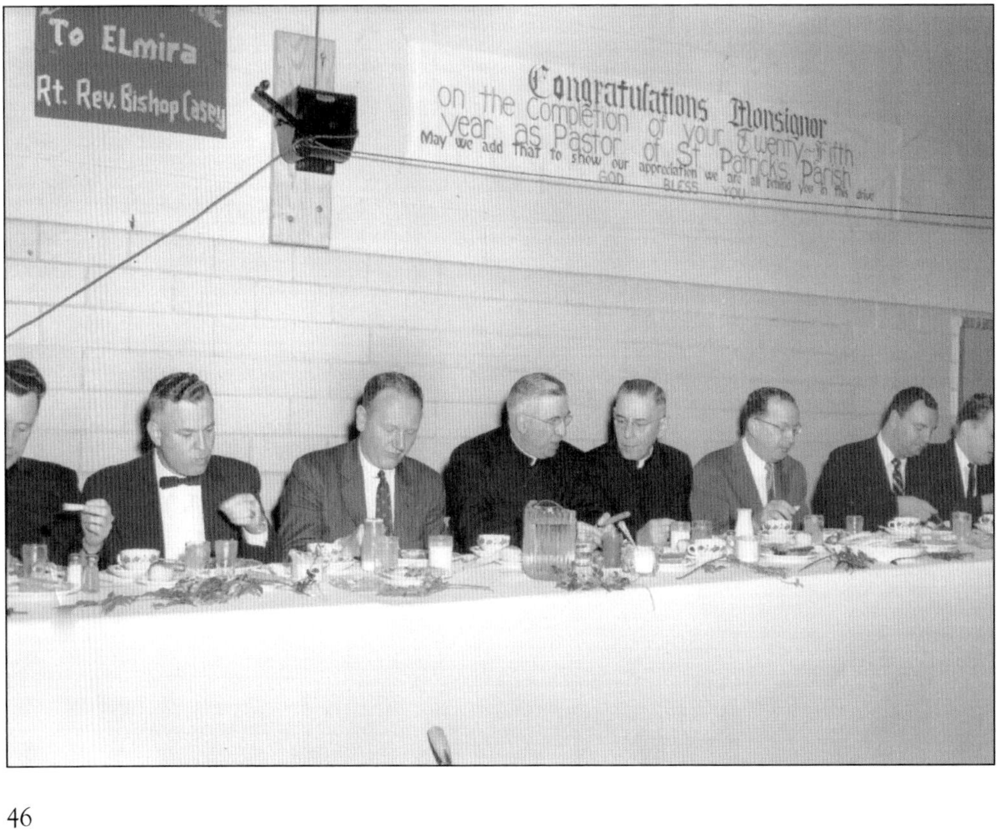

Around 1905, the Italian population of the city began to grow as immigrants came to work for the railroads. Fr. Ernest Ziegan and the Italian community arranged to conduct mass in St. James Hall, the auditorium in St. Patrick's School. In 1909, construction of a two-story brick building with a basement auditorium began. St. Anthony's opened in 1911. Fires damaged the church in 1921 and 1933, but the fire of 1947 substantially destroyed the whole building. This photograph is from sometime before 1947. (Courtesy of Parish Archives.)

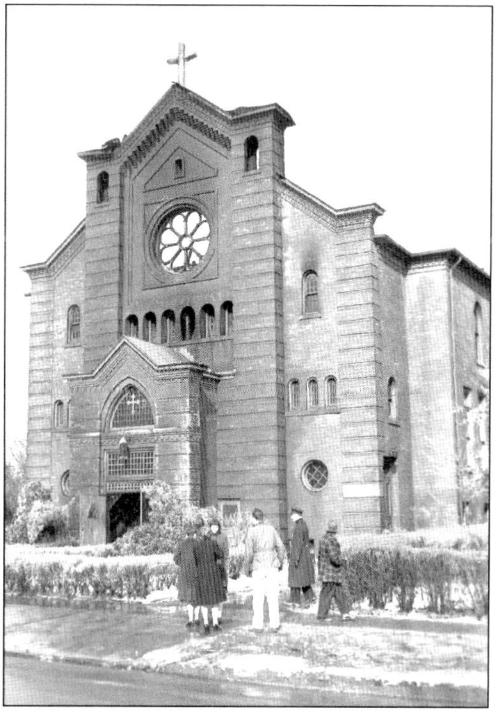

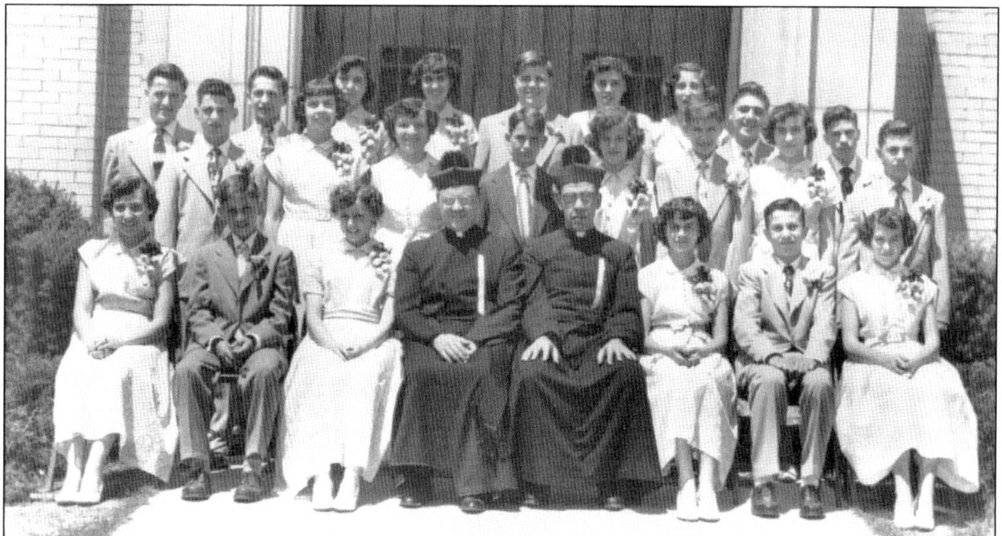

When St. Anthony's opened in 1911, the church was on the second floor and the school occupied the first floor. At its first commencement in 1912, there were two children in the graduating class. The class of 1951 posed for this photograph. Shown here are, from left to right: (first row) Rosemarie Antuzzi, Robert Chalk, Joan Canzonesi, Rev. Albert L. Simonetti, Rev. Nicholas P. Alletto, Teresa DiSanto, Nicholas Rossi, and Helen Saravullo; (second row) James Cleary, Rosemary Getola, Marietta Pilla, Robert Sophia, Charlotta Ward, Peter Romani, Ann Marie Tomara, and Charles Ponzi; (third row) Philip Vella, Daniel Mandell, Carmella Cafolla, Ermina Capozzi, William Riley, Mary Ann Rullo, Theresa Fabrizio, Anthony Della Salla, and William Dandrea. (Courtesy of Parish Archives.)

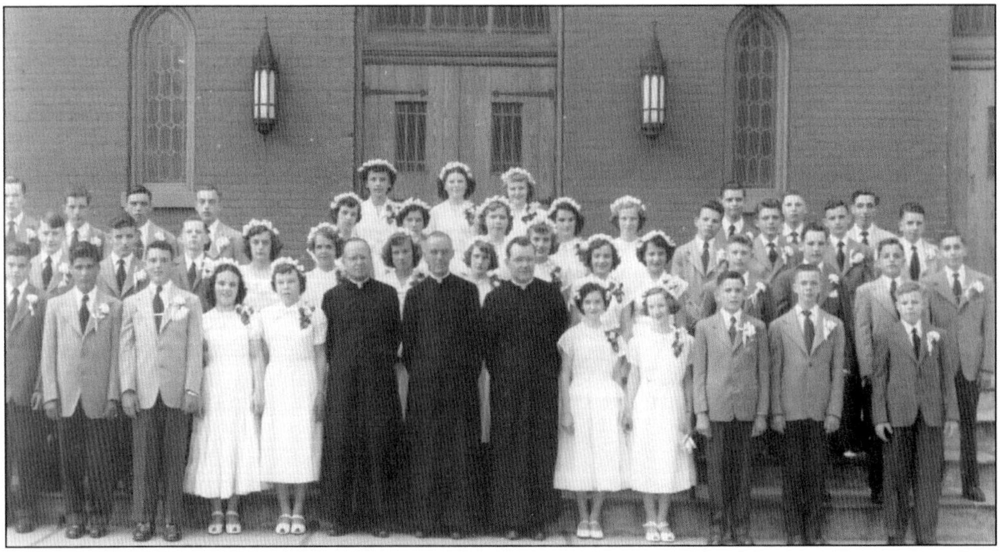

St. Mary's parochial school dates from around 1880. A new brick building was constructed in 1898, with 335 registrations. Fr. Thomas Toole, pastor from 1944 to 1958, twice enlarged the parish school facilities, adding a gymnasium and auditorium in 1952. Pictured here are members of the 1949 St. Mary's School graduation class. (Courtesy of Parish Archives.)

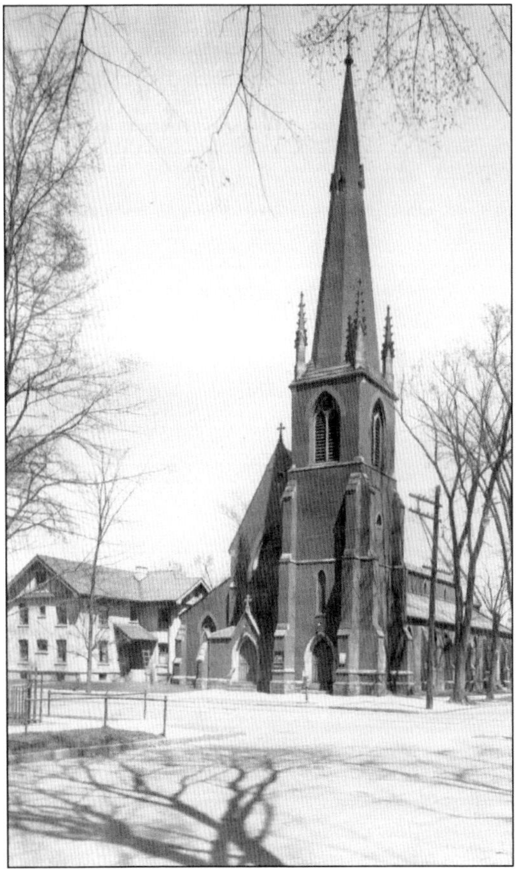

Trinity Episcopal Church was organized in 1833. The report from the *Gospel Messenger* stated, "The prospects of this new parish are in a high degree favorable and, if the services of an active and devoted clergyman could be had for it, it would afford an abundant harvest to his labors. It is expected that measures will be immediately taken to erect church." A new church was consecrated in 1837, replaced by the current building in 1858 under the leadership of Rev. Andrew Hull. The magnificent all-brick steeple is 11 stories high. This photograph is from around 1915. (Courtesy of Trinity Episcopal Church.)

A beautiful and prominent memorial at Trinity is the Arnot Memorial Chapel. Consecrated on November 28, 1882, it was the gift of Marianna Arnot Ogden. The brick and stone building, built in the 13th-century style, has a sundial above the chancel window, lending the building the look of an old English parish church. (Courtesy of Trinity Episcopal Church.)

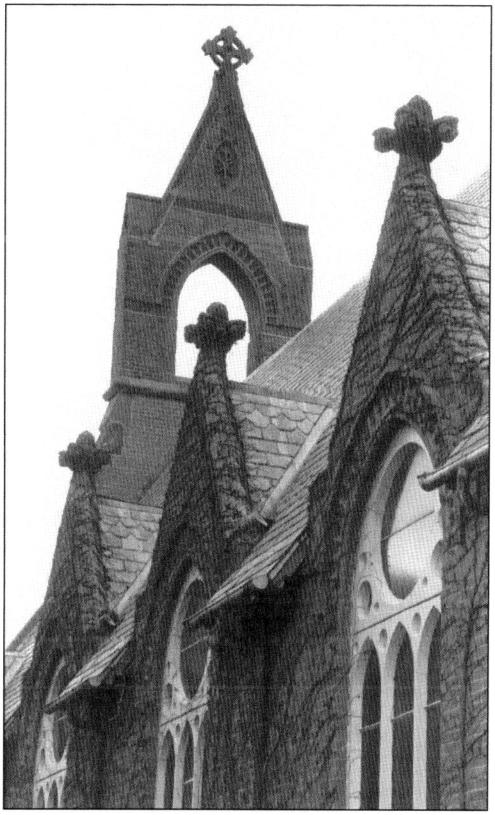

The Reverend Henry E. Hubbard served Trinity from 1917 to 1953. His service to young people was noteworthy. During his tenure as scoutmaster, 62 boys advanced to the rank of Eagle. He used his own summer place on Cayuga Lake as a camp for the youth. He also built impressive basketball teams that took many trophies. He saw to it that all age groups had some activities, from 2¢ suppers to dances. It was a real "community church," in that no one was asked if he or she were a parishioner in order to partake in the events. (Courtesy of Trinity Episcopal Church.)

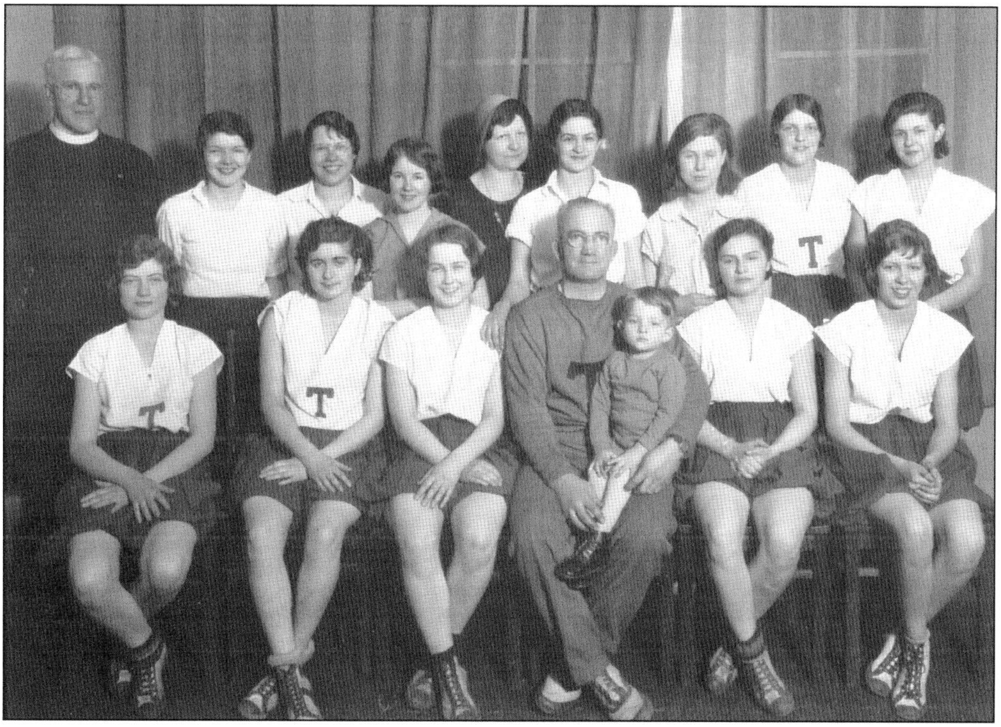

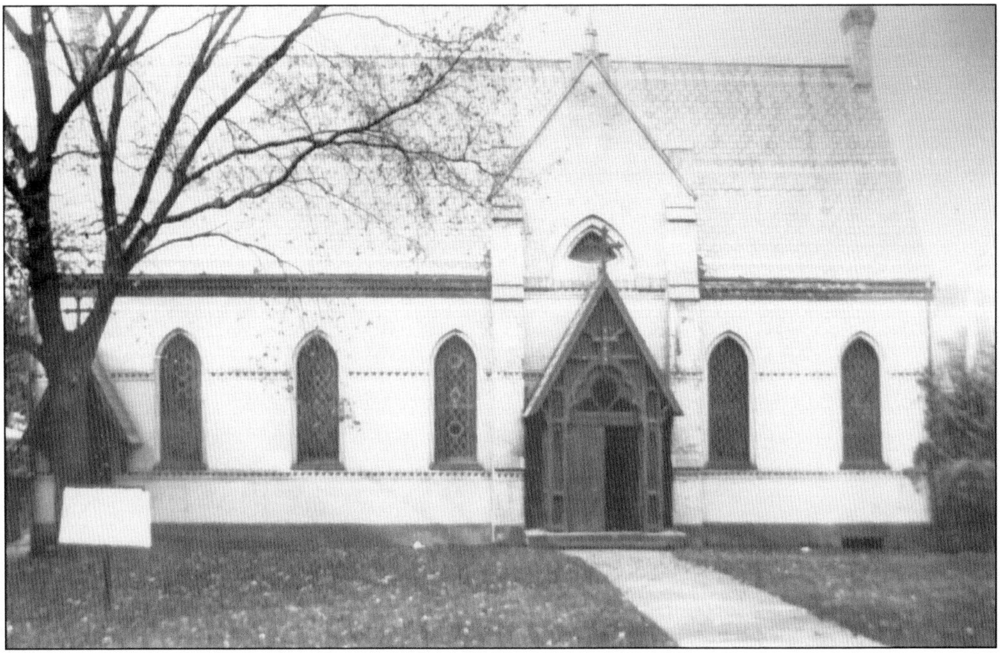

Grace Episcopal Church Parish was founded on May 9, 1864, by 47 families who moved from the Mother-Church in Elmira, Trinity Parish. The separation was caused by issues connected with the Civil War. The first church of Grace Parish was consecrated on Epiphany, 1866, and served the parish until 1906, when it was replaced by the current building. A fine of $1 was imposed on any member failing to attend vestry meetings, and a subscription list was started for church purposes. (Courtesy of Grace Episcopal Church.)

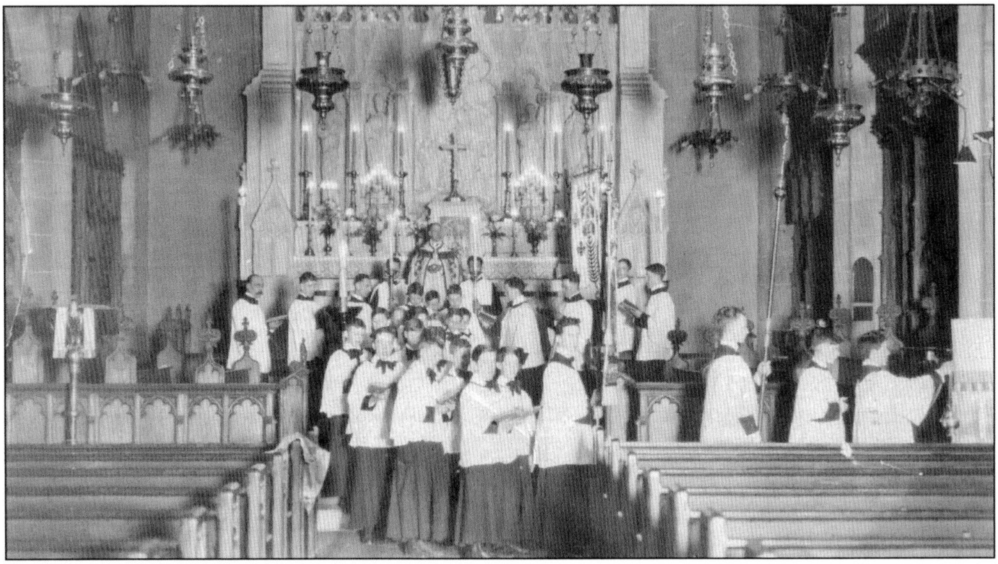

The present building was designed by the Reverend Frederick W. Burge of Westfield, New York, architect, with Otis Dockstader of Elmira as associate architect. The beautifully designed nave of the church is 95 feet in length, the span is 30 feet, and the breadth, including aisles, is 56 feet. The height from the floor to the spring of the roof is 44 feet and, to the ridge of the ceiling, about 50 feet. (Courtesy of Grace Episcopal Church.)

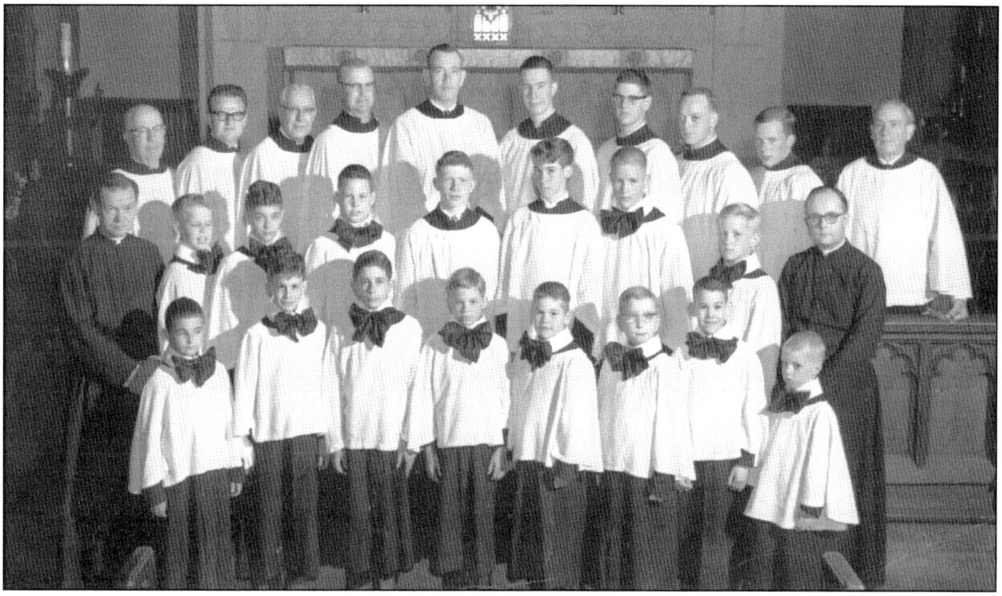

The Grace Church choir of boys and men was organized in 1908. William H. Morvan took charge of the choir in 1912. As recounted in local newspaper the *Telegram* of October 5, 1924, Morvan, in answer to the question, "Why are so many Episcopal Church choirs made up of boys and men instead of women and men?" said, "Boys in a church are not just a fad . . . the quality of the boy voice renders it especially fit for use in the services of the church. . . . The maintaining of boy choirs and choir schools has been one of the ideals of the Anglican (English) church for centuries." (Courtesy of Grace Episcopal Church.)

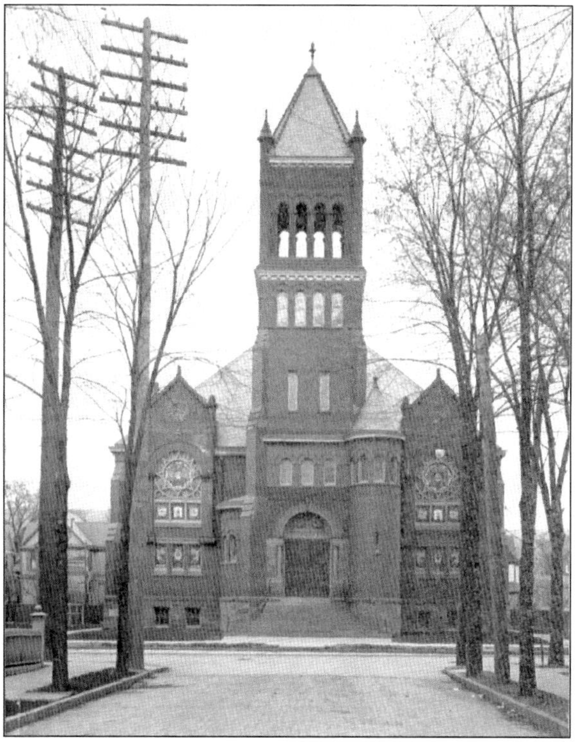

On October 1, 1874, it was resolved to form a German Evangelical church. Members met in the Central Baptist Church until the decision was made in 1876 to construct their own building. The cornerstone was laid in September 1877. The present church, shown here around 1906, was built in 1898, and the first service was held on August 8, 1899. Today, the "German Church" is the First United Church of Christ, the result of a 1957 merger of the Congregational and Evangelical and Reformed groups. (Courtesy of the First United Church of Christ.)

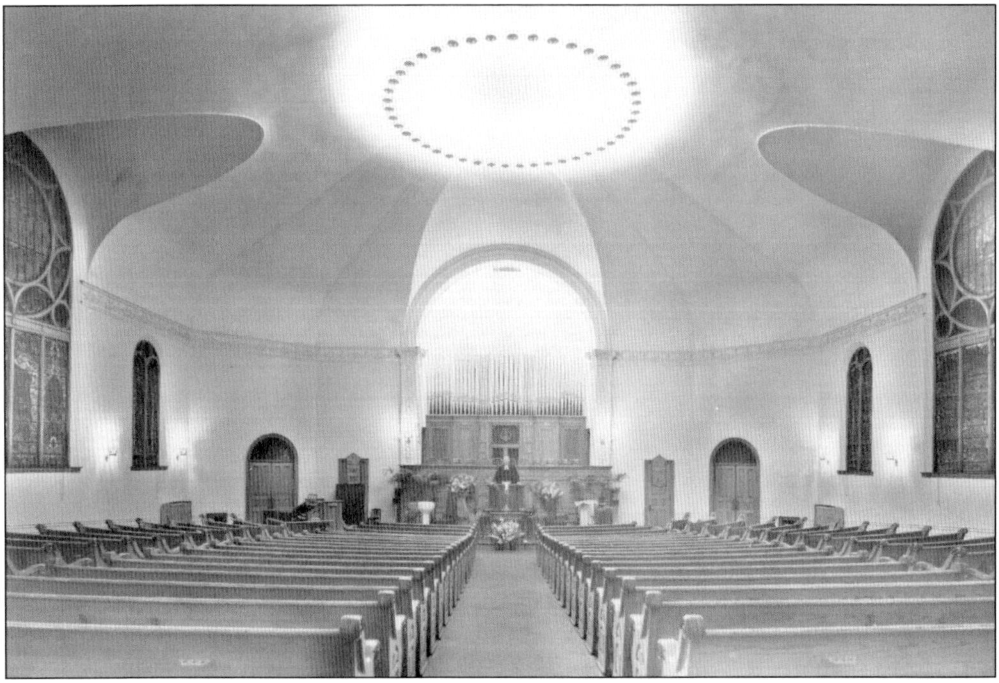

The dedication of the new building was held on August 8, 1899. Among the ministers present was Rev. Thomas K. Beecher. A sermon in German was preached by Rev. Theodore H. Braun of Corning. His subject was "The Corner Stone." Pictured is the church sanctuary around 1937. (Courtesy of the First United Church of Christ.)

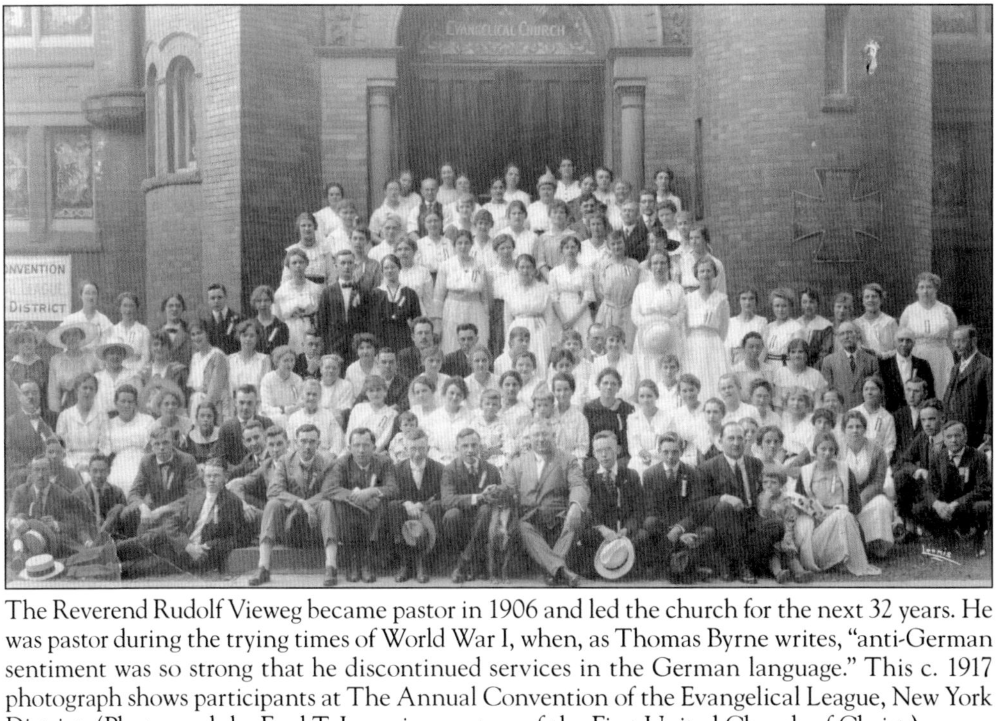

The Reverend Rudolf Vieweg became pastor in 1906 and led the church for the next 32 years. He was pastor during the trying times of World War I, when, as Thomas Byrne writes, "anti-German sentiment was so strong that he discontinued services in the German language." This c. 1917 photograph shows participants at The Annual Convention of the Evangelical League, New York District. (Photograph by Fred T. Loomis, courtesy of the First United Church of Christ.)

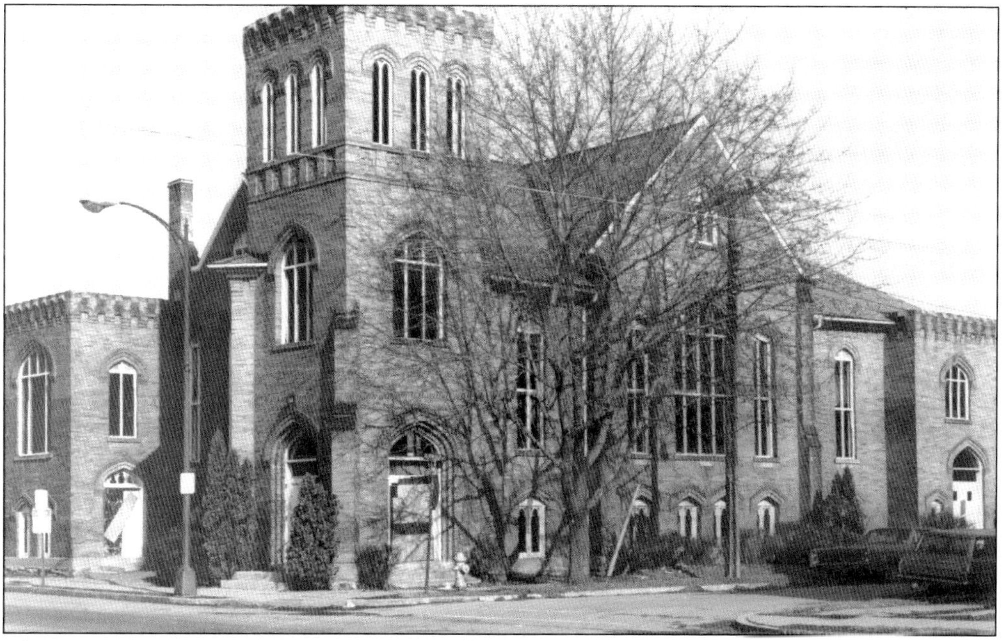

The religious movement known as the Disciples of Christ, or Christian Church, was born in 1809 in Kentucky. When people from that area came to Elmira in the 1890s, they felt a need to establish a church. On October 20, 1895, 36 people signed a charter to organize one, and they incorporated in 1898 as the First Church of Christ of Elmira, Disciples of Christ, with a membership of about 200. They purchased an old two-story brick building on the corner of South Main and Partridge Streets, which they had been renting for $3,000. A new church building was completed on the site in 1906 (and demolished after the Flood of 1972). Shortly after the building opened, the minister resigned and the congregation found itself in considerable financial difficulty. Through the efficient guidance of Rev. Charles M. Kreidler and the efforts of dedicated members, the church regained financial stability. The building is shown in the undated photograph above. The c. 1918 image below shows the choir, with Reverend Kreidler seated behind the pulpit and organist Edna McKane at the organ. (Courtesy of Central Christian Church.)

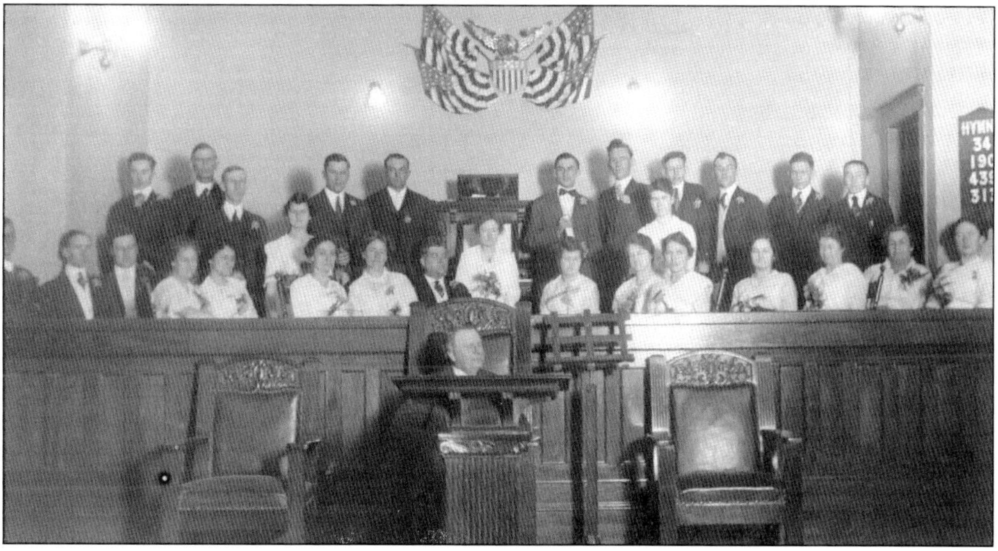

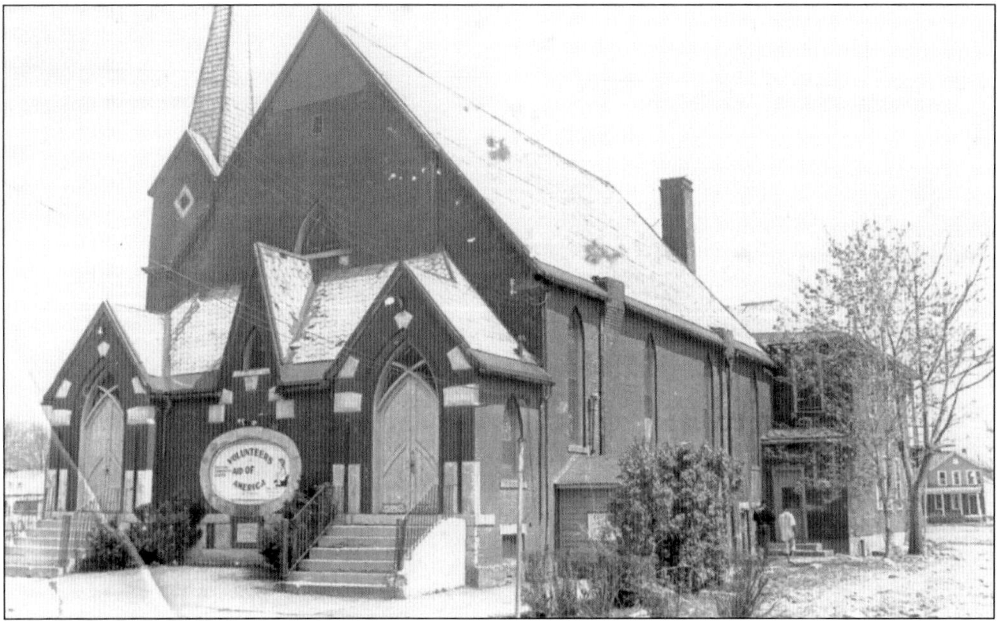

The Congregation B'nai Israel's founders erected a white frame building on High Street between East Water and John Streets. At the time, 29 members were assigned seats, and the service was a traditionally Orthodox one. The original building was replaced in 1886 by the High Street Temple, shown here. In 1950, the temple was sold to the Volunteers of America. In 1951, the cornerstone was laid for a new temple at the corner of West Water Street and Guinnip Avenue. (Courtesy of CCHS.)

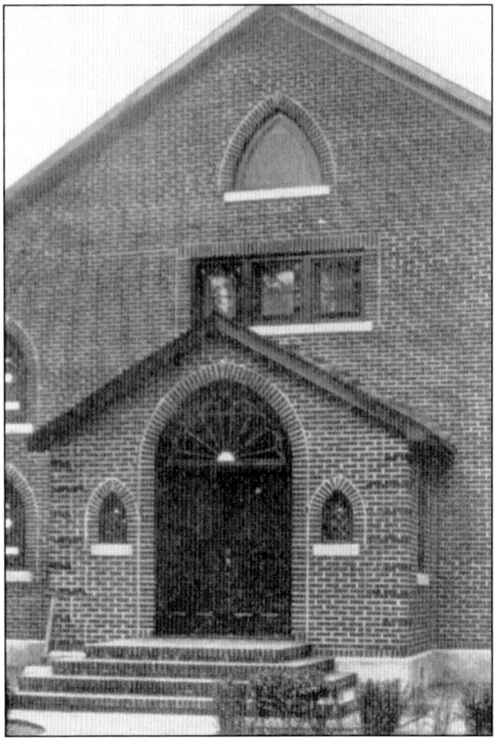

As the years passed, more Jews arrived in the community. Over time, differences arose, and the Jewish community split. In 1883, the Congregation Shomer Adassh Benia Niestad (Shomray Hadath) was formed. When the opportunity arose, they bought the white frame building on High Street from B'nai Israel. In a 1983 story in the *Star Gazette*, Ruth Golos said, "they moved the synagogue with teams of horses. . . . [T]hey had to cut down a tree to move it" to Orchard Street. That synagogue remained the home for the congregation until 1956, when it relocated to West Elmira. Pictured is the Orchard Street Synagogue around 1940. (Courtesy of CCHS.)

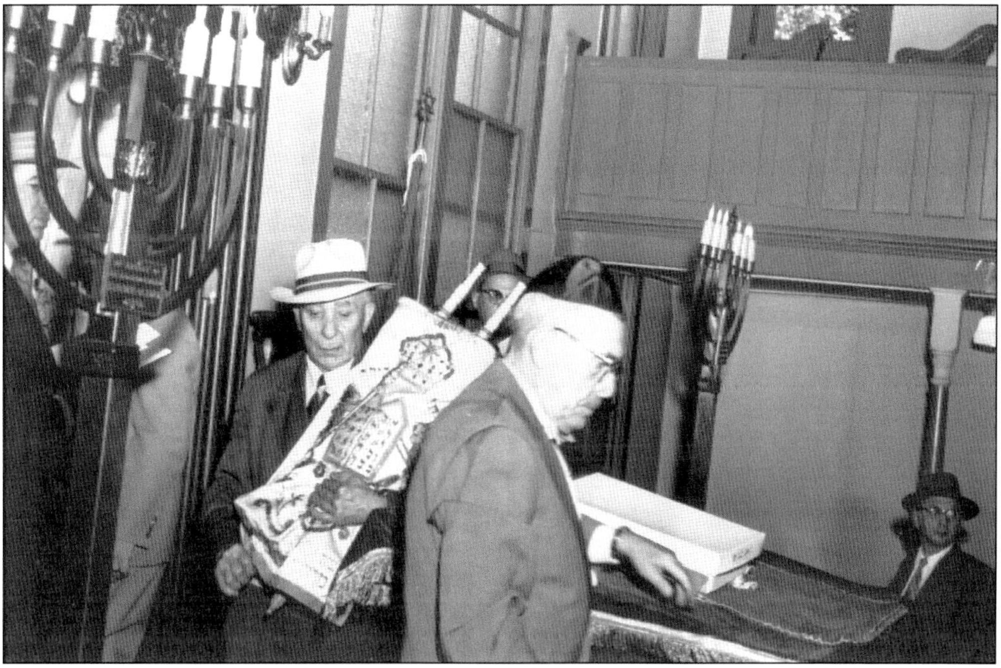

Under the leadership of Rabbi James I. Gordon, with Archie Sadinsky as president, the Orchard Street Synagogue was replaced by a new building at West Water Street and Cobbles Park. Shown above is the removal of the Torah from the Orchard Street building, carried by Phillip Schecter with Cantor Aaron Etkind. Below, Morris Fidelman (in front) leads the procession bringing the Torahs into the new synagogue around 1957. (Courtesy of Congregation Shomray Hadath.)

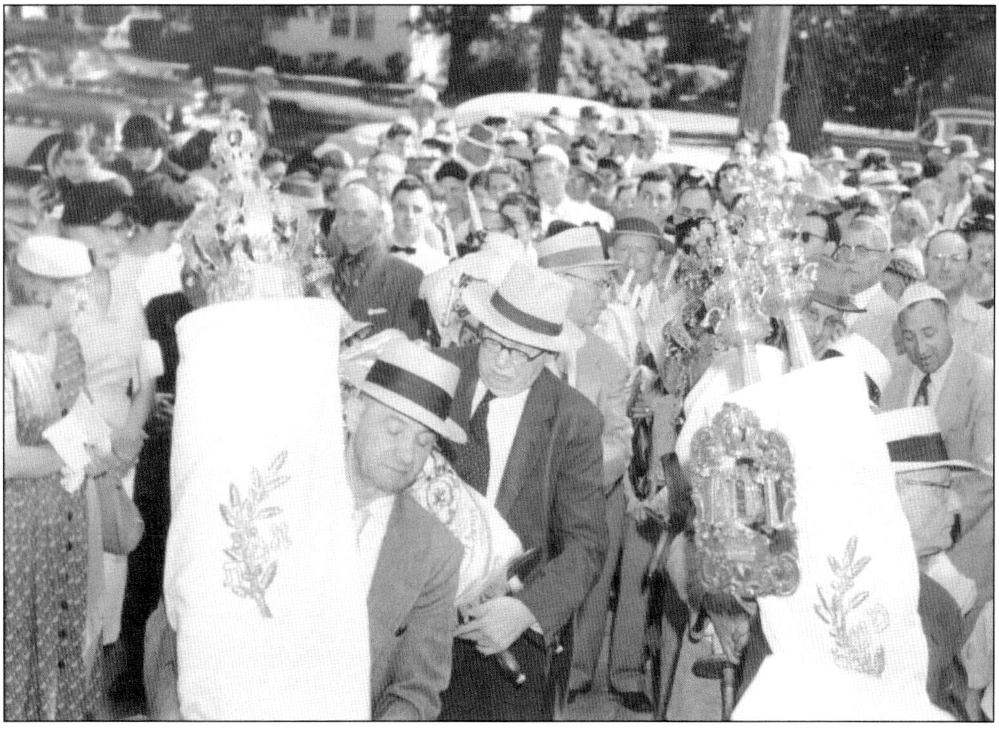

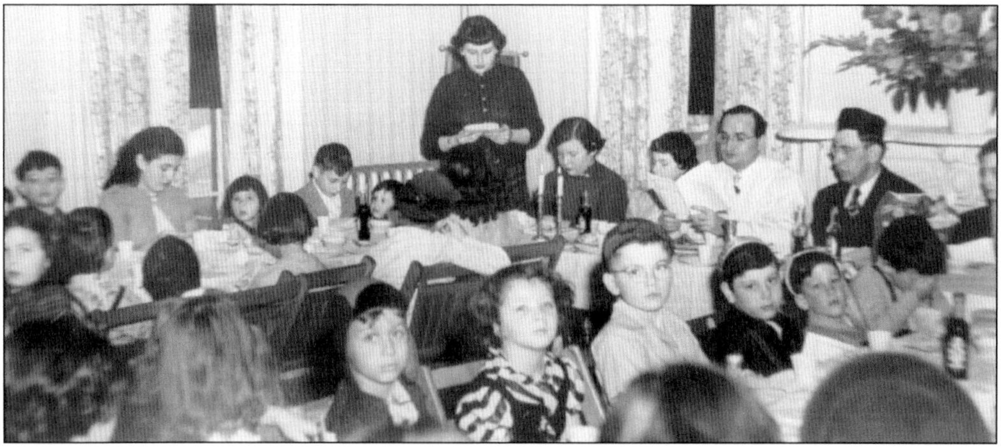

The Pesach Seder is a Jewish ritual feast that marks the beginning of the Passover holiday. It is performed by a community or multiple generations of a family and involves a retelling of the story of the liberation of the Israelites from slavery in ancient Egypt. Shown here is a Seder being held around 1950 at the Orchard Street Synagogue with Rabbi Norman Siegal (left) and Rev. Elmer Appel (right). (Courtesy of Congregation Shomray Hadath.)

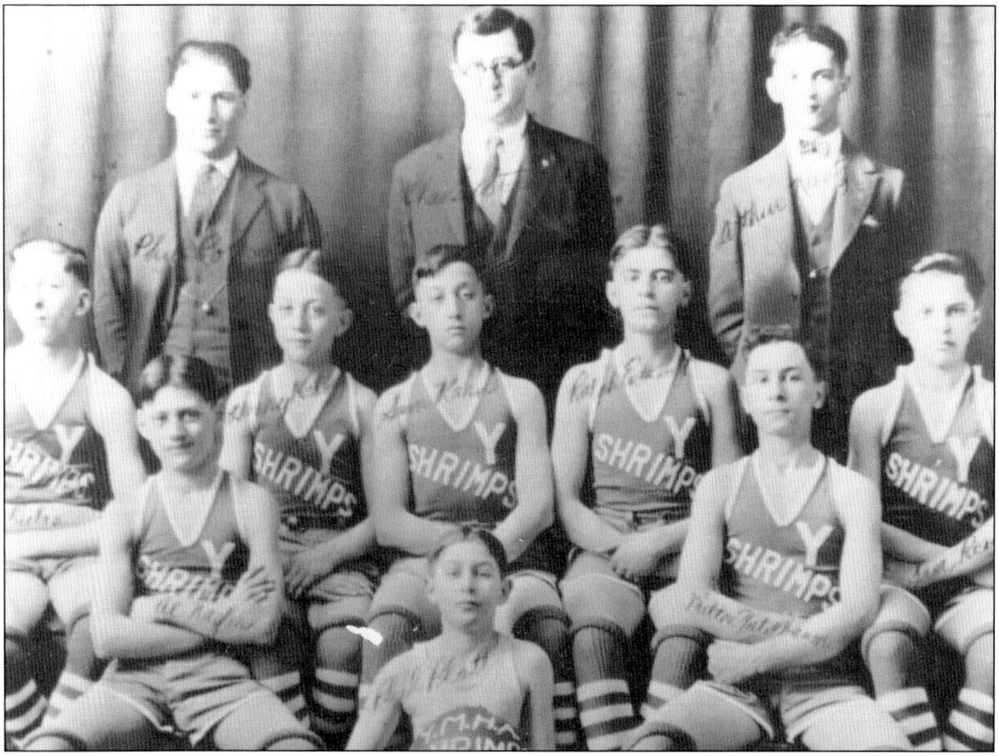

The Young Men's Hebrew Association, located on the corner of Madison and Market Streets, sponsored a variety of activities for the youth of the Jewish community. The Shrimps, shown in the 1924–1925 season, competed in city leagues. Pictured are, from left to right, (first row) Al Nagler, Phil Platt, and Milton Tatelbaum; (second row) Maurice Rubin, Heshie Kahn, Sammy Kahn, Ralph Etkind, and Sam Rosenheck; (third row) Phil Rothstein, Charles Epstein, and Arthur Kantz. (Courtesy of Congregation Shomray Hadath.)

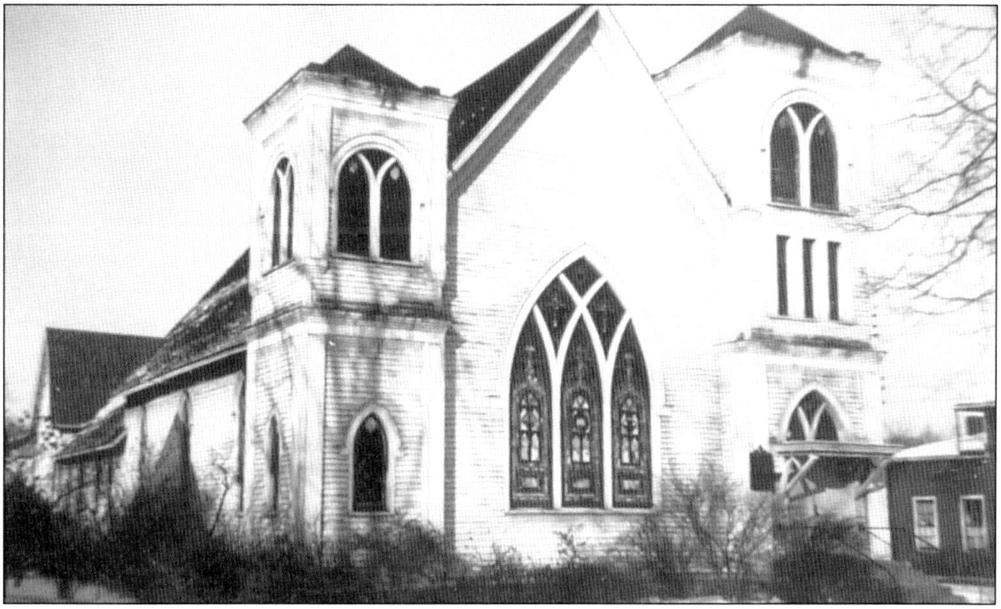

The Chemung River was an obstacle for churchgoers in the 19th century. The Presbyterians had a number of congregations south of the river. In 1882, the Franklin St. Presbyterian Church was organized. In 1957, that church merged with South Presbyterian Church to form Westminster Presbyterian Church, which relocated to the Maple Avenue site. The church is shown here around 1946. (Courtesy of CCHS.)

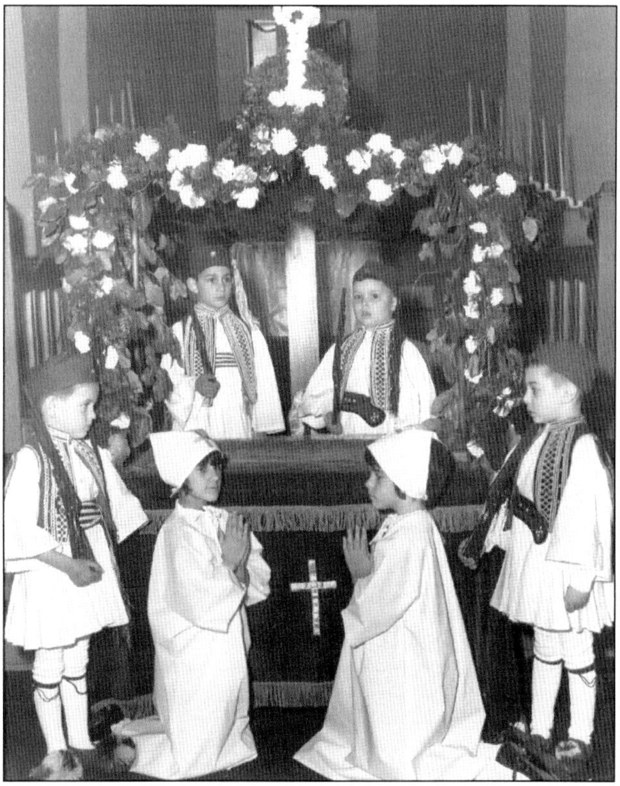

Elmira has a small Greek community, many members of which established homes on the south side of the city. In 1965, the Greek community purchased the former Franklin St. Presbyterian Church building. As Thomas Byrne writes, "In 1969, Mrs. Penelope Patros, widow of Thomas Patros, gained the privilege of naming the church St. Athanasios Greek Orthodox Church in honor of her deceased husband's patron saint." Pictured here in an Easter ceremony from around 1967 are, from left to right, (first row) unidentified, Stella Sidone, Gia Vichos, and Andy Patros; (second row) John Sindone and Danny Stevens. (Courtesy of Andy Patros.)

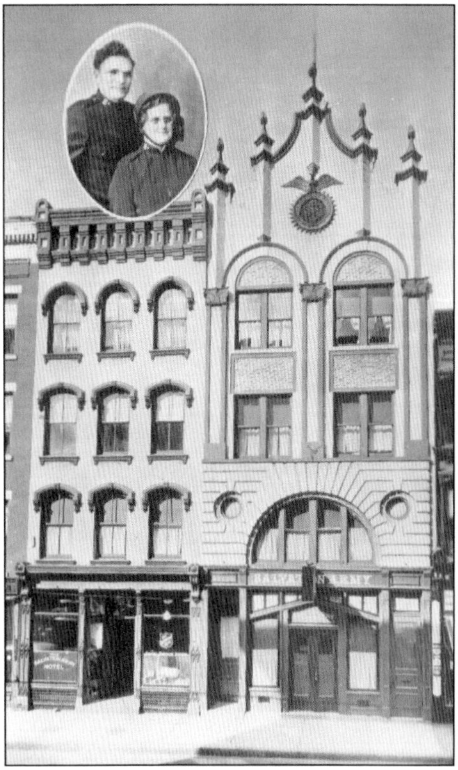

"Well, we're here and we mean to stay!" These were the words uttered by Captain Woodyard (pictured inset with his wife) in his opening address, June 10, 1884, when the Salvation Army officially opened in Elmira. In 1905, seeking a permanent and well-equipped home for its work, the group purchased the lot and four-story building at 153 Baldwin Street and an adjoining, unimproved lot. A four-story building was erected in the same year on the vacant lot and connected to the other structure. (Courtesy of Clarisa Fife.)

The chapter was busy in the 1920s and 1930s. There was a well-organized Sunday school, an anti-smoking league for boys, a Band of Love for little girls, Girl Guards, Boy Scouts, Young People's League, Y.P. Band, and a Senior Band. During the Depression, every noon a meeting was held at the Baldwin St. Citadel. The song "There's a Song For The Days That Are Trying" became known as the Depression Chorus. Pictured here are members at work around 1933. (Courtesy of Clarisa Fife.)

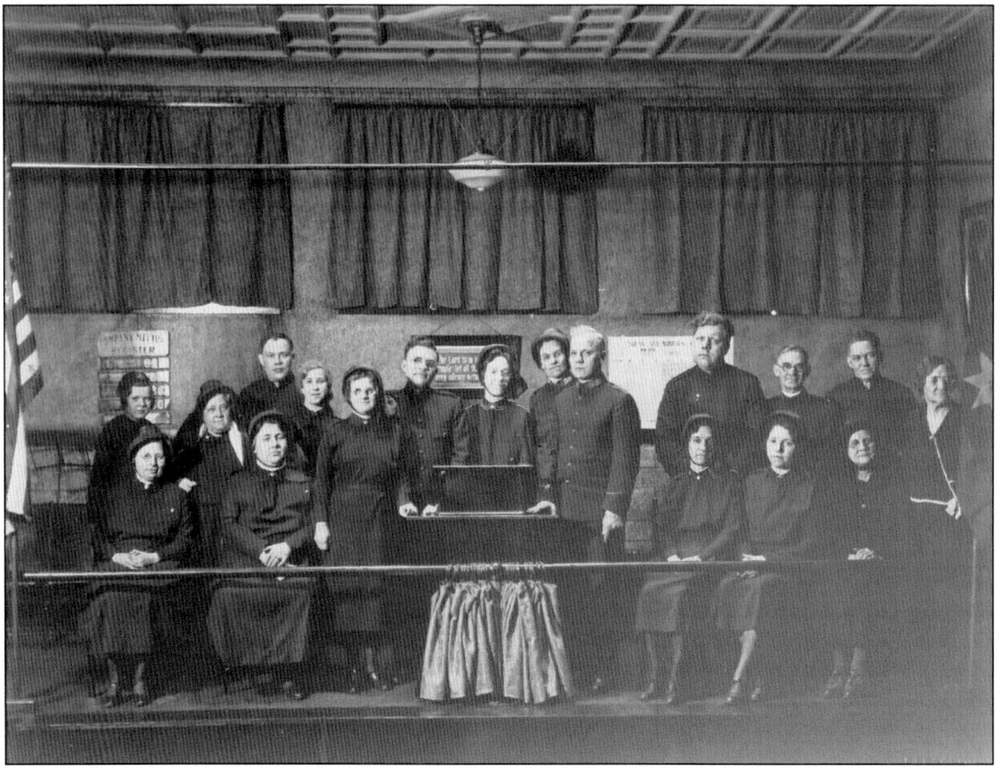

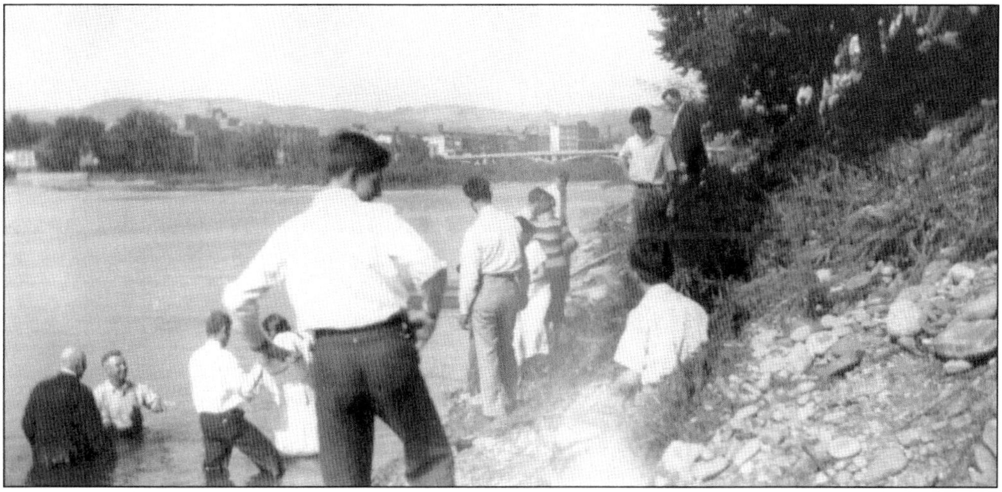

The Gospel Tabernacle laid its cornerstone in 1934 on Henry Street, where Tops Market is currently located. Pictured here is the pastor of the Gospel Tabernacle performing a baptism on the south side of the Chemung River around 1935. (Courtesy of John Arikian.)

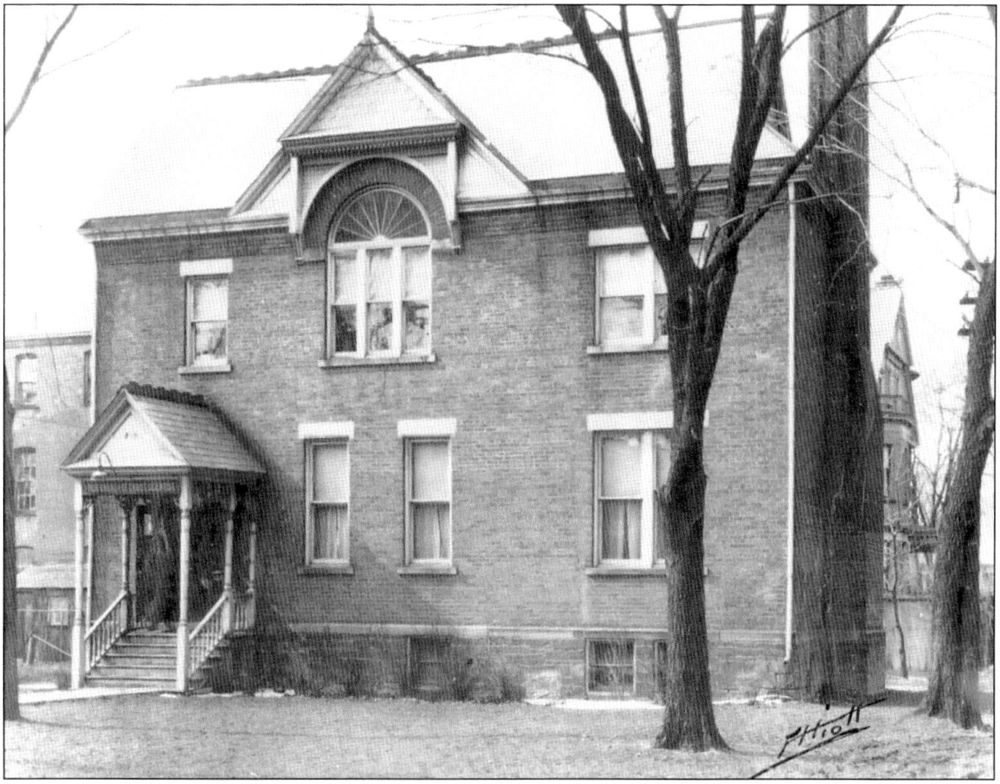

First Church of Christ, Scientist in Elmira was born on Wednesday evening, March 6, 1901, when eight believers gathered to consider the advisability of holding public services. It was decided to begin at once, and the first service was held the following Sunday evening. The Christian Scientists have had several homes. Their first permanent home, at 214 W. Gray Street, was purchased in 1909, the result of a generous gift. It is shown here in a 1922 photograph. This served until 1924, when the Diven residence was acquired. (Courtesy of CCHS.)

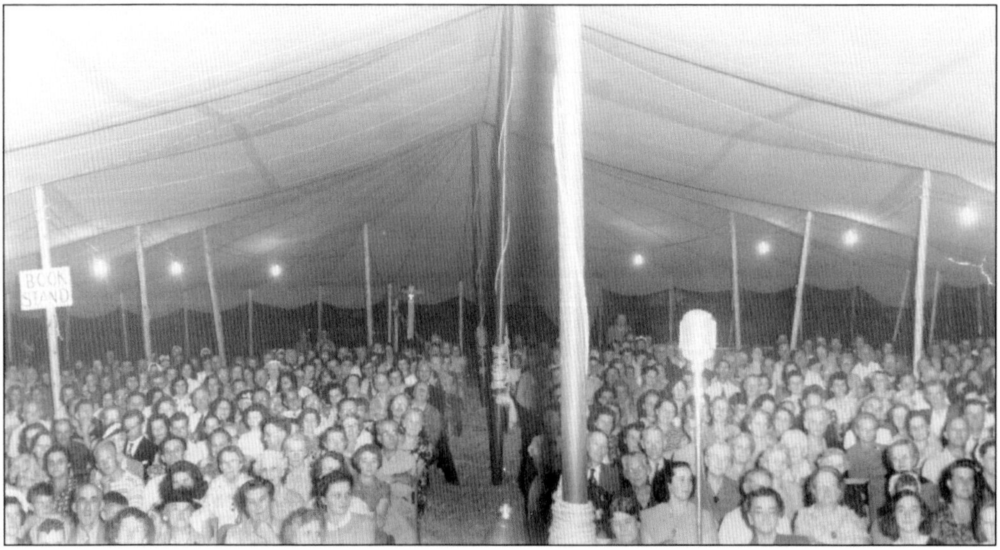

Peter and John Bedzyk rented the Springstead Shirt Factory, at 115 East Henry Street, to begin a church. On August 18, 1944, 25 people attended the first service of the Pentecostal Tabernacle. The offering was $6.50. The church seated 125 with camp meeting benches. People pledged and paid 60¢ for used theater seats. A series of tent meetings was held on College Avenue starting in 1947. The Reverend Richard Vinyard held a healing campaign in a "tent cathedral" located on the corner of East Miller and Falk Streets from July 21 to September 4, 1950. (Courtesy of Elmira Christian Center.)

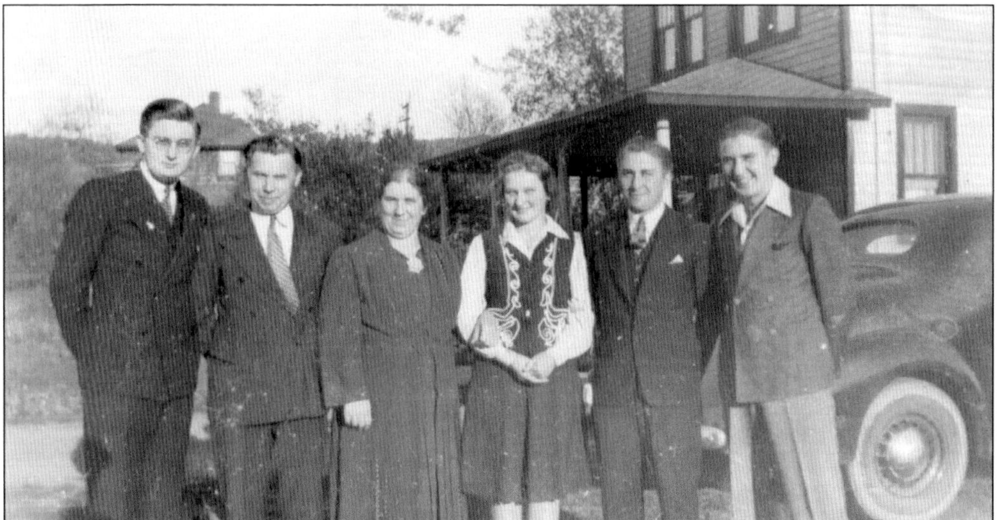

Brother John Bedzyk, founder of the Pentecostal Tabernacle, wrote of his parents, "My father (Mike) had three bad habits: gambling, drinking and beating up my mother. God sent a former priest to Elmira to preach the gospel. A number of Ukrainian families found the Lord, including my parents." When the Pentecostal Tabernacle obtained its first building in 1950, Mike Bedzyk mortgaged all of the property he owned and, according to his son, did much of the remodeling of the property that became the church. When the church expanded in 1955, Mike Bedzyk again mortgaged his property. Pictured from left to right are John Bedzyk, Michael Bedzyk Sr., Anna Bedzyk, Helen Bedzyk, Peter Bedzyk, and Michael Bedzyk Jr. (Courtesy of Elmira Christian Center.)

Three

THE ARNOT OGDEN MEMORIAL HOSPITAL AND ST. JOSEPH'S HOSPITAL

Physicians of Elmira, from the establishment of the village, had realized the need for a public hospital. In 1836, Chemung County and the Chemung County Medical Society were formally established. The Elmira Academy of Medicine was formed in 1852 to discuss cases and share medical knowledge. Drs. Silas O. and Rachel B. Gleason opened the "Water Cure" on Elmira's East Hill in 1857. They delivered the Clemens' children and provided care during their summer stays. The dismal conditions at the Elmira Prison Camp and the railroad boom, which resulted in "boxcar surgery," confirmed the need for organized care.

The Elmira Academy of Medicine sought to build Elmira's first general hospital in 1871, but an unstable economy thwarted fundraising. In 1887, Marianna Arnot Ogden, a patient of Dr. William Wey of the academy, gave Elmira its first general hospital. She was the eldest daughter of John Arnot, a pioneer Elmira merchant and banker. In 1875, at age 50, she married William Butler Ogden of Ogden, Utah. He was the first mayor of Chicago and the first president of the Union Pacific Railroad. He died two years after the wedding. When Marianna Ogden decided to endow the hospital, a friend persuaded her to make it a memorial to her family as well. Thus the name Arnot Ogden Memorial Hospital.

In 1873, a three-story Victorian building was erected on the east side of Elmira. Christened The Academy of Our Lady of Angels by its founders (the Sisters of St. Mary of Namur), it gained prominence as a training school for young women. In 1905, the academy closed and the building became vacant. In 1907, two prominent Elmira citizens, Dr. Daniel P. Murphy, a local surgeon, and his cousin, attorney John J. Hassett, working with Bishop Bernard J. McQuaid of Rochester and Mother Agnes, the superior of the Sisters of St. Joseph, purchased the property for a much-needed second hospital in Elmira. Renovations began in 1908 for its transformation into St. Joseph's Hospital. This was the first time in the 258-year history of the St. Joseph Order that its sisters would own and operate a hospital.

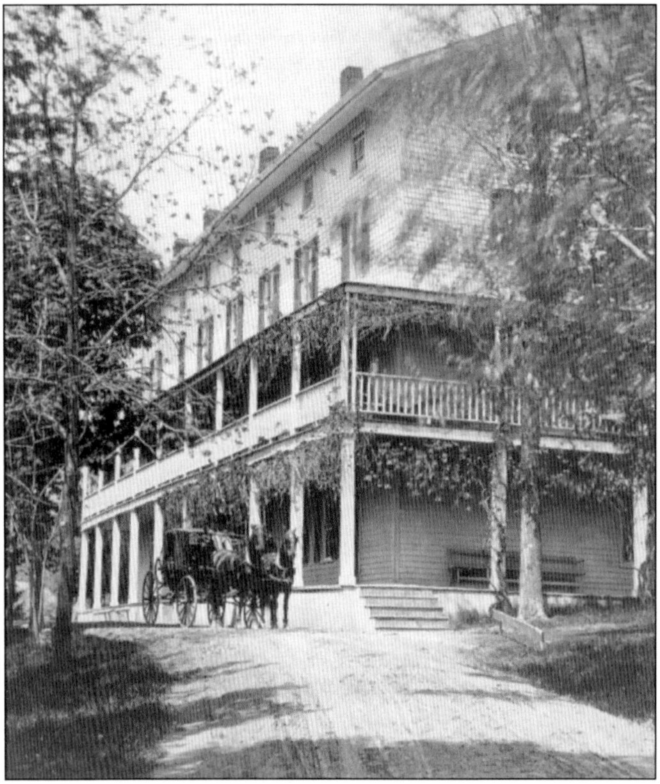

The Gleason Sanitarium (originally called the Elmira Water Cure) was established in 1852. It operated for 50 years, dispensing "eclectic" medicine, with an emphasis on hydropathy, or hydrotherapy, as it is known today. (Courtesy of CCHS.)

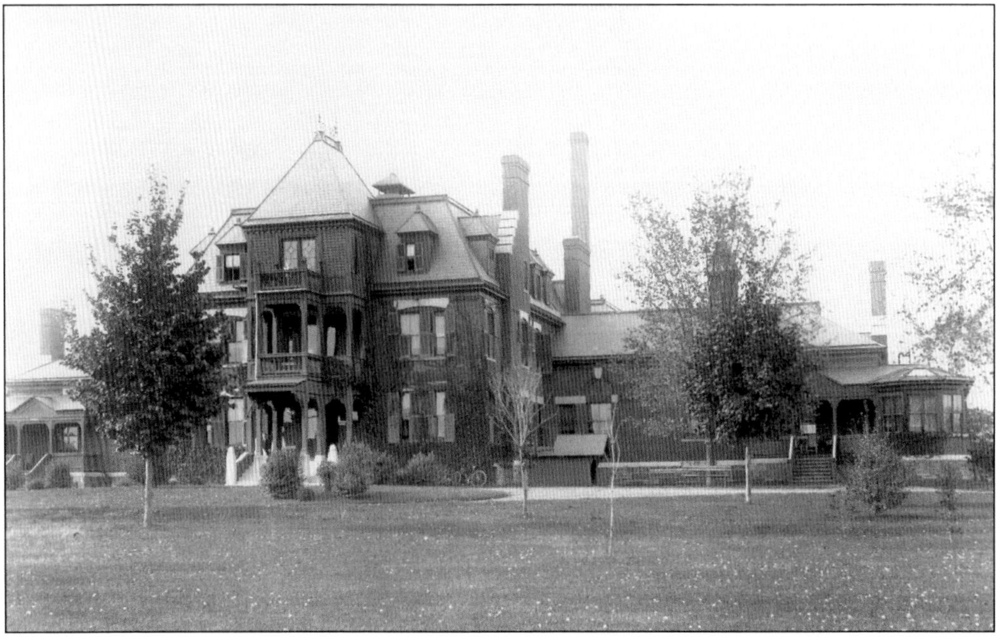

The new Arnot Ogden Memorial Hospital opened on December 20, 1888. It had 25 beds, and the staff consisted of three nurses, a matron, and four other employees. In its first year, there were 97 admissions and one birth. Some concern was expressed that the hospital was "so far out into the country." (Courtesy of CCHS.)

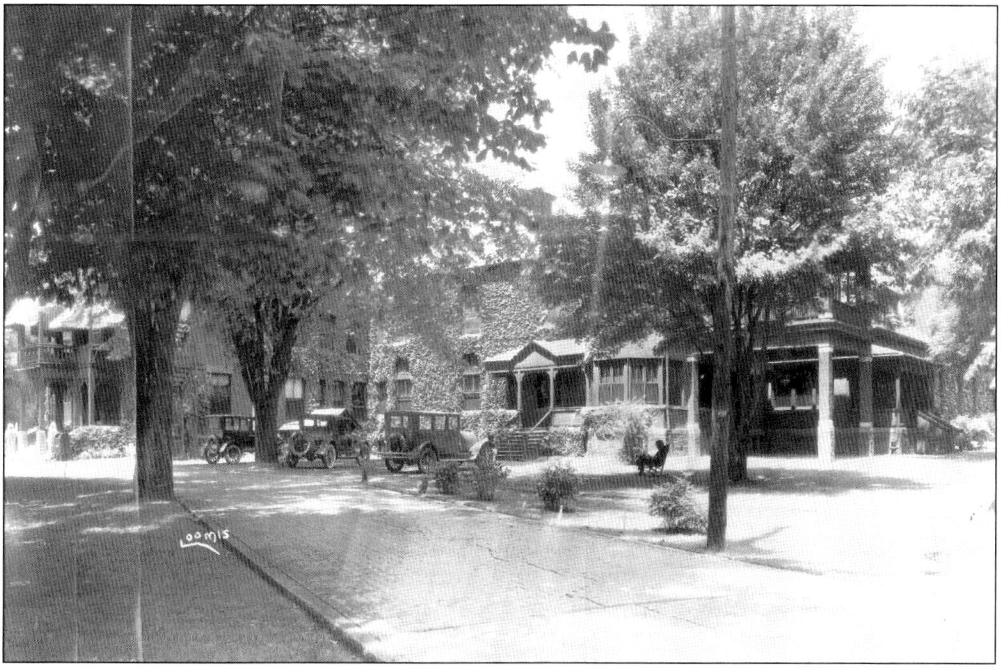

In the 1880s, public opinion considered hospitals a last resort, since, for the most part, they were crowded, dark, and unsanitary. The Arnot Ogden, however, was bright, clean, open, and situated amid wooded surroundings. The hospital is shown here around 1910. (Courtesy of CCHS.)

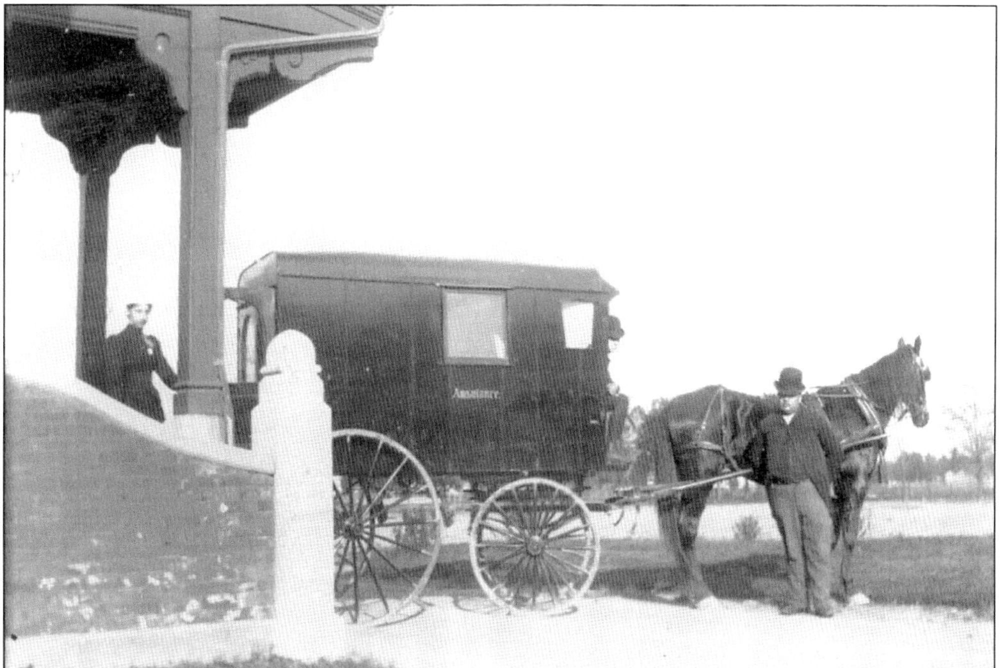
With the opening of the hospital, ambulance service became important. The hospital was located on the outskirts of the city, posing the problem of the transportation of patients. Pictured here is an ambulance at Arnot Ogden Memorial Hospital around 1895. (Courtesy of CCHS.)

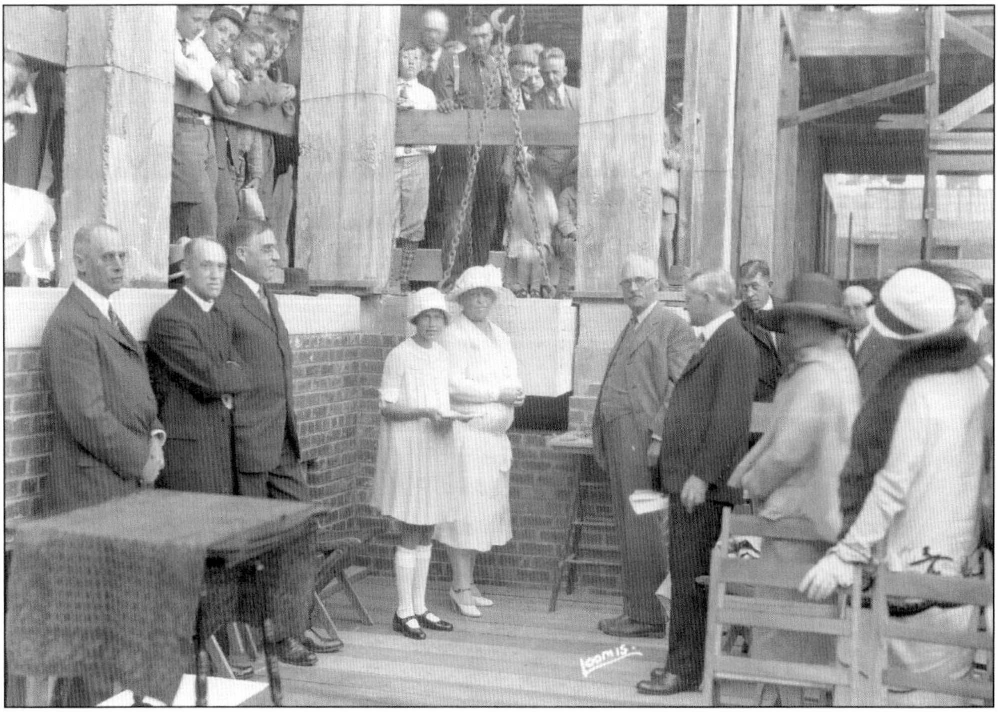

The Arnot family gave $370,000 in endowments to establish the hospital as a voluntary, nonprofit institution. On September 14, 1926, the cornerstone was laid for a new building, the result of the first public appeal for building funds. Shown here are, from left to right, Mayor Donald Heller, Rev. Frederick Henstridge, Dr. Arthur Booth, Betty (Elizabeth) Falck, Sarah Wey Tompkins, Frederick H. Johnston (builder), and E.E. Buchanan, president of the hospital. (Courtesy of CCHS.)

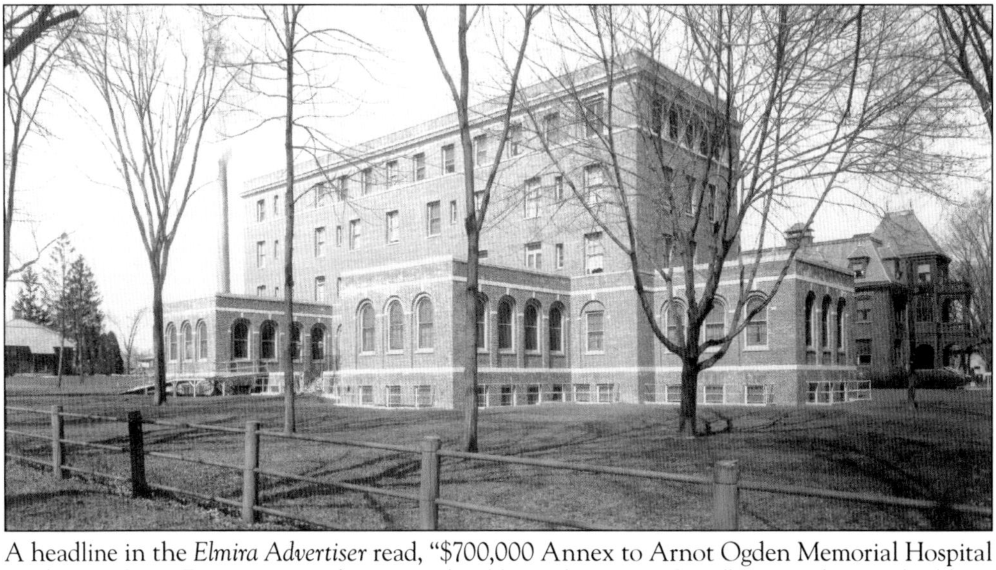

A headline in the *Elmira Advertiser* read, "$700,000 Annex to Arnot Ogden Memorial Hospital is Thrown Open For Inspection by General Public." There were four floors in the new building. The first floor had an emergency room, sunroom, and terrace. The second floor was devoted to obstetrical work, the third floor had 20 patients' rooms, and the fourth floor was for children. (Courtesy of CCHS.)

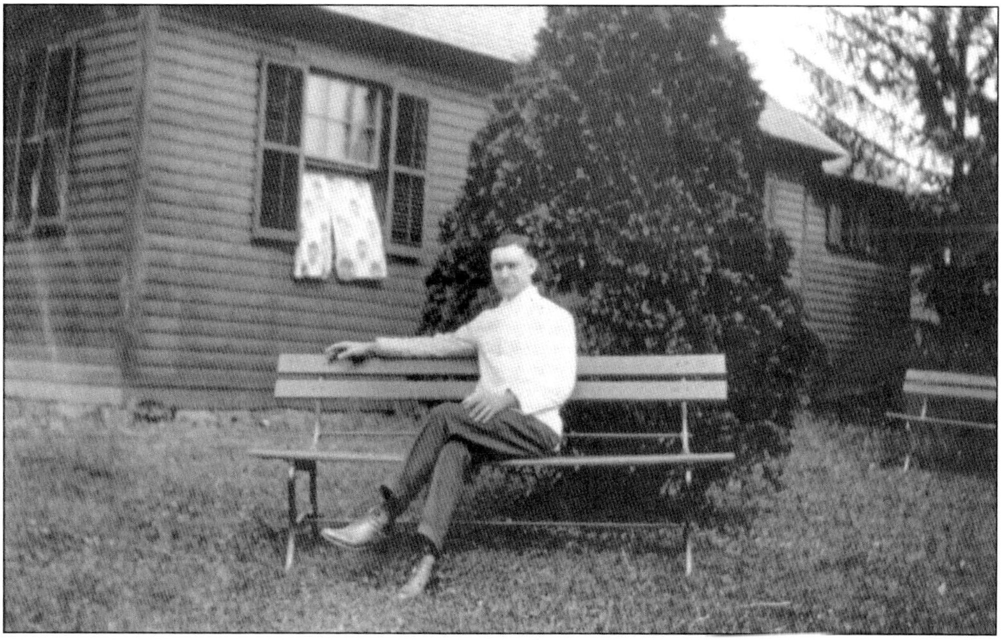

Diphtheria and typhoid outbreaks swept Elmira at the time of the 1889 flood. In that year alone, there were 55 diphtheria cases in the city. In 1895, a major epidemic of typhoid fever claimed 71 lives. With time, better municipal sanitation and testing techniques began to address these problems. In 1889, a seven-bed "isolation cottage" was built away from the main hospital to house people with contagious diseases. The cottage is shown here around 1890. (Courtesy of Arnot School of Nursing.)

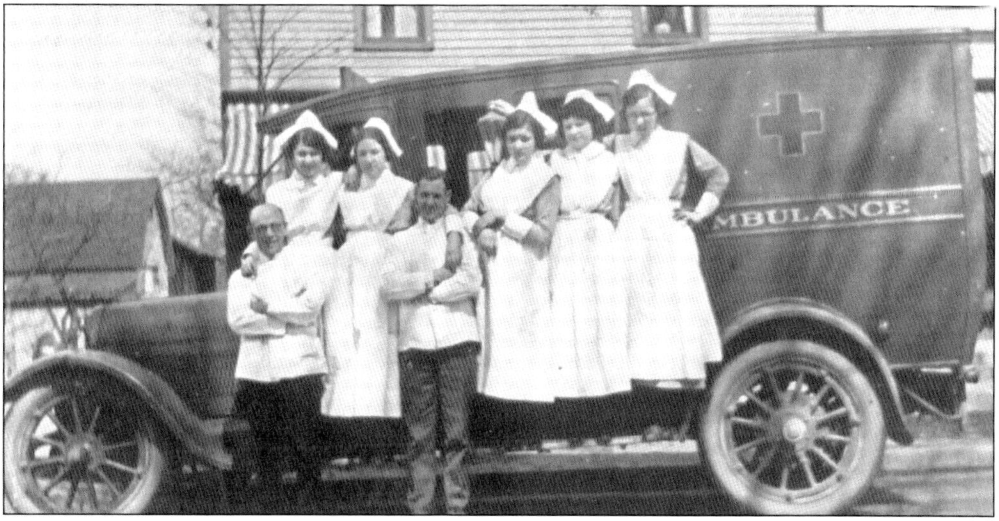

The School of Nursing of the Arnot Ogden Memorial Hospital was established in July 1889. Called a "Training School for Nurses" at the time, it was one of the earliest such schools in the country. The initial class had three students. From the first prospectus of the school: "Candidates will be required to bring with them to the hospital three dresses of washable material, six white aprons, five inches from the bottom of the skirt with bib eight and one half inches across the bottom . . . they must wear noiseless shoes." Shown here is the 1926 graduation class. (Courtesy of Arnot School of Nursing.)

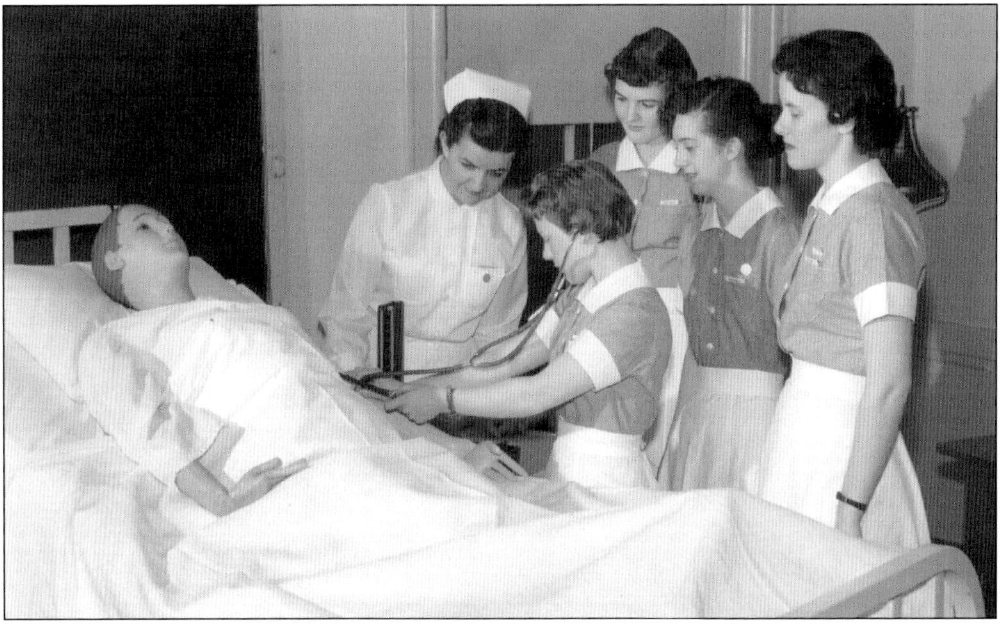

Future nurses receive training with Mrs. Chase (the mannequin) on taking blood pressure. Tuition in 1940 was $100 a year for the five-year college-hospital course. The students received board, lodging, and a reasonable amount of laundry work from date of entrance. Today, the total educational cost for the 105-week program is $30,552, without room and board. (Courtesy of Arnot School of Nursing.)

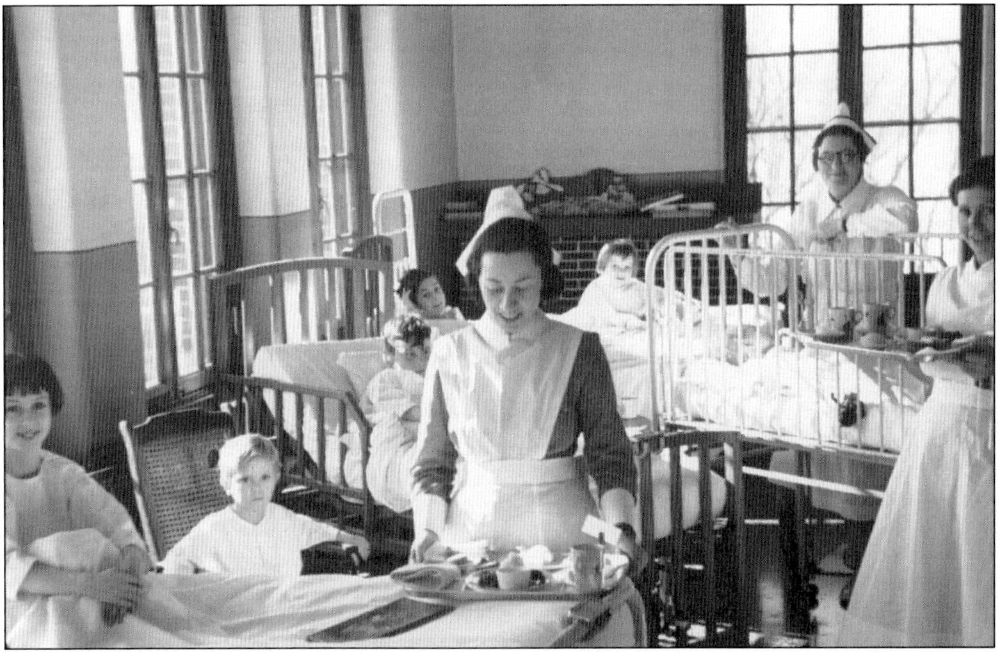

The sunroom, playroom, recreation center, and health center in the children's department were designed to create a place where children could meet other boys and girls and forget about their illnesses. The concept was intended to provide an incentive for "perfect" conduct. (Courtesy of Arnot School of Nursing.)

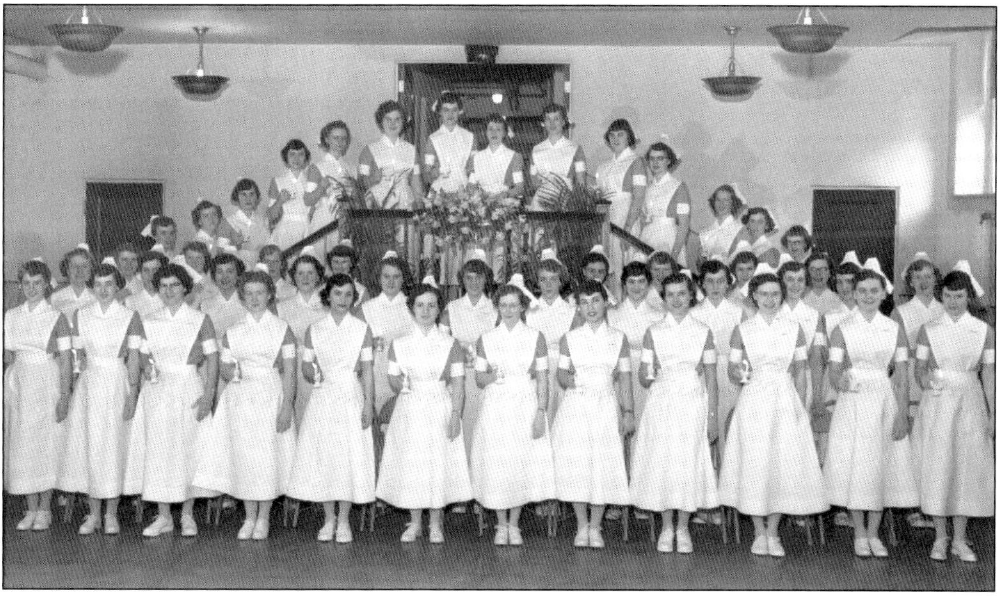

A capping ceremony followed the probationary period until 1956. Beginning with the class of 1959, caps were a part of the uniform at the beginning of the freshman clinical experience. This photograph shows a candlelight ceremony from 1953 for sophomores who were members of the class of 1955. (Courtesy of Arnot School of Nursing.)

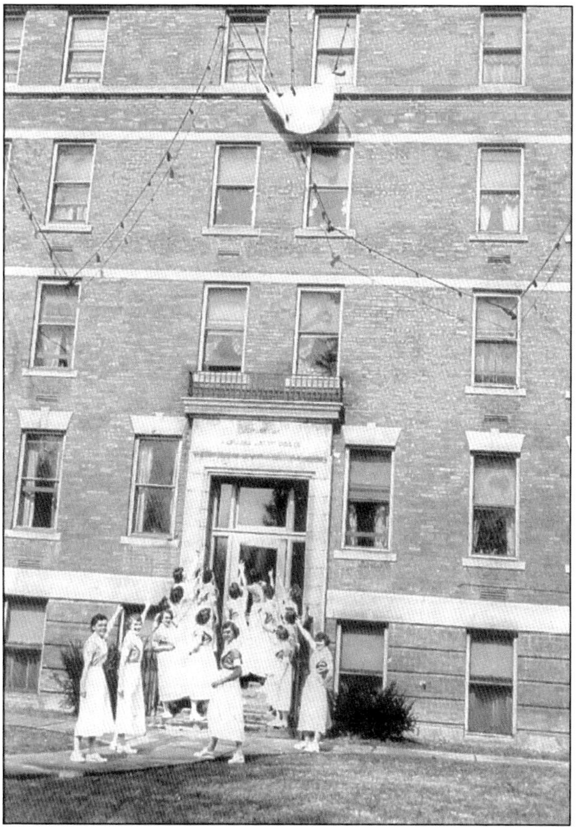

Uniform styles have changed throughout history, from two-piece dresses with a bib, to one-piece dresses, to tops with pants or a dress. Students wore black stockings throughout the year of 1949. Seniors wore white stockings for the first time in 1950, while underclassmen continued to wear black stockings. The class of 1955 celebrated "Black Stocking Day," when they could change to white stockings. (Courtesy of Arnot School of Nursing.)

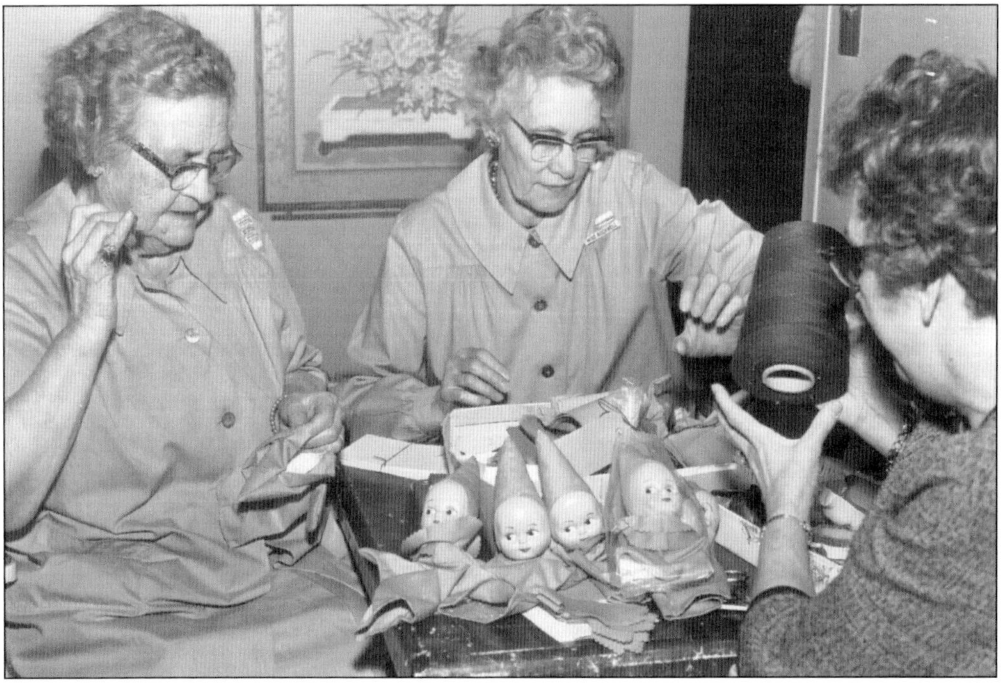

It began with a tea. On October 3, 1953, women representing 73 community organizations shared a cup of tea and decided that a hospital auxiliary should be formed. One purpose was to assist patients and visitors. In 1958, Pinkie the Puppet arrived on the scene. Pinkie's dressing was the handiwork of a "Sewing Bee." This adorable puppet is a gift from the auxiliary to each child admitted to the hospital. In 2002, blue puppets were added for the boys. (Courtesy of Marge MacPherson.)

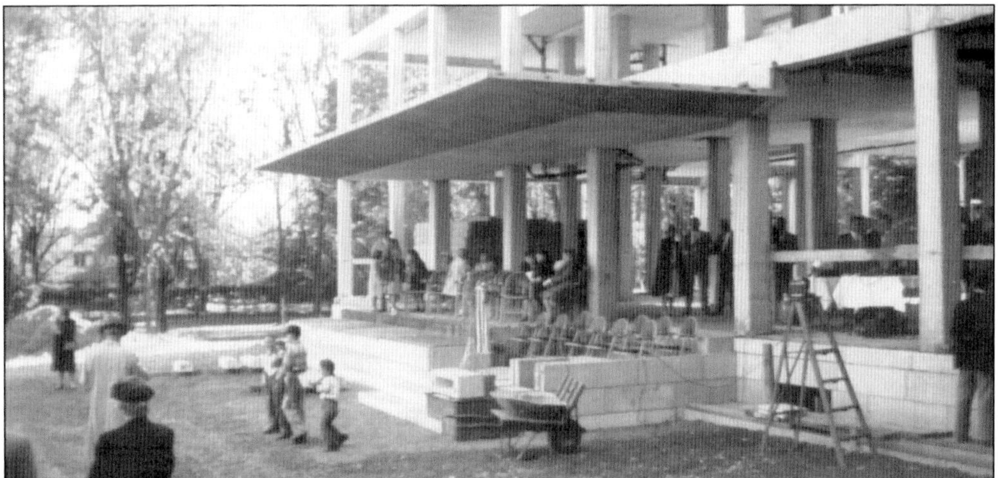

The Arnot Ogden Memorial Hospital has experienced steady growth since its founding. In 1951, demands had outgrown capacity and an appeal was made to the public, which raised $1.5 million. The original structure was demolished to make way for a new eastern complex. Capacity increased to 271, and two new twelve-bed nurseries and a six-bed premature nursery were opened. The new complex was built by Streeter Associates; coauthor Archie Kieffer was the master mason. The cornerstone was laid in 1954, and the building was dedicated in 1955. This photograph is from around 1954. (Courtesy of the Arnot School of Nursing.)

Catholics of Elmira had long desired a hospital under the direction of Sisters. When John J. Hassett learned about the opportunity to purchase the Academy of Our Lady of the Angels, he consulted with Dr. Daniel P. Murphy (shown here). Dr. Murphy promised the help of his medical colleagues to support the project. His sincerity and eloquence convinced Mother Agnes Hines of the need for the hospital. (Courtesy of St. Joseph's Hospital.)

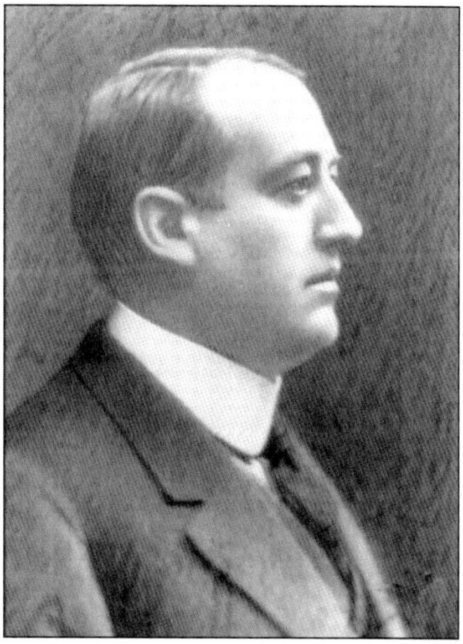

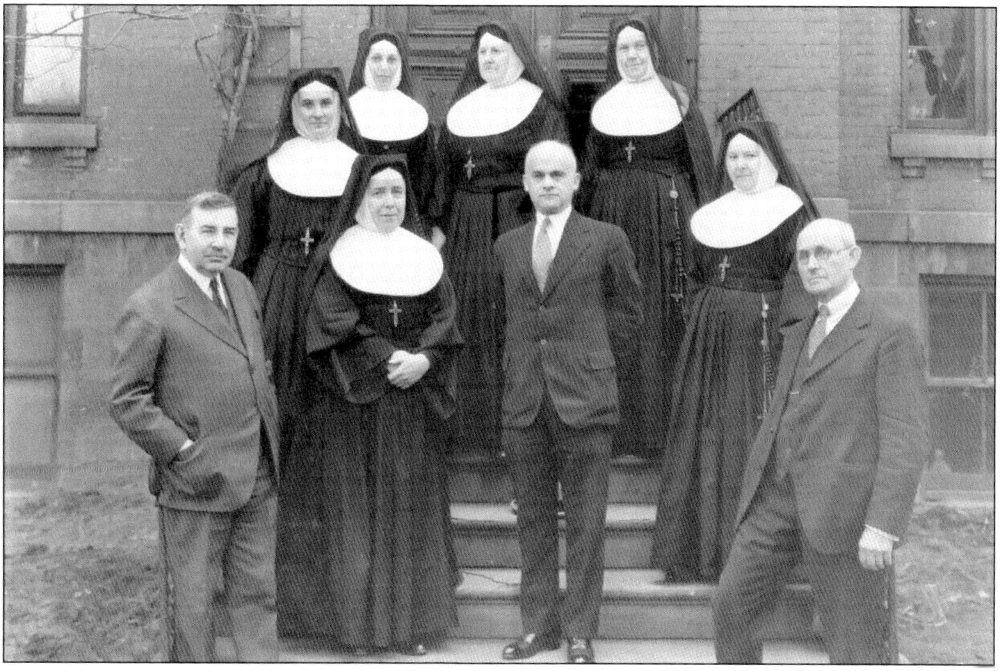

The Sisters of St. Joseph were a teaching order, having never operated a hospital. Rev. Mother Agnes Hines went to the chapel and prayed that God would direct her and that the Holy Spirit would enlighten her to select the right Sister to head the daunting project. It came to Mother Agnes that, "the first Sister to enter the chapel to pray will be the one." Sister Rose Alice was the next nun to pray in the chapel, and she would serve as the administrator until her death in 1939. Pictured here around 1931 are the founding Sisters and some of the first physicians. They are, from left to right, (first row) Dr. Nathan Soble, Sr. Rose Alice Conway (administrator), Dr. Abraham Lande, Sr. Mary John Monaghan, and Dr. George Case; (second row) Sr. Hedwiga Fetchner, Sr. Ruth Schicker, Sr. St. Ann Murphy, and Sr. Jerome Owen. Not shown are Sr. Caroline Gueter and Dr. Daniel Murphy. (Courtesy of St. Joseph's Hospital.)

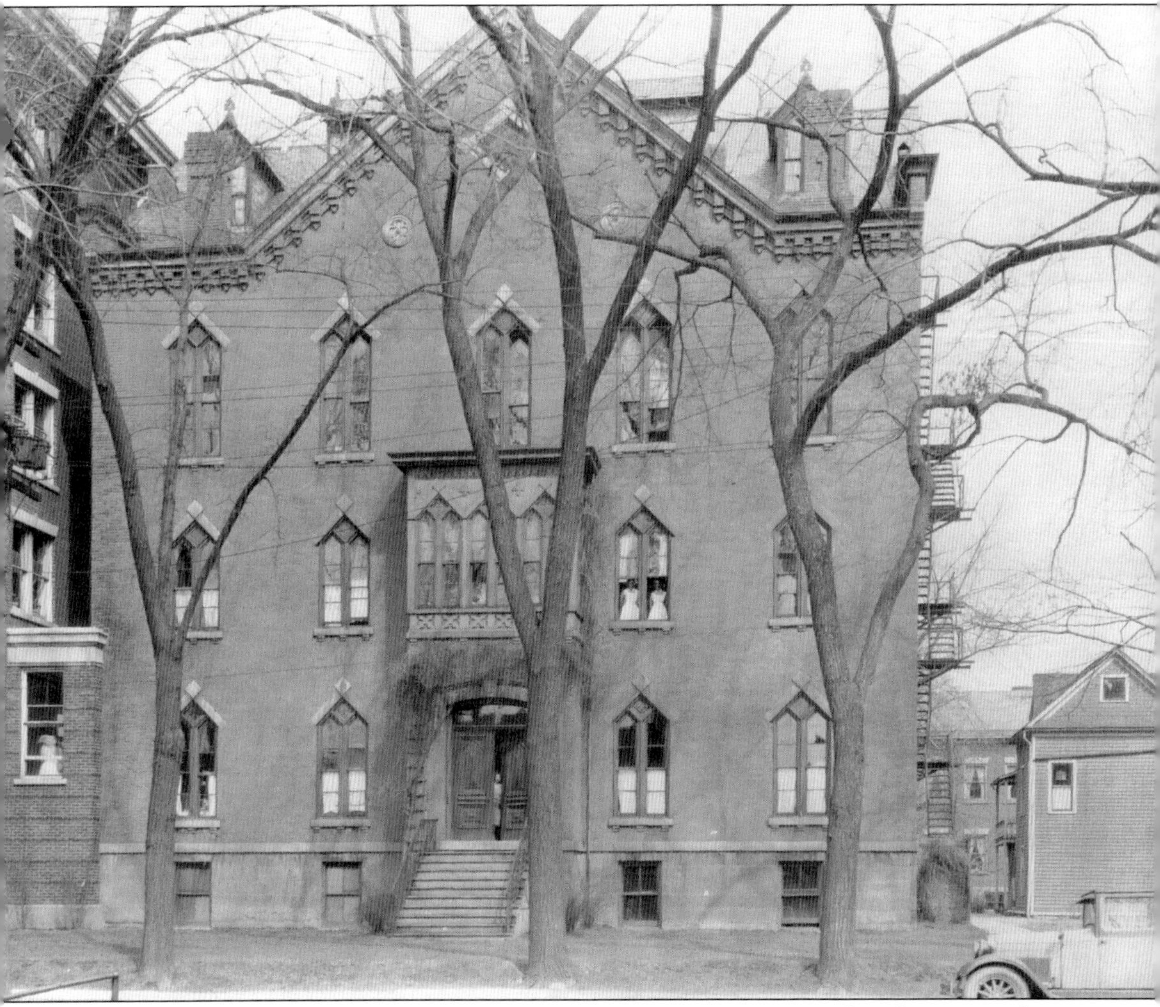

The Academy of Our Lady of the Angels, located next to St. Peter and Paul's convent, became the site for St. Joseph's Hospital. Title to the property was transferred to the Sisters of St. Joseph in 1907 for $10,000. A cottage on the corner of Market Street and Dewitt Avenue was bought for $3,000 as a nurse's residence. Money was raised to renovate the academy into a hospital facility with four floors and a total of 35 beds. The hospital opened on September 24, 1908, and is shown here around that same year. (Courtesy of St. Joseph's Hospital.)

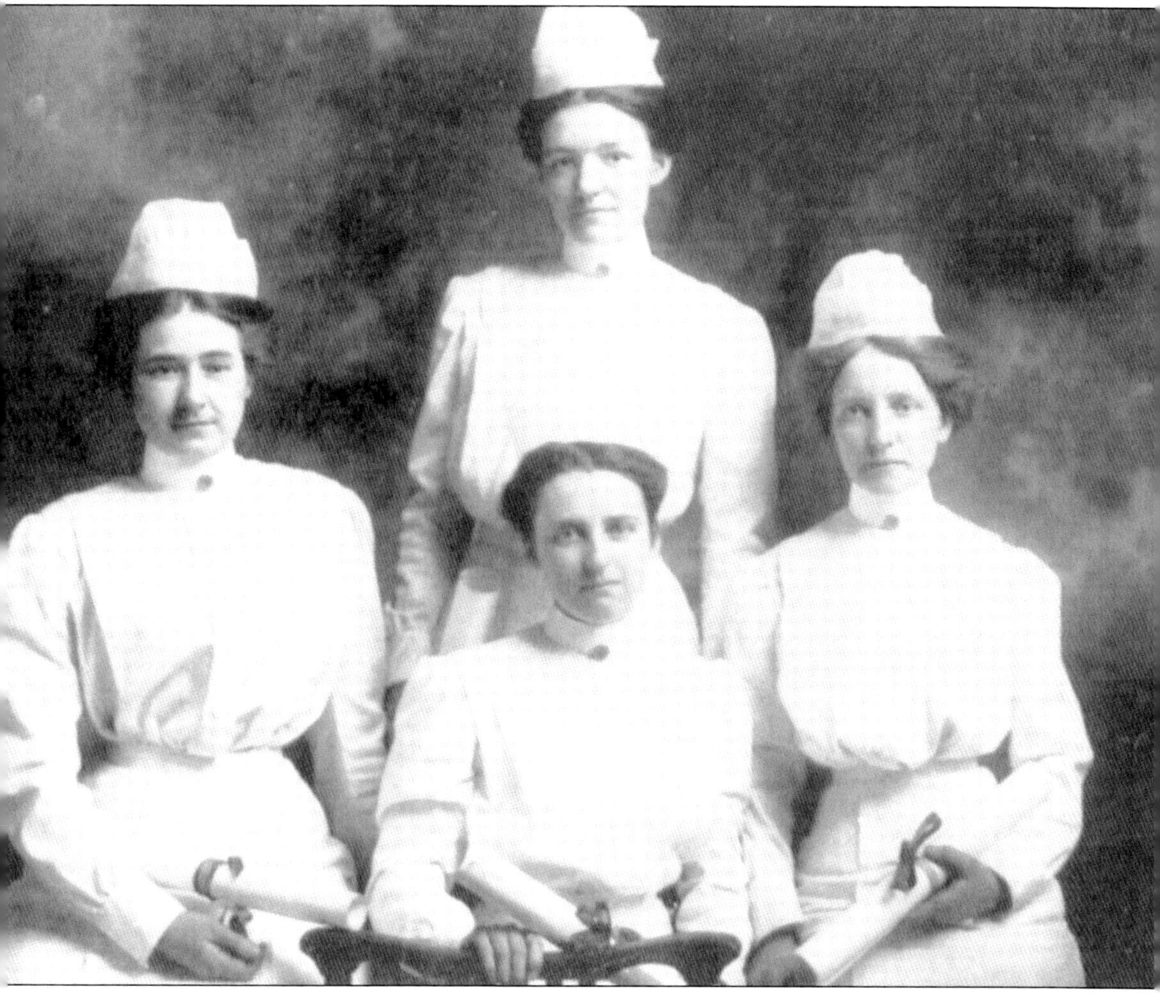

Edward J. Dunn (1866–1927) was one of St. Joseph's greatest benefactors and the man for whom Dunn Field is named. In his will, Dunn left the hospital one-tenth of his estate. With this gift, the hospital directors were able to erect a residence for student nurses and for the nuns, including a memorial chapel, and to complete the medical wing. Pictured here are the first graduates of the St. Joseph's School of Nursing, the class of 1911. Seated from left to right are Josephine Tyrasinski, Lena MacInerney, and Catherine Sullivan. Harriett Keavin is standing. (Courtesy of St. Joseph's Hospital.)

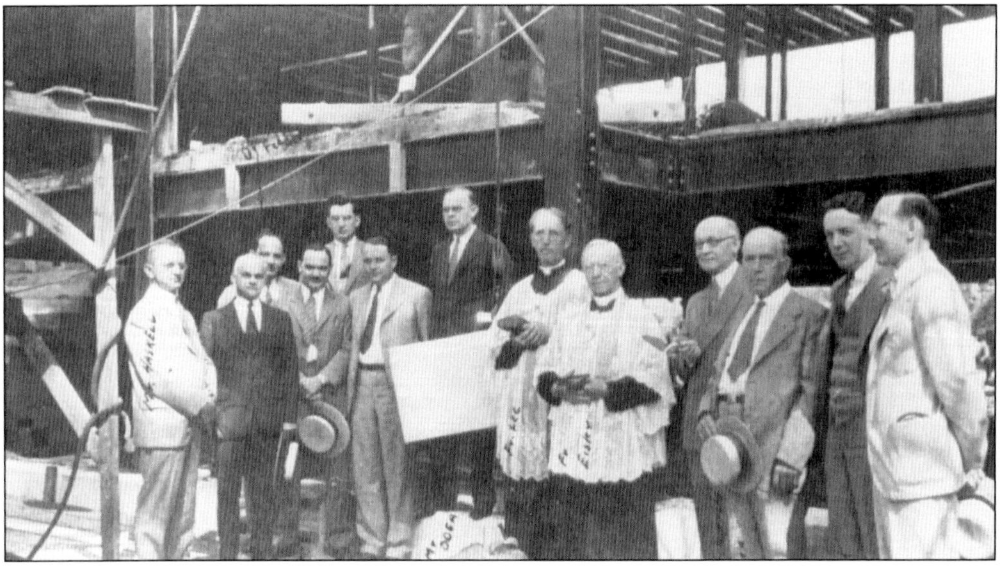

The ceremony for blessing the cornerstone of the medical building was held on June 2, 1931. Attending the ceremony are, from left to right, Harry Haskell, Dr. Abraham Lande, Dr. Joseph M. Feder (partially hidden), Dr. Andrew Blash, Dr. John R. McLaughlin (in back), Leo E. Considine, Cornelius O'Dea, Monsignor Lee, Father Eisler, Thomas B. Fitzgerald, Daniel Sheehan, Dr. William J. Cusick, and Dr. J. Harold Hunt. (Courtesy of St. Joseph's Hospital.)

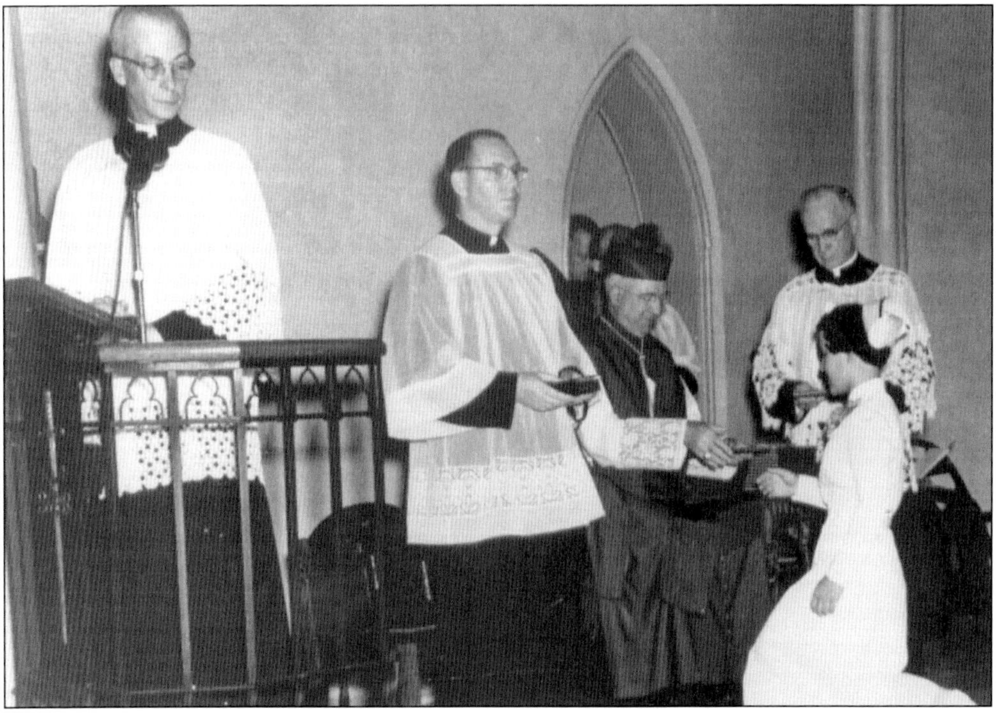

Graduation from the St. Joseph's School of Nursing was held at St. Peter and Paul's Church, and was considered a very special occasion. Shown here around 1957 are, from left to right, Father McGhan, Father Manley, Bishop Casey, Patricia Callahan, and Father Hynes. (Courtesy of Archives of St. Joseph's Hospital.)

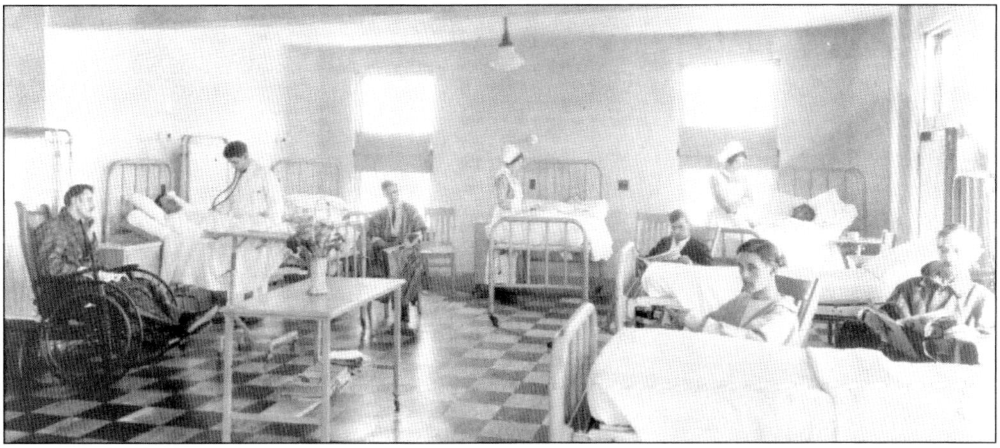

By 1919, Bishop Thomas Francis Hickey saw the need for more space at the hospital. Under the leadership of Edward J. Dunn, $125,000 was raised for a new, six-story surgical building. Bishop Hickey broke ground on July 16, 1922. In 1923, the new building opened, accommodating 150 patients. Pictured here is the Surgical Ward No. 3 as it appeared in 1926. (Courtesy of St. Joseph's Hospital.)

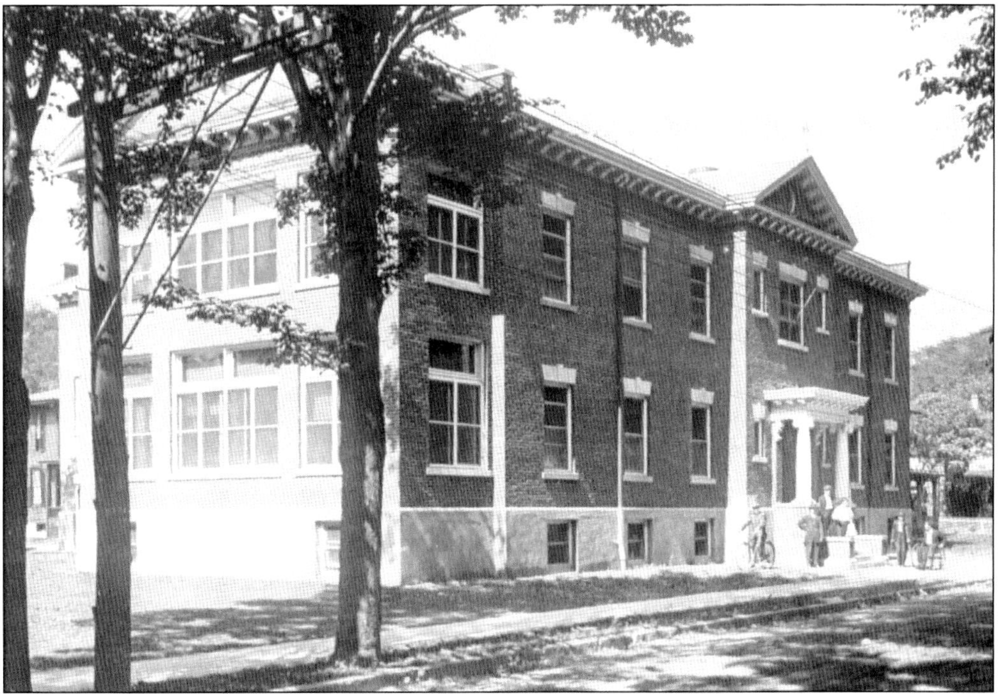

St. Joseph's Hospital admitted 385 patients in 1909 and delivered one baby. A laundry building was added in 1910, and within a few years, construction of a two-story brick building on High Street was under way. It opened in 1914, consisting of medical and surgical beds on the first floor and a maternity division on the second. The annex increased bed capacity to 75. The building was demolished in 1975. (Courtesy of St. Joseph's Hospital.)

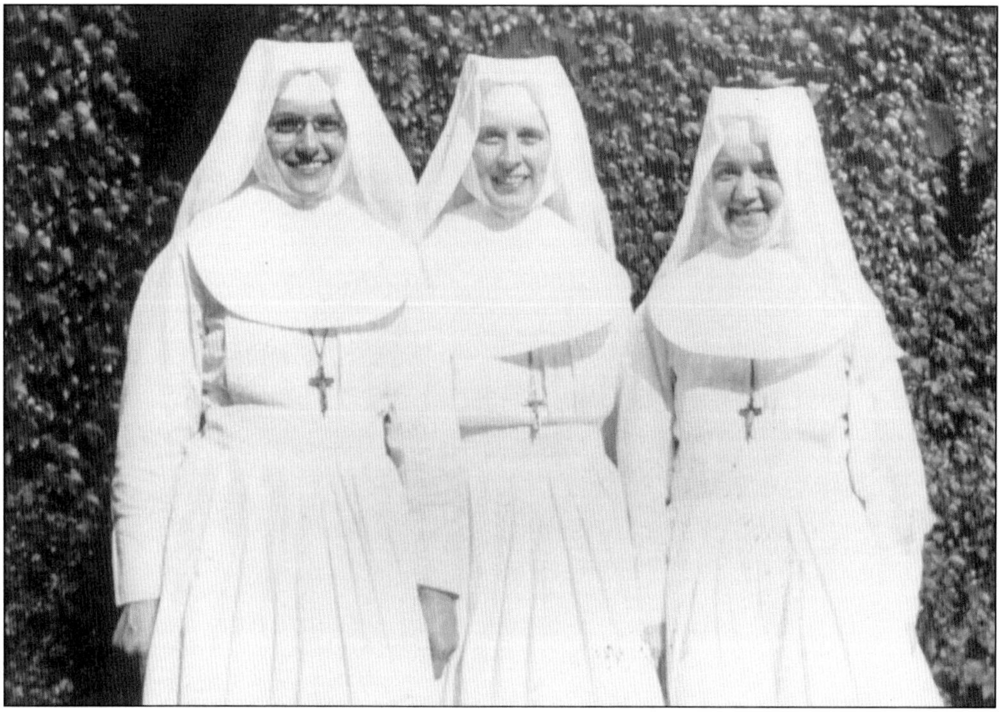

This 1945 photograph shows the customary uniform for the nurses at St. Joseph's Hospital. White was also worn by most of the staff. In 1969, the style was changed to a more contemporary look. (Courtesy of St. Joseph's Hospital.)

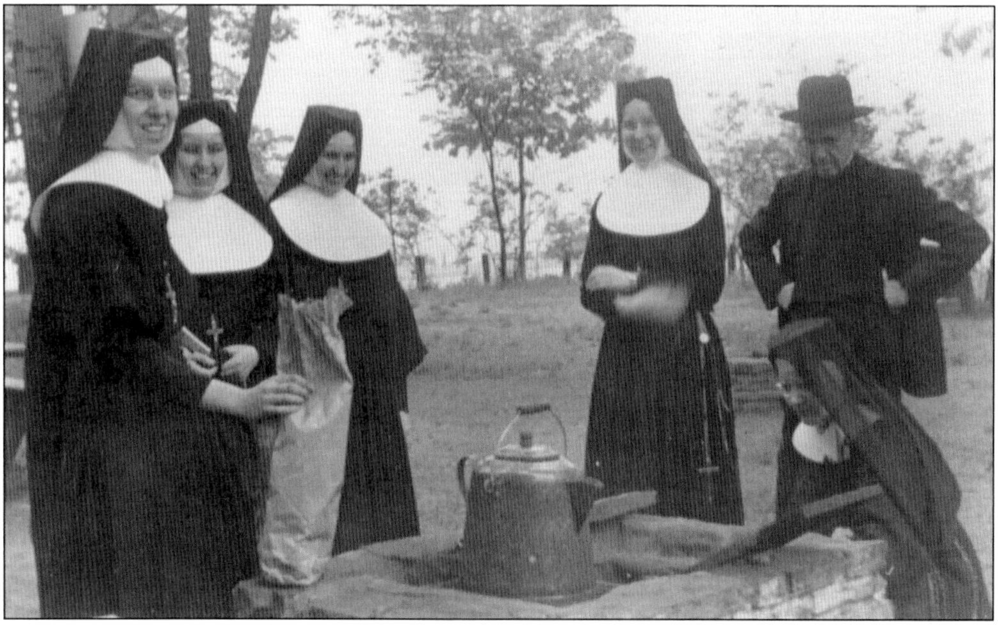

All work and no play makes teaching a challenge. This 1955 photograph shows the faculty of St. Joseph's School of Nursing relaxing at a picnic. From left to right are Sister Joseph Margaret, Sister Marie Gregory, Sister Marie Michael, Sister Karen, and the Reverend Michael Hines. (Courtesy of St. Joseph's Hospital.)

Four

Education and Recreation

When the first board of education was organized in 1859, there were five "public" schools and a number of private ones. The new school district had 16 teachers and 1,200 students ages 4–21. As the community grew, so did the number of schools, which were located in different areas of the city. Many folks still refer to their elementary school by its number. The schools and their numbers are as follows: School No. 1, Thomas K. Beecher; No. 2, Arthur W. Booth; No. 3, Parley Coburn; No. 4, George M. Diven; No. 5, George Washington; No. 6 was never given a name, but its site became the Elmira Vocational School; No. 7, Riverside; No. 8, Harry Lagonegro; No. 9, Edward Hardy (demolished); No. 10, J. Sloat Fassett; No. 11, Harry N. Hoffman (demolished).

Baseball in Elmira dates back to the Civil War, when the Chemung Unions played against some of the prisoners at the Elmira Prison Camp in 1865. Professional baseball was introduced in 1888 with the "Babies." In 1931, the Elmira Colonels were purchased by the St. Louis Cardinals, beginning Elmira's connection with the major leagues.

Elmira's baseball park has been known as Dunn Field since 1921, when Edward J. Dunn purchased several acres in the area known as Recreation Park. He paid off all park debts and gave the land to a board of Elmira baseball directors. In 1928, Babe Ruth and Lou Gehrig played before an estimated 8,000–10,000 people, according to the *Chemung Valley Reporter.*

History of Tioga, Chemung, Tompkins, and Schuyler Counties, published in 1879 said of Eldridge Park, "It was an experiment throwing these choice grounds open to the public. It is a compliment to the taste and good sense of the public that this confidence is not abused." Created by Dr. Edwin Eldridge, the park became a very special place to Elmirans and visitors from around the country. Private property designed for a public purpose, it was purchased by the city in 1889 after Dr. Eldridge's untimely death in 1876. The park has evolved over the years. In the 1920s, it helped make Elmira the "fun city." The dance pavilion (a former railroad station) could hold 3,000 people. No intoxicants were allowed. The casino was a great attraction, as were the bear pits, and eventually the roller coaster, merry-go-round, the whip, and the midway. One could say that Eldridge Park was the Six Flags of its day.

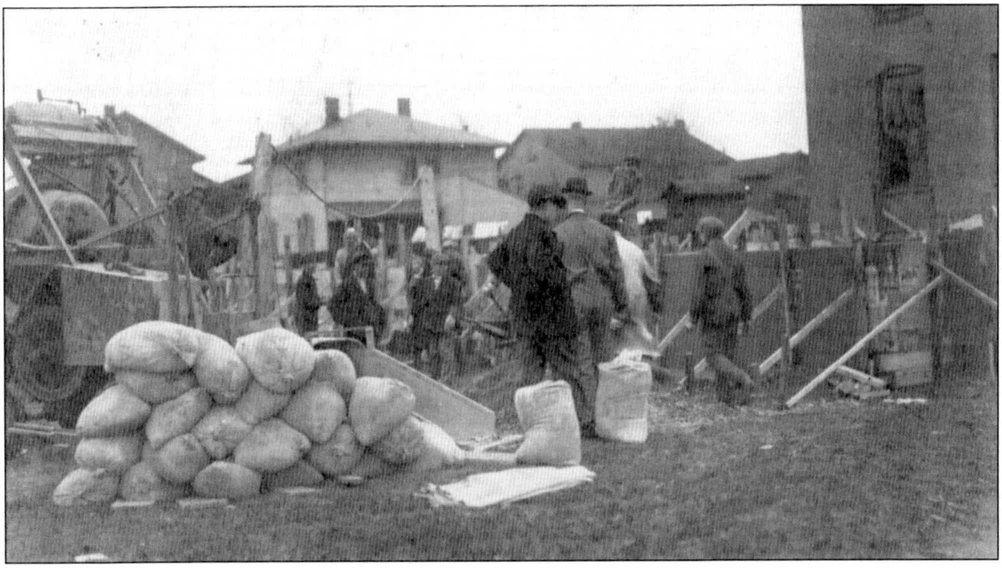

School No. 1 was built in 1868 on land purchased from the John W. Wisner estate. The cost of construction was $25,000 for a two-story, red-brick building without lights, steam heat, or running water. In January 1934, the original building was razed and replaced by the current building, which was named after Thomas K. Beecher, the first minister of Park Church. The photograph was taken around 1934. (Courtesy of CCHS.)

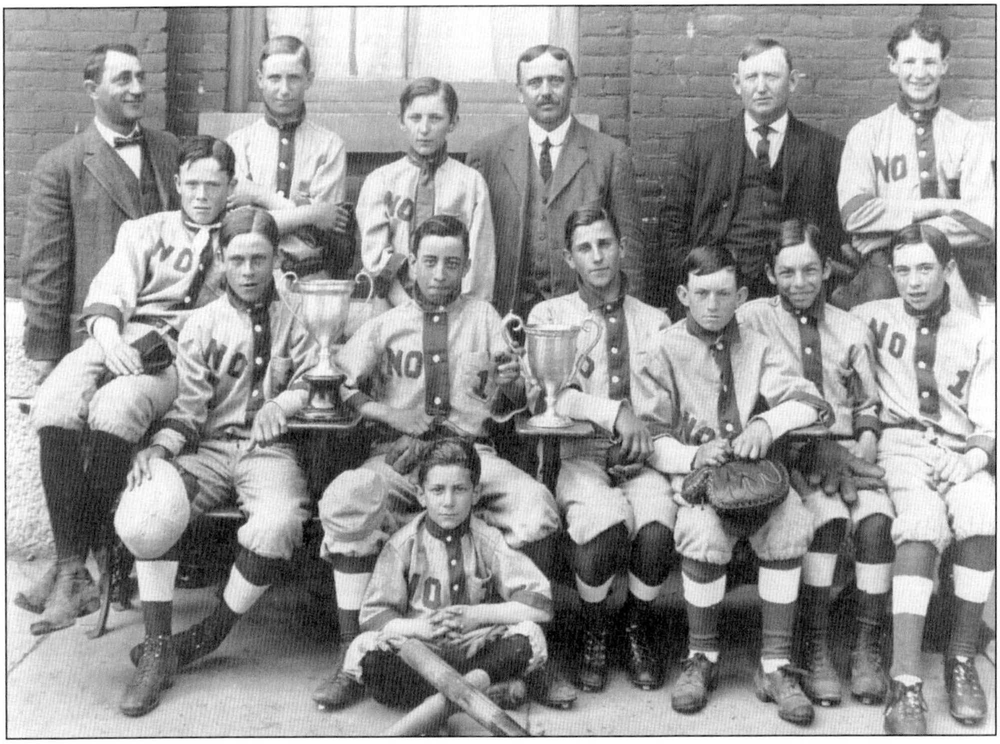

In 1908, professional baseball returned to Elmira after a 13-year absence. By 1914, the Elmira team had its first championship. The various schools also had teams. Shown here is School No. 1's baseball team around 1912. (Courtesy of Thomas K. Beecher School Library.)

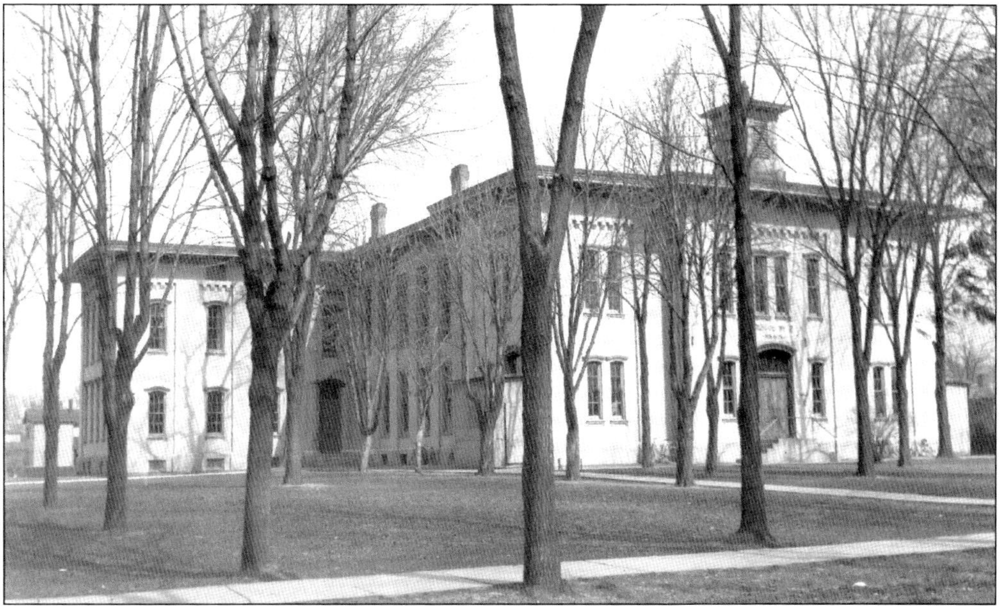

School No. 2 was built in 1869. Arbor Day ceremonies were important at the future Booth School, as described in *A Century of Public Education in Elmira, 1845–1945*: "With fife and drum, with military precision, left, right, left, right, out of the building, onto the lawn, into a circle—to plant a tree—a tree in memory of Longfellow, Whittier or some other of the country's great. Little Susie . . . wanted, oh! So badly a Longfellow tree because Longfellow's whiskers were prettier; but they had a Whittier tree." (Courtesy of CCHS.)

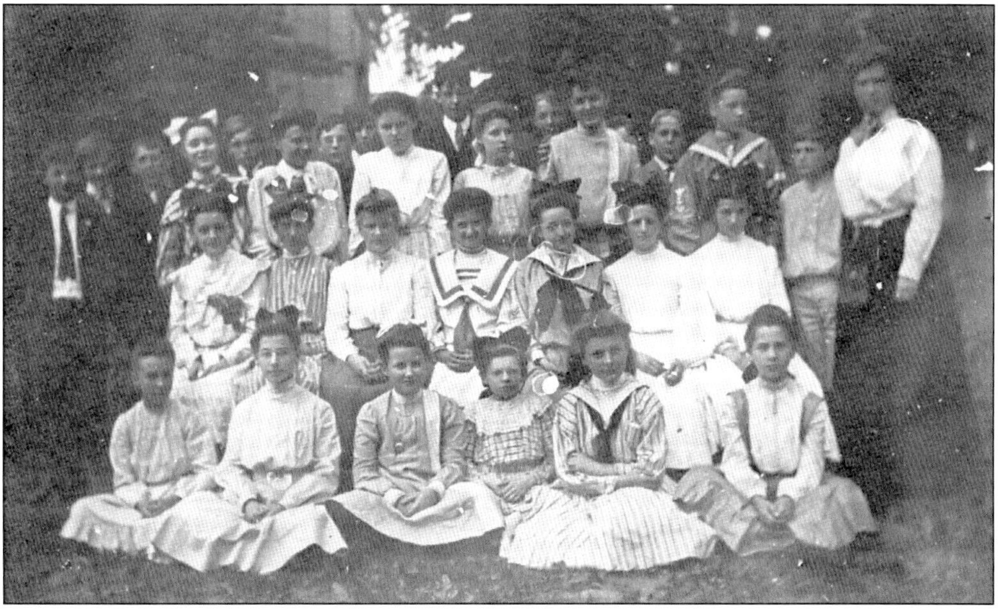

In 1898, the superintendent of schools reported to the board of education that, "drawing is hardly appreciated by the people of the country." The drawing supervisor had one box of paints for the whole city. On the other hand, it was reported, "the experiences in vocal music . . . are having an elevating and refining effect" on the character of the pupils. This 1902 photograph shows the fifth-grade class at School No. 2. (Courtesy of CCHS.)

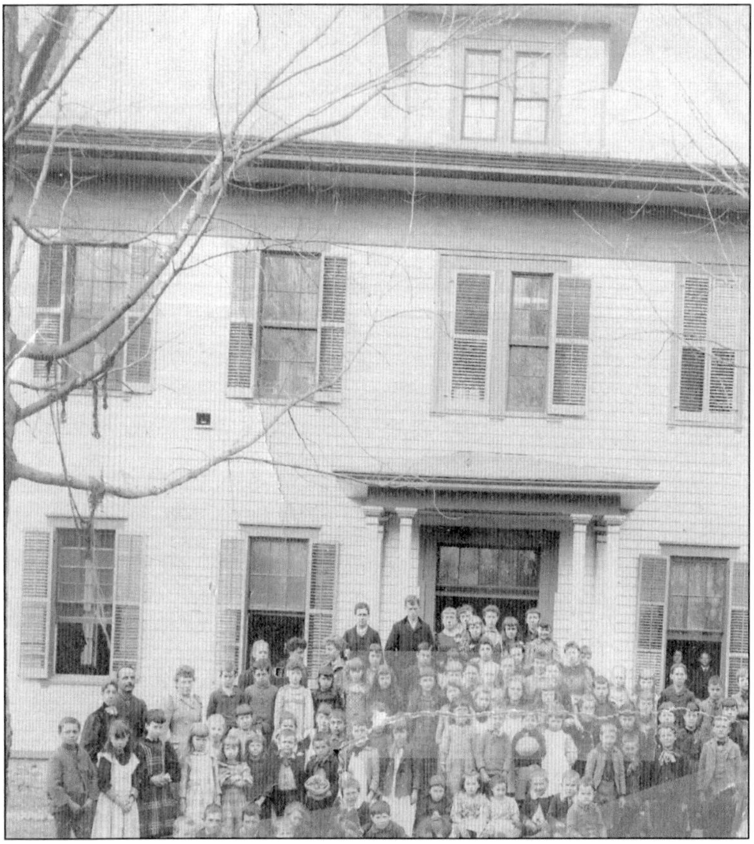

School No. 3 was the only school on the south side. It was originally located on Pennsylvania Avenue and Sly Street in 1838. In 1845, it was relocated to the Updegraph House (shown here) at 113 East Hudson Street at a cost of $1,200. It remained there until 1871, when a new building was erected behind the current Parley Coburn School. (Courtesy of CCHS.)

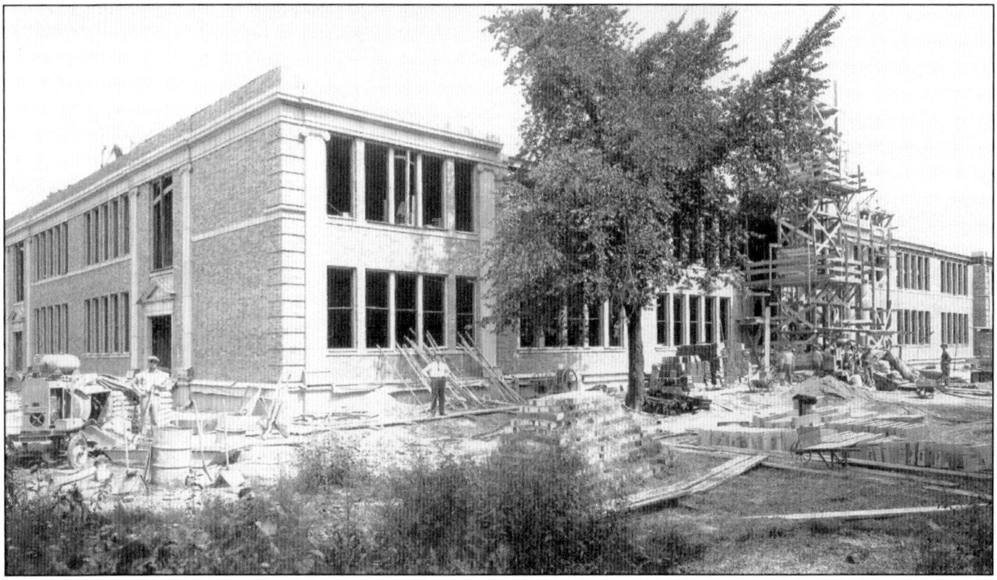

The new Parley Coburn building was the first of the new type of school. It had a large kindergarten room, a gymnasium, an auditorium, a cooking room, and shops, a restroom for teachers, and large, airy classrooms, among them the ideal three-room library group. (Photograph by Fred T. Loomis, courtesy of CCHS.)

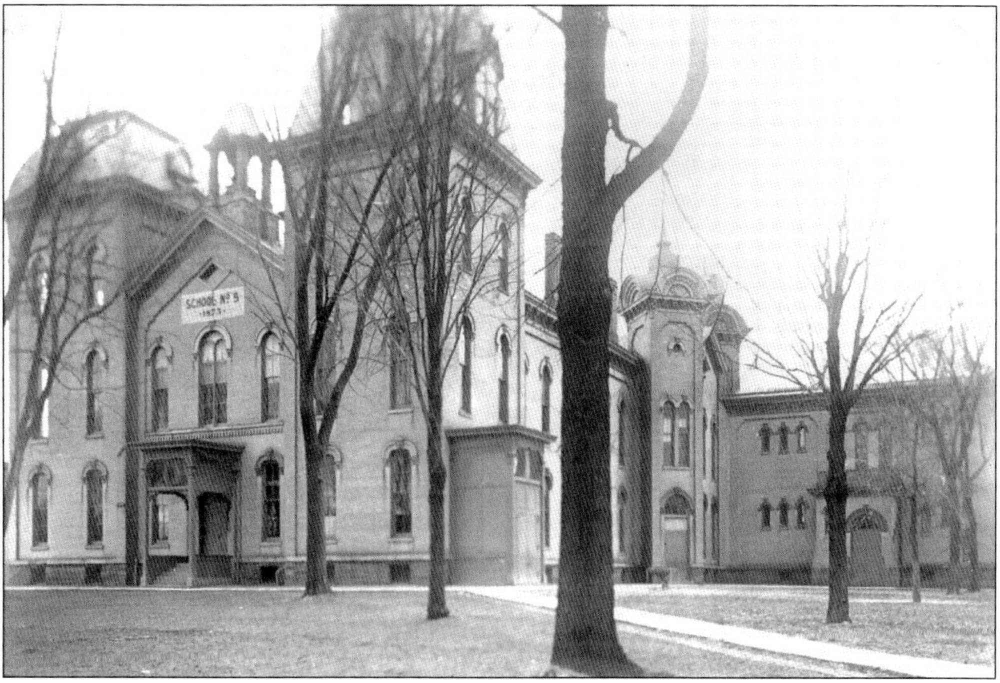

Built in 1873, No. 5 School could boast of the city's first female principal, Hannah Rhodes, who served in 1882. In those days, the principal was known as the principal teacher and earned about $150 per month. (Courtesy of CCHS.)

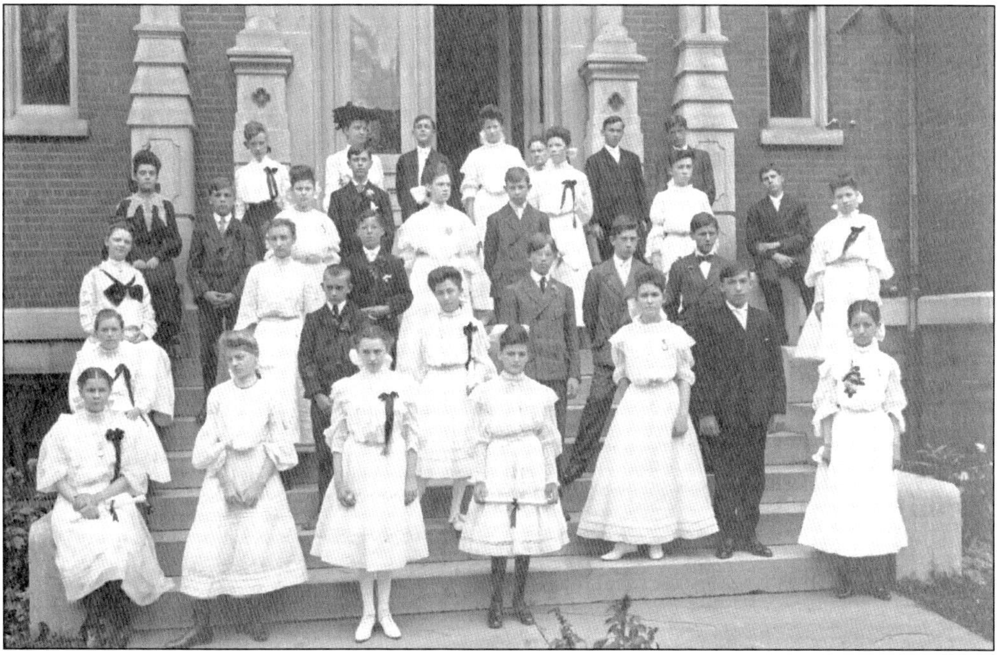

There were three schools on the site of present-day Diven School. In 1875, parents of District 4 pupils complained of "new fangled" ideas, since in that period vaccinations became compulsory. Graduation from School No. 4 was always an exciting day, as seen in this 1905 photograph. (Courtesy of CCHS.)

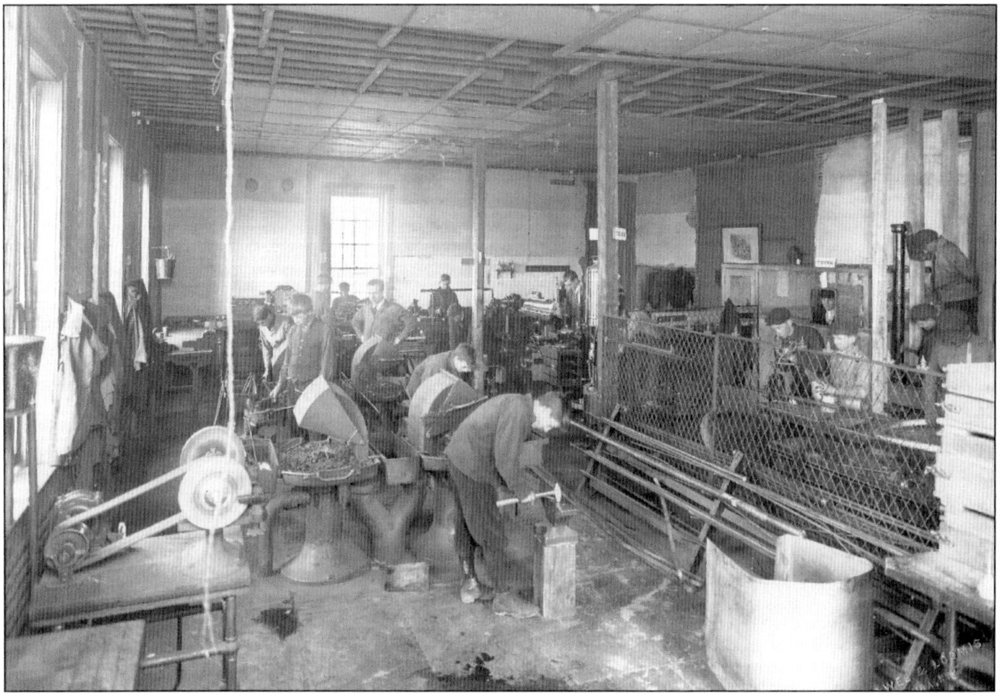

The Elmira Vocational School (1913–1953) was located in the building that had been School No. 6, near the DL&W Railroad (721 Lake Street). There, boys were taught pattern and cabinetmaking, woodworking, plumbing, heating, and drafting. They spent three hours in their vocational area and three hours on related bookwork. The school received local, state, and federal funds. (Courtesy of CCHS.)

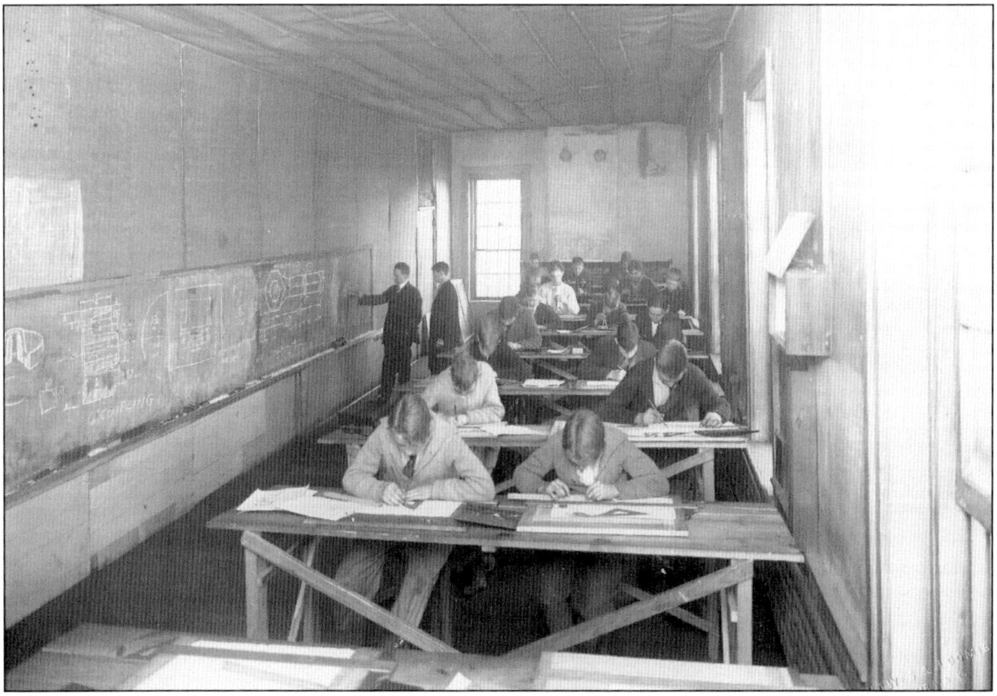

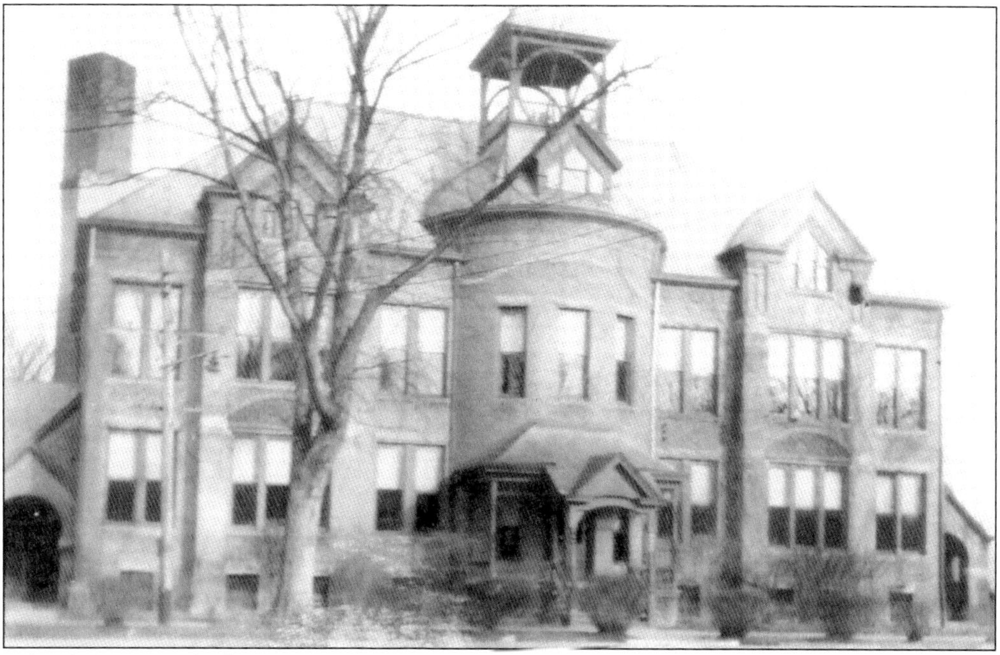

School No. 7 was built in 1890 to relieve the overcrowding at No. 3. Fire drills were introduced in the system around 1900. School No. 7 had a homelike entrance, and the janitor installed a bell to be rung for a fire alarm. An official visited at Riverside and unsuspectingly rang the bell. Much to his surprise, he was almost overwhelmed by a sudden onslaught of pupils believing there was a fire drill. (Courtesy of Riverside School Library.)

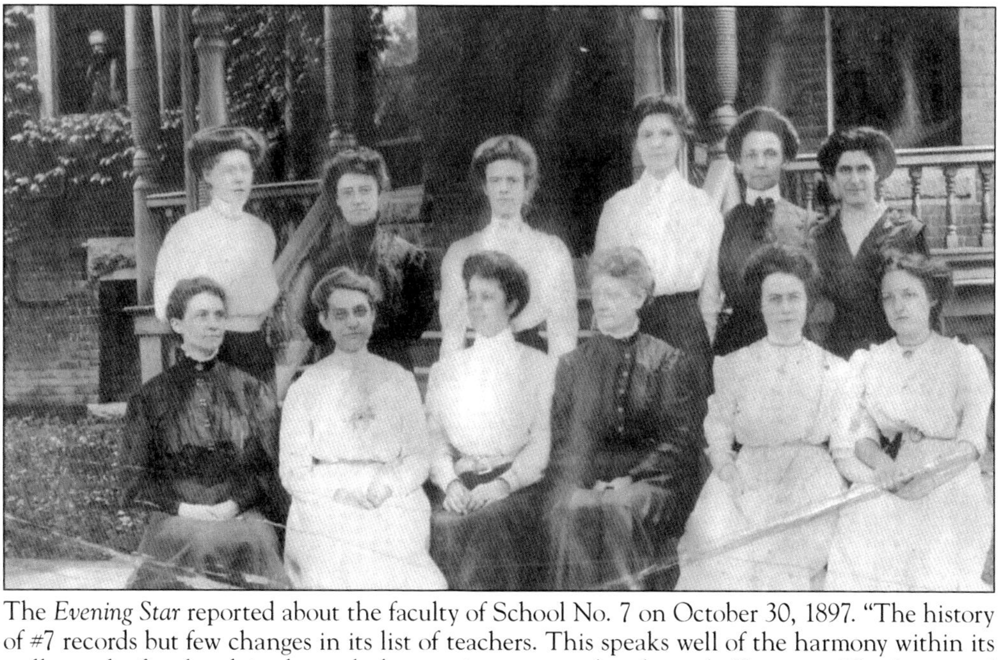

The *Evening Star* reported about the faculty of School No. 7 on October 30, 1897. "The history of #7 records but few changes in its list of teachers. This speaks well of the harmony within its walls . . . the first break in the ranks by marriage occurred at the end of last year. This happened when the working force was numbered 13 and there still is a hesitation as to whether that number shall be declared lucky or unlucky." (Courtesy of Riverside School Library.)

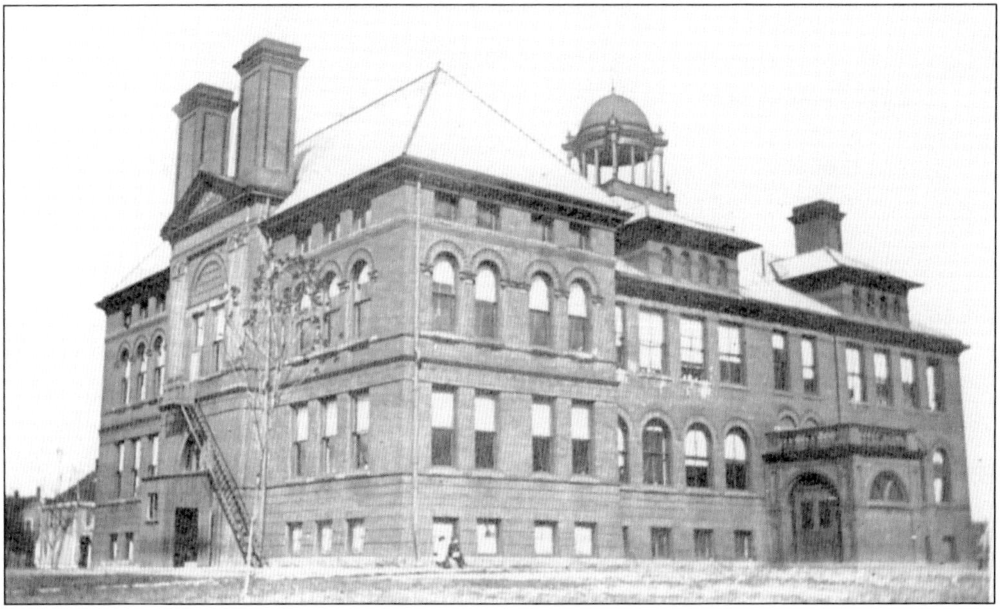

School No. 9, shown here in the early 1900s, was built in 1896. Edward Hardy was the principal from 1901 to 1942. According to *A Century of Public Education in Elmira, 1845–1945*, "Early in his principalship the school grounds, once a swale with rocks and cat-tails were filled, graded and made into a playground the envy of all the south side. The tall oaks and elms now surrounding the grounds were carried in from nearby woods by his boys and planted on Arbor Days and other festive occasions." (Courtesy of CCHS.)

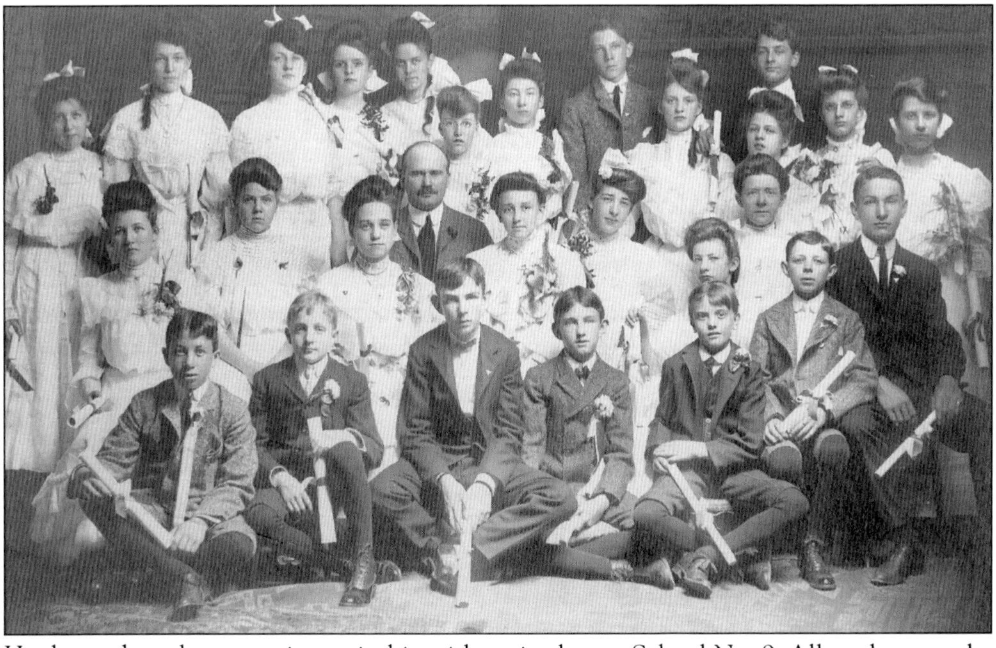

Hardy conducted an experiment in his arithmetic class at School No. 9. All work was to be done mentally and orally, without a pencil. Tests were given before and after the experiment to determine the extent of growth during the month. Principal Hardy poses here with the class of 1904. (Courtesy of CCHS.)

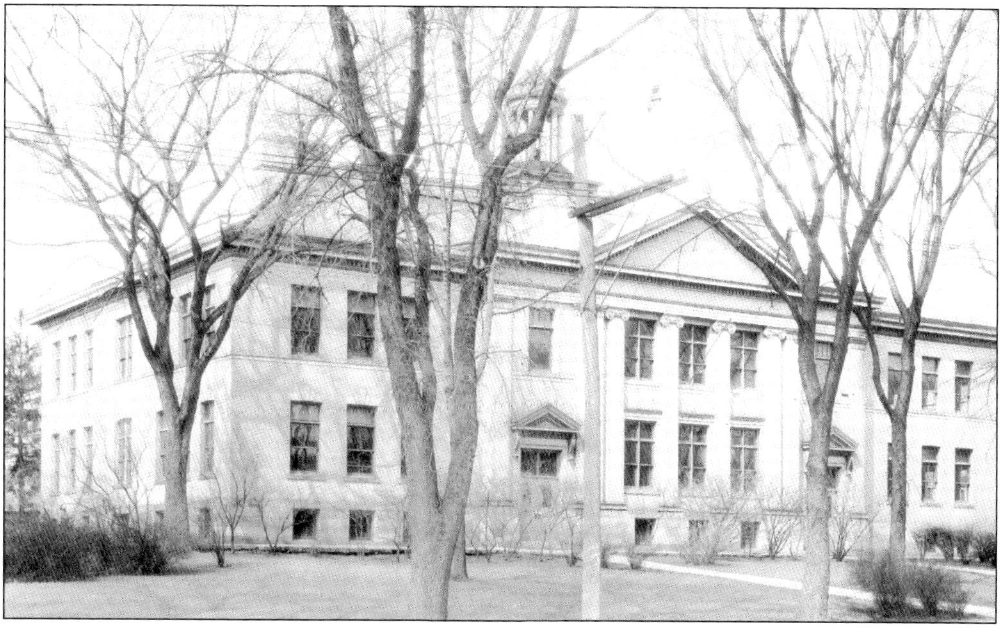

Built in 1907, School No. 11 was, for a long time, known as the "Silk Stocking" School because those building new homes in the district were "possessors of a fair degree of the world's goods." In the early years, female teachers in training were warned to wear their hair up and their skirts down. Next to the principal in his office was a "bunch of switches tied over the desk, right handy for good use." (Photograph by Fred T. Loomis, courtesy of CCHS.)

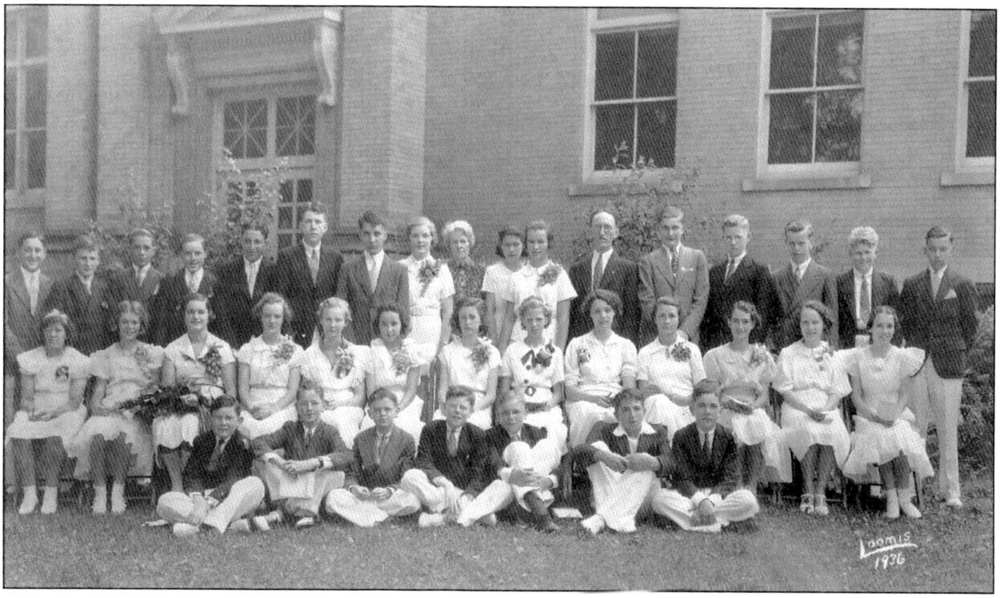

No. 11 School was the first in the Elmira Public School system to have a kindergarten, which was introduced in 1913. It was the first successful project of the Parent Teacher Association. The board of education did not support the concept, so the PTA purchased the equipment for the room and hired a qualified teacher for the first three months, after which the board assumed responsibility. Shown here is the 1936 graduation class of No. 11 (Hoffman) School. (Photograph by Fred T. Loomis, courtesy of CCHS.)

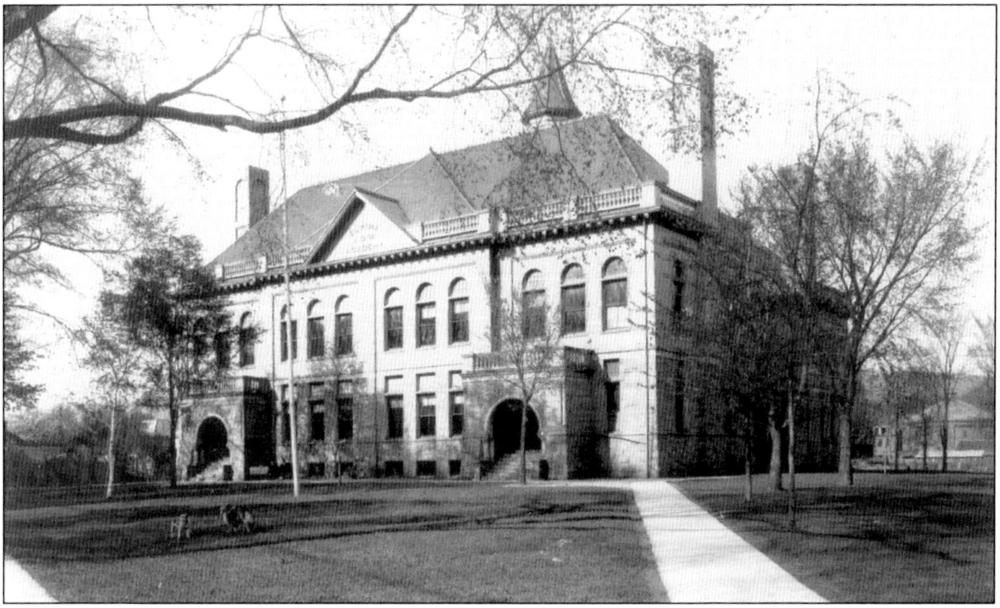

The Elmira Free Academy (EFA) began in 1836 as a private school. With the creation of the board of education in 1859, and the school's incorporation by the regents in 1863, the old academy ceased to exist and high school education became the responsibility of the taxpayer. The first EFA opened in 1862. The second building (pictured here around 1890) was built in 1890, and a third, much larger school was built in 1913 (the current Ernie Davis Middle School.) (Courtesy of CCHS.)

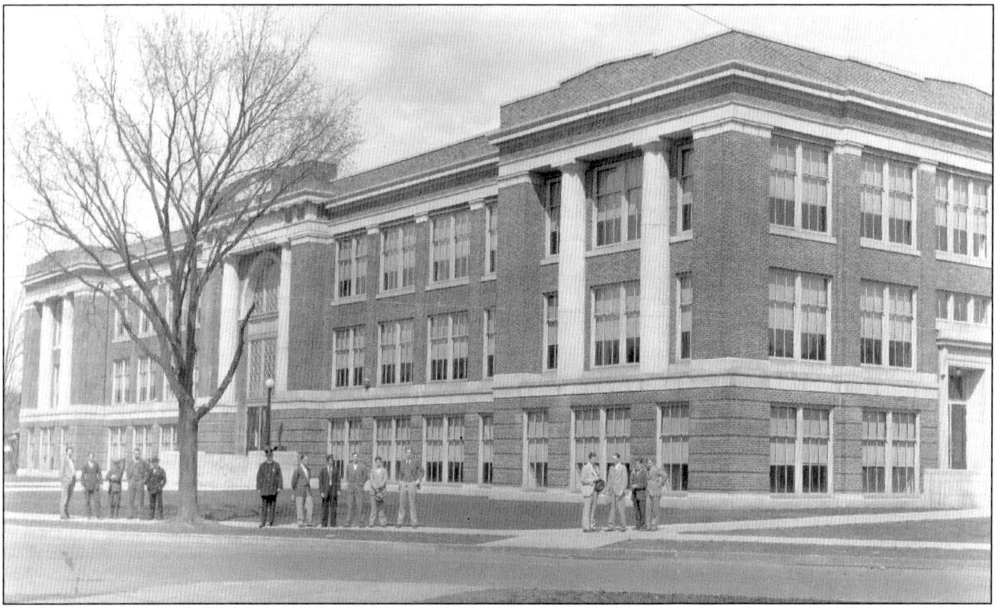

The new Southside High School opened on January 28, 1924. Designed by Pierce and Bickford Architects, it cost $520,376. It was the first high school with six grades. Frank M. Edson was the first principal, serving until his death in 1932. He was replaced by Clifford F. McNaught. The structure remained unchanged until a gym was added on the south side in the early 1960s. The building is now the Chemung Co. Human Resource Center. (Courtesy of CCHS.)

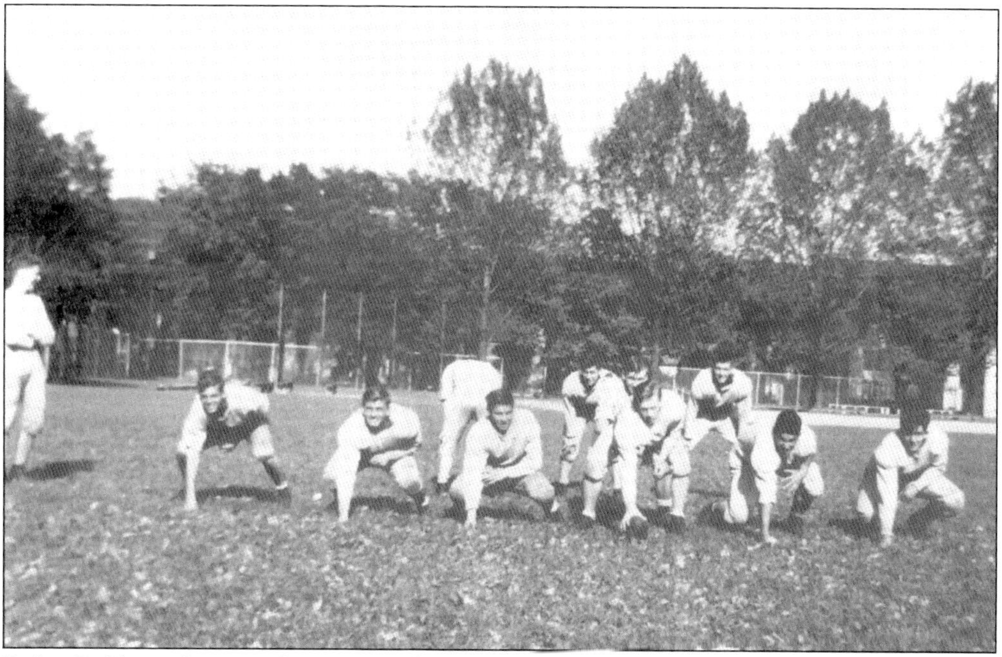

Parker Field was the scene for 48 years of sports history in Elmira. It opened in 1925 as the Elmira Athletic Field. It was later known as the Harper St. Athletic Field and, in 1937, became Parker Field in honor of longtime Elmira Free Academy principal Francis R. Parker. It was dedicated in 1948 when a monument and floodlights were installed. In 1963, the largest crowd ever to watch an Elmira football game—7,199—came to see Southside High outlast EFA, 21-13. The field ceased to exist after 1973, when the site was sold for a housing project. These 1946 images show the Elmira High School football team practicing at Parker Field. Pictured below from left to right are football coaches Bill Wipfler, Vic Impecato, and Carl Pillard. (Courtesy of CCHS.)

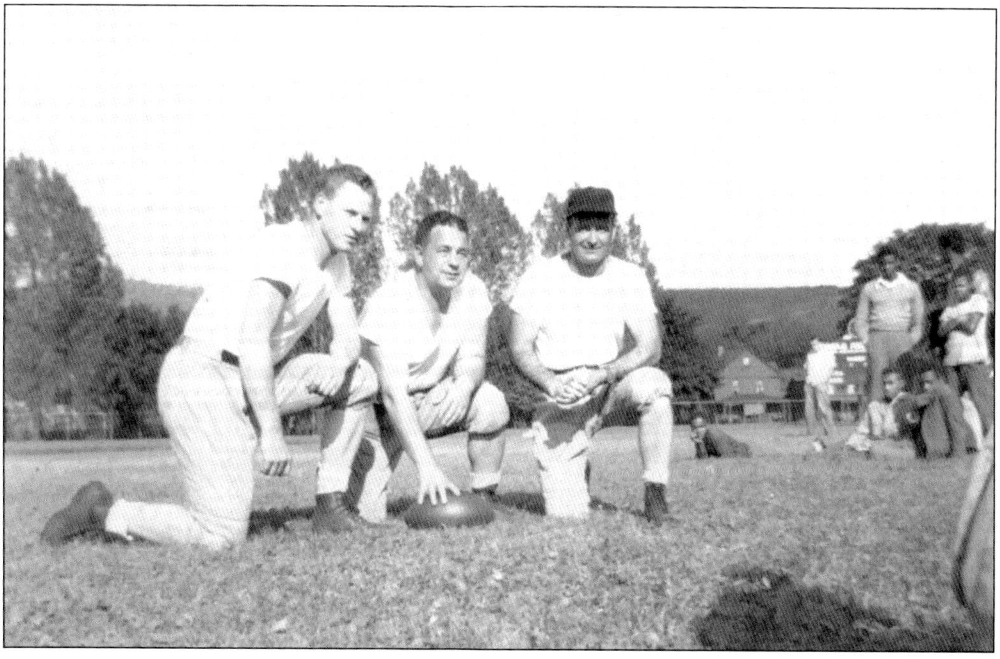

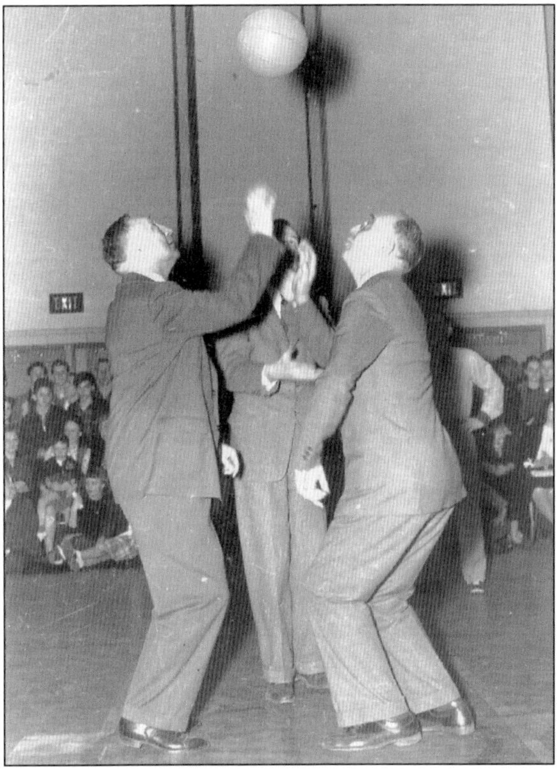

Intracity competition in sports was introduced to the Elmira School District in 1947. As the basketball season got under way, Southside principal Clifford McNaught (left) and Elmira Free Academy principal Dr. Albert Helmkamp (right) have a jump ball, marking the first intracity basketball game around 1947. (Courtesy of CCHS.)

In 1958, the Elmira Free Academy basketball team capped a two-year, 52-game winning streak with the Section 4 title. Ernie Davis's basketball coach, Jim Flynn, believed he was a better basketball player than football player. Shown here are, from left to right, (first row) John Peckally, Bob Hill (scorekeeper), Mike O'Connor, and George Williams; (second row) Tony Spallone, Joe Bednarek, Aden Galpin, Jack Moore, Coach Flynn, Ernie Davis, Ralph Quatrano, Leo Hughey, and Bill Blash. (Courtesy of CCHS.)

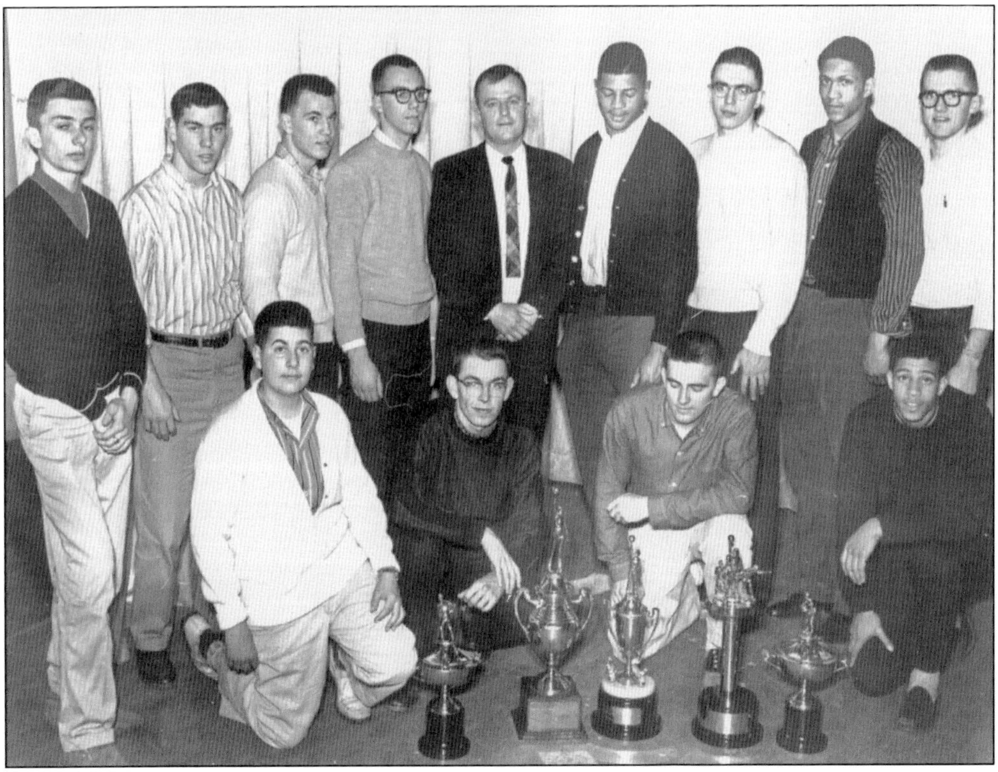

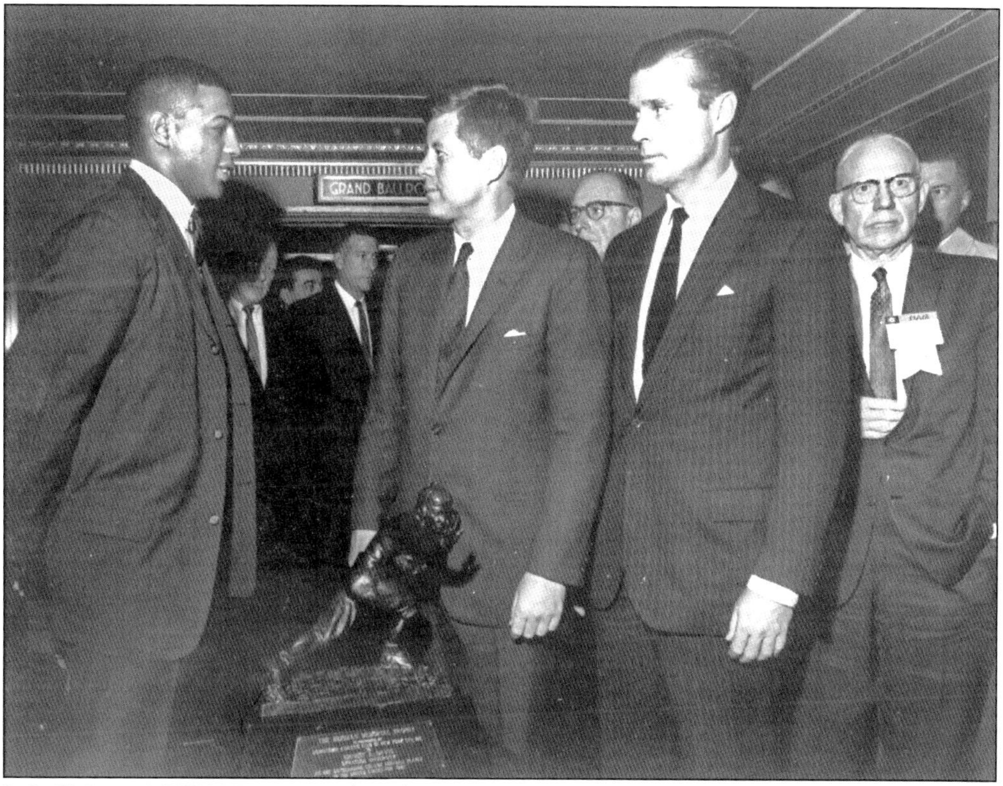

In Jeff Merron's ESPN Page 2 article "The Express in Real Life," Ernie Davis described his meeting with Pres. John F. Kennedy upon winning the Heisman Trophy in 1961: "We're standing in the anteroom talking when the doors open and here comes the president. He walked up and introduced himself, 'Hi, I'm Jack Kennedy'. We chatted and the president remarked what an honor it was to win the Heisman Trophy. A picture was taken and we left." Davis was diagnosed with leukemia and died on May 18, 1963, at age 23. (Courtesy of CCHS.)

Professional baseball began in Elmira in 1888 when the Central League was formed in response to the growing popularity of the sport. Elmira's team was called the Babies. They finished sixth in a league of twelve that year. The team is shown here around 1888. (Courtesy of the National Baseball Hall of Fame.)

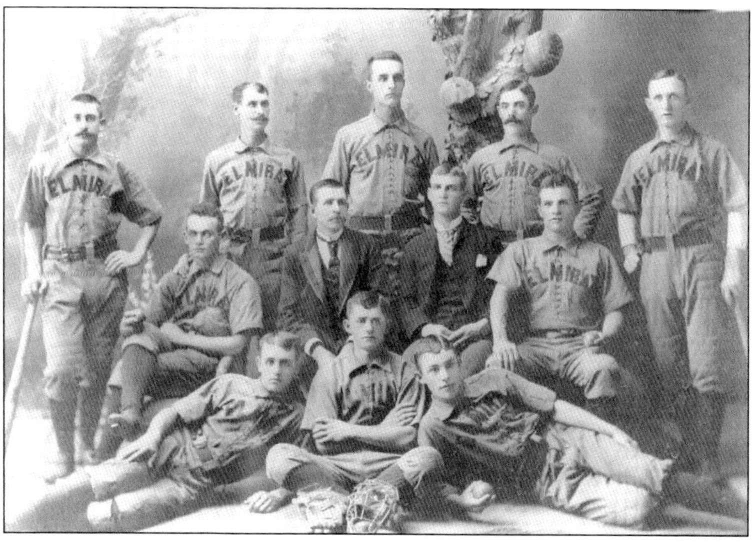

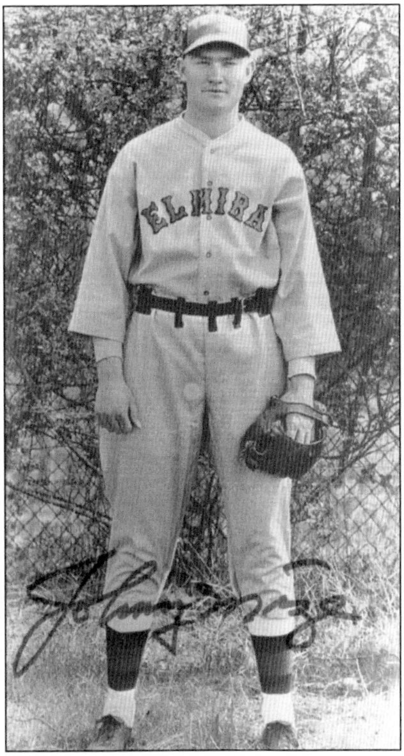

"The Big Cat," Johnny Mize (1913–1993) played for Elmira in 1932. He played in 106 games, batting .326 with 8 home runs. Mize played in the majors from 1936 to 1953, ending his Hall of Fame career with the Yankees. At his 1981 induction, Mize introduced himself to Marty Chalk (vice president of the Elmira Pioneers) and told him that his baseball career took him to many places, but that Elmira was his favorite. He particularly liked Moretti's Restaurant, and his favorite spot was The Patch. (Courtesy of the National Baseball Hall of Fame.)

Dunn Field, located on the southeast side of the city, was one of the nation's best minor league ballparks. The site where Dunn Field is located was assembled by Edward J. Dunn. Late in 1938, The Dunn Field Corporation and the federal Public Works Administration began work on a new stadium, which was completed in early 1939. Floodlights were installed on June 12 of that year. This c. 1940 aerial photograph shows the stadium before the development of the current residential area surrounding it. (Courtesy of CCHS.)

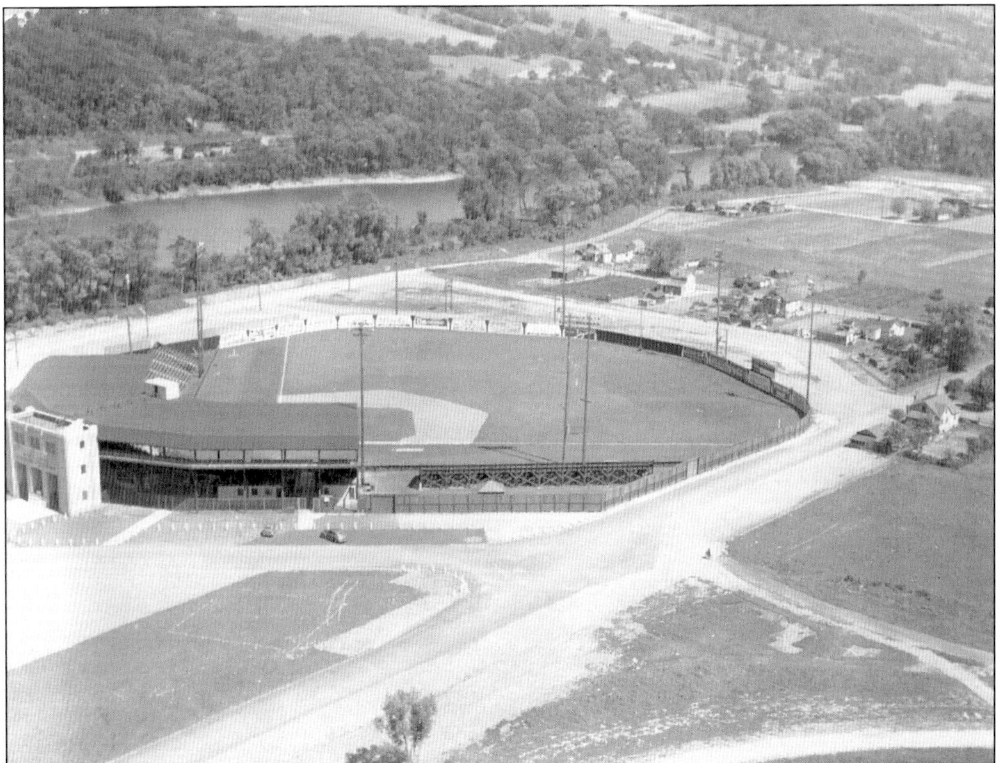

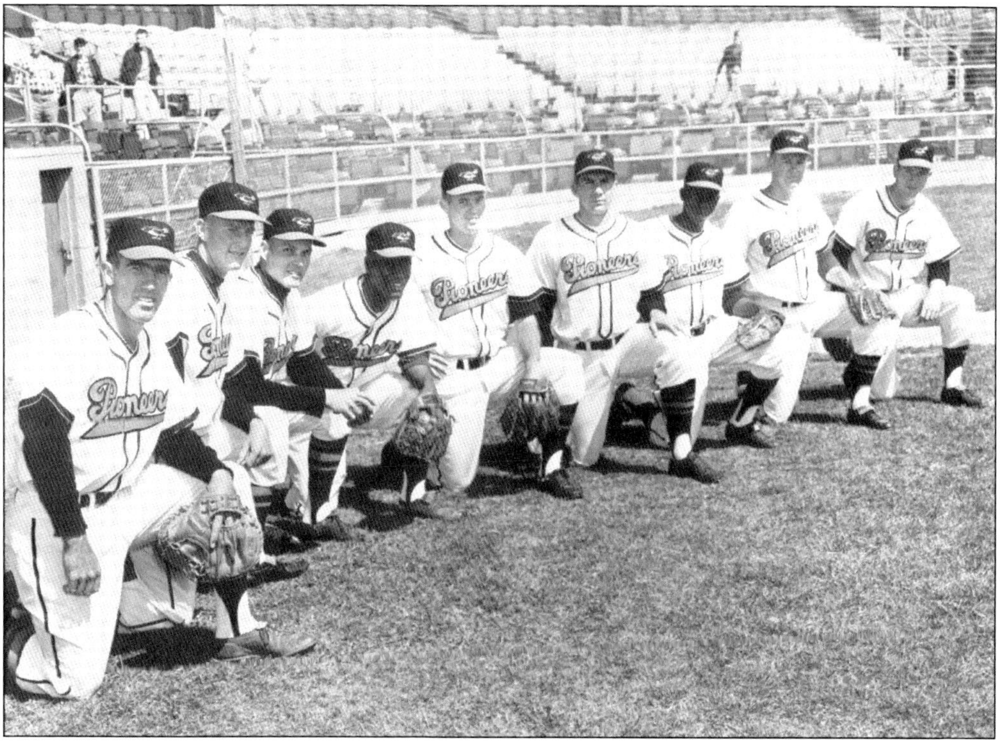

The period from 1962 to 1968 has been called the golden age of baseball in Elmira. The Baltimore Orioles were the major league affiliate. The Pioneers went to the playoffs five times and won the championship twice. The 1962 championship squad sent four players to the majors (ML). Players from that team shown here are, from left to right, Andy Etchebarren C (ML), Dick Henderson 1B, Jim Vadas 2B, Mickey McGuire SS (ML), Nellie Cochran 3B, Lloyd Fourroux LF, Joe Pulliam CF, Jim Liggett RF, and Dave McNally P (ML.) (Courtesy of Art Wellington.)

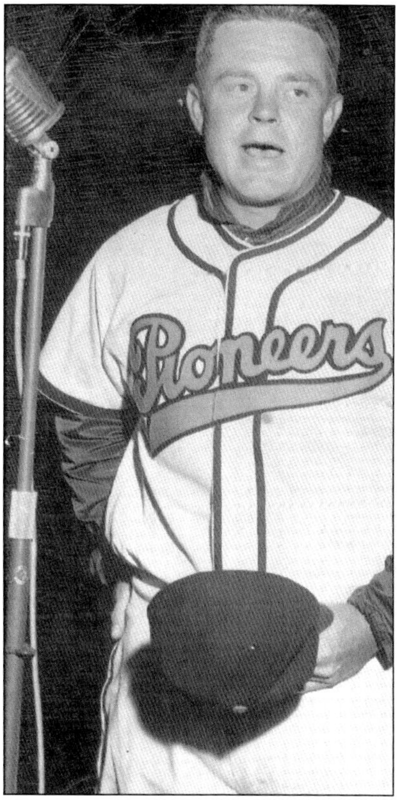

Was Earl Weaver (The Banty Rooster) Elmira's best manager? He won one pennant, finished second the other three times, and won the Eastern League Governor's Cup in 1962. He managed Elmira from 1962 to 1965. (Courtesy of CCHS.)

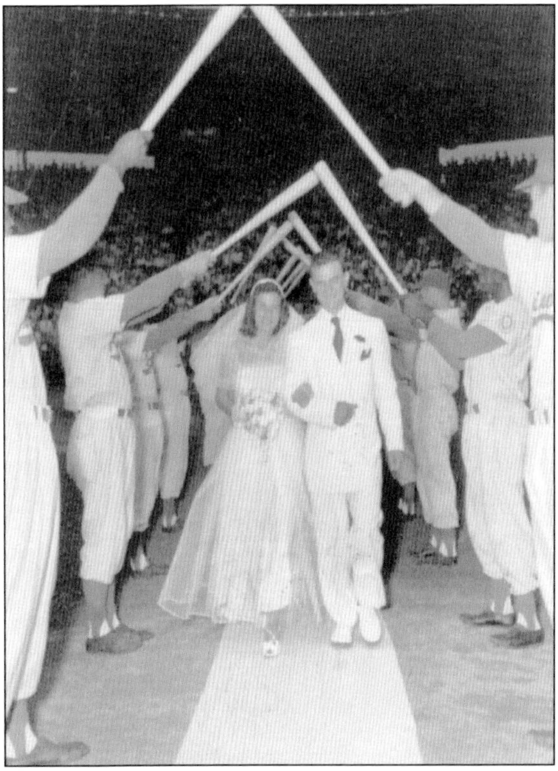

Don Zimmer began his professional baseball career in 1949 and never looked back. He broke in to the major leagues in 1954. Since 1971, he has managed or coached every year. In 1989, as skipper of the Chicago Cubs, he was named Manager of the Year. Zim, while playing for the Elmira Pioneers, married his high school sweetheart at home plate on Dunn Field on August 16, 1951. Jean (Soot) Zimmer wrote to the authors, "Dunn Field and Elmira will always have a place in our hearts" (May 24, 2012.) (Courtesy of The Elmira Pioneers.)

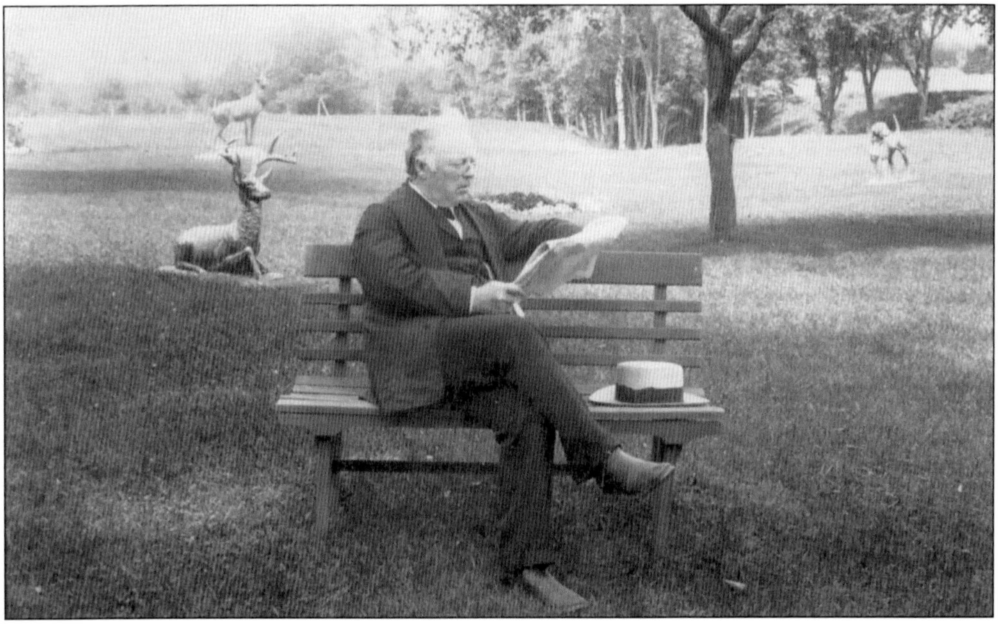

Dr. Edwin Eldridge came to Elmira in 1857. He purchased and developed the park and surroundings that bears his name today. Ausburn Towner wrote, "He made it a garden of beauty, with his own eye and taste directing the grading and filling, the planting of trees and formation of artificial ponds and lakes" The park was private property but open to the public. He died unexpectedly in 1876, and the city purchased the property in 1889. (Courtesy of CCHS.)

On October 2, 1875, at the inaugural meet at the Driving Park racetrack at Eldridge Park, American Girl, a 13-year-old mare, dropped dead in the middle of the race. Newspaper accounts say a rainbow appeared. The Driving Park Association, moved by the tragic event, elected to build a statue of the horse. The statue was destroyed by vandals in 1980. (Courtesy of CCHS.)

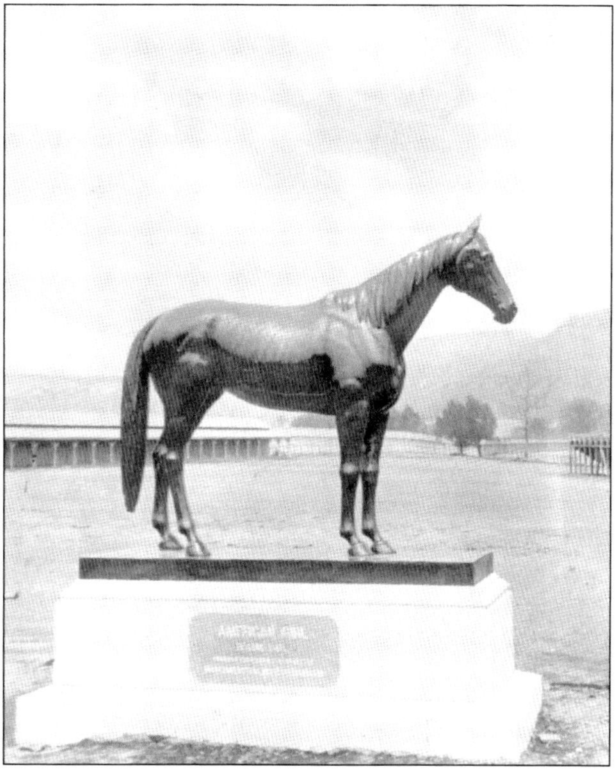

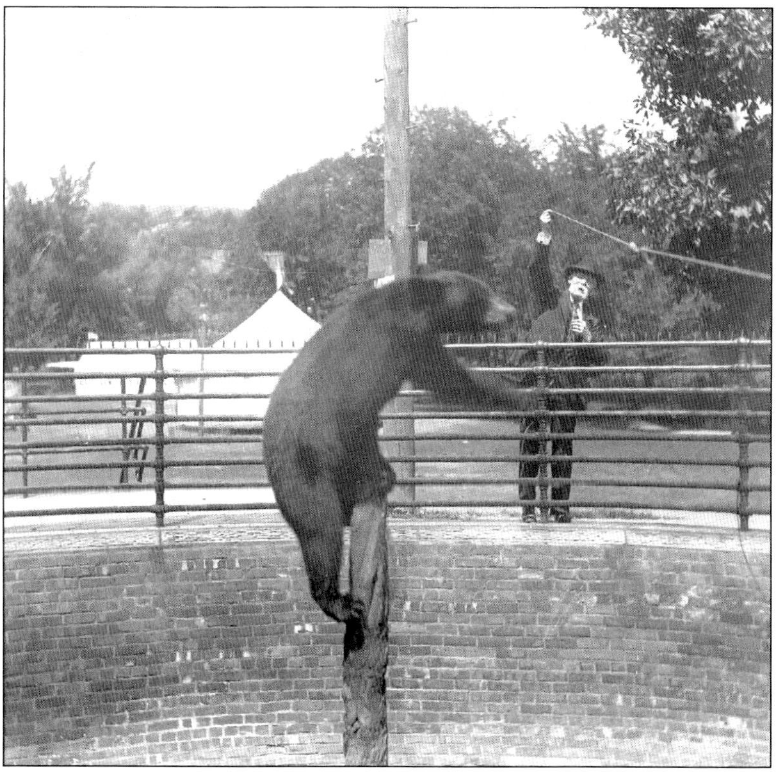

The Bear Pit had its heyday from 1907 to 1910. In addition to three brown bears, the facility also had deer and some monkeys. By 1924, only one bear remained, although traveling shows took place there. This photograph is from around 1902. (Courtesy of CCHS.)

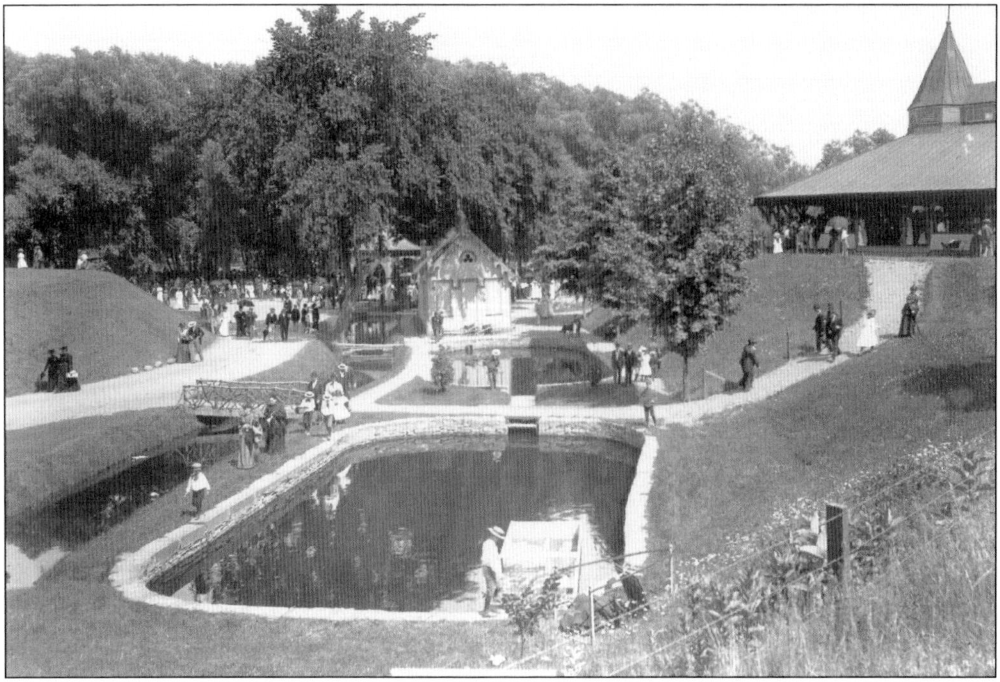

The Dance Pavilion was built about 1890 as a station for the Erie Railroad. It shut down as a station in 1910, when train service was discontinued. Architecturally, it was the most significant building in the park. (Photograph by Elisha and Charles Van Aken, courtesy of CCHS.)

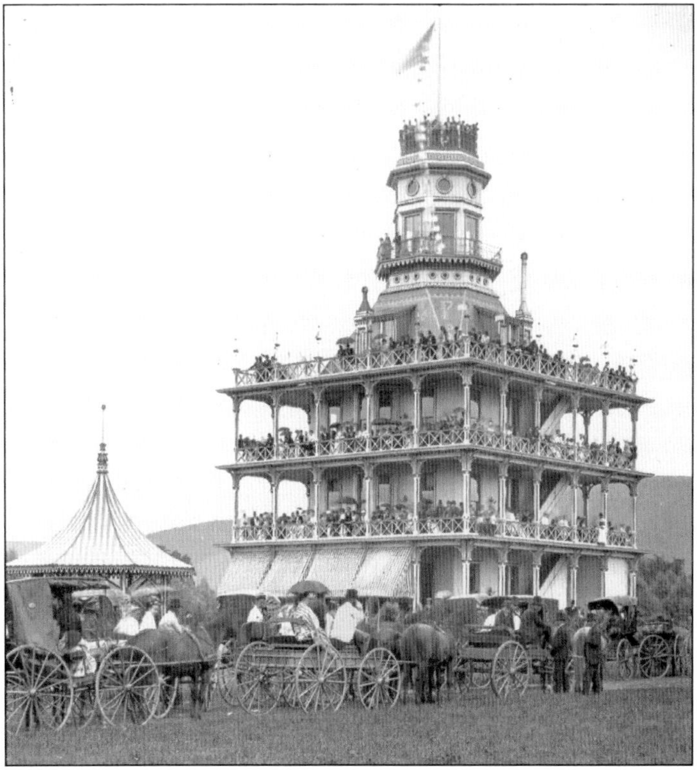

The Casino, shown here around 1890, was one of the principal attractions when the property was owned by Dr. Eldridge and for some years after his death in 1876. It had a restaurant (but did not serve alcohol), a dance floor, an ice cream parlor, and an observation tower. Folks crowded the pinnacle to see the lake exhibitions and fireworks. Most fascinating was Dr. Eldridge's mechanical mermaid, which would rise and disappear in the lake when a concealed cord was pulled. (Courtesy of CCHS.)

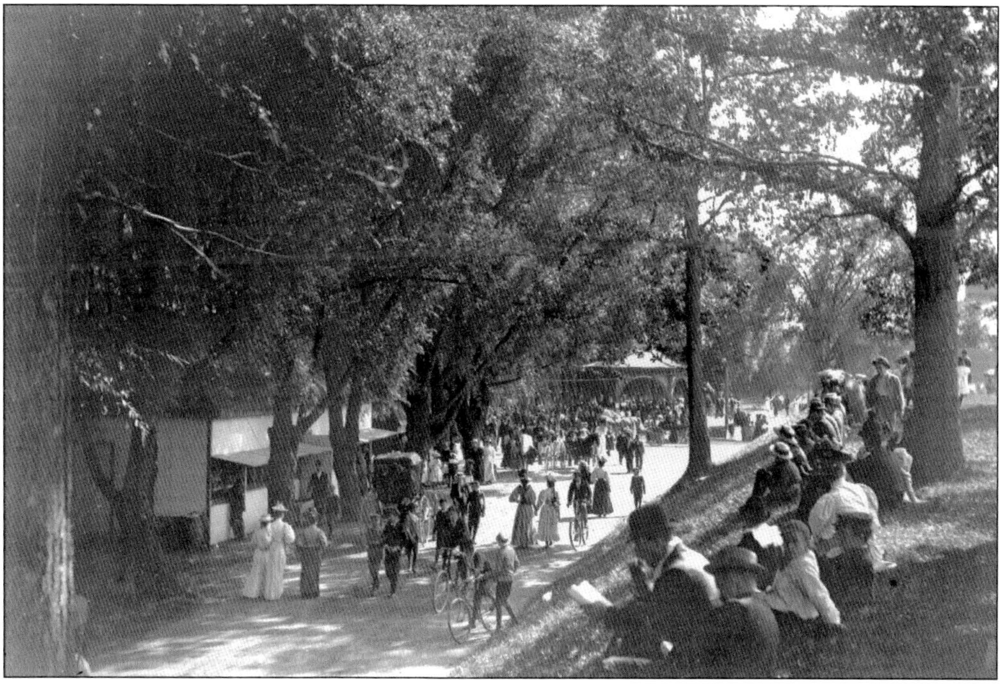

The midway at Eldridge Park was developed in 1900. The original midway, shown above, lasted until 1939, when it was replaced by a more modern midway with an Art Deco design (below). Eldridge Park provided a variety of entertainment. People like to remember the roller coaster, Kiddieland, bumper cars, the dragon boat, and the whip. (Above, courtesy of CCHS; below, courtesy of *Elmira Star Gazette*.)

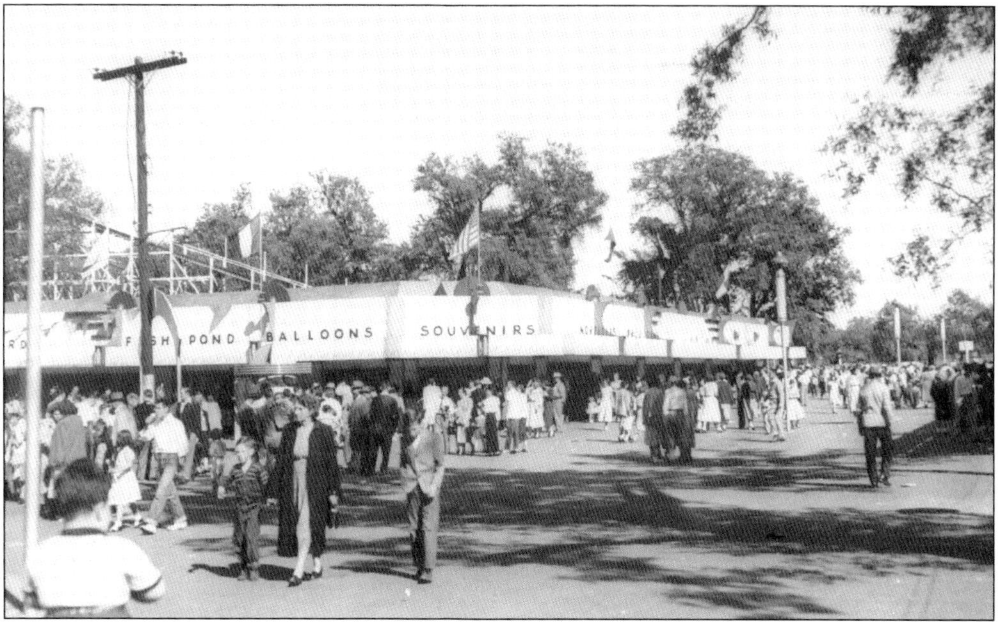

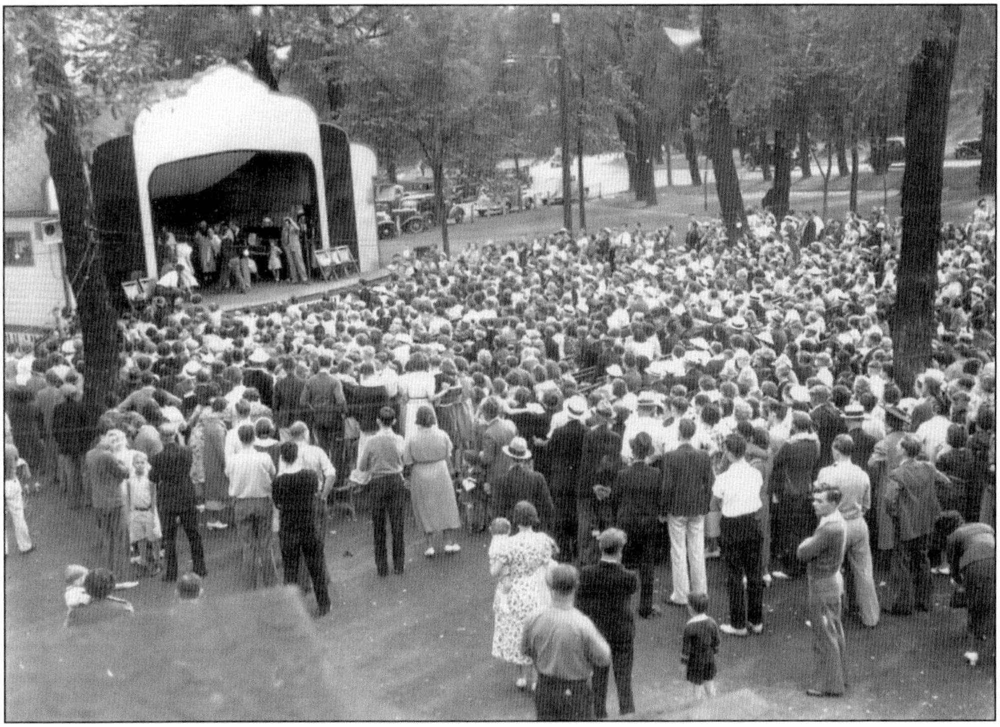

The Eldridge Park Talent Parade was built about 1940 by Art Kendall Jr., apparently at the urging of City Park superintendent Fred Wright. It reflected the diversity of activities at the park after the Depression. With the arrival of Jay Parker as director of public relations, the peak years for the stage were 1952–1976. Talent shows, musical entertainment, beauty pageants, and circus acts could be seen there. (Courtesy of CCHS.)

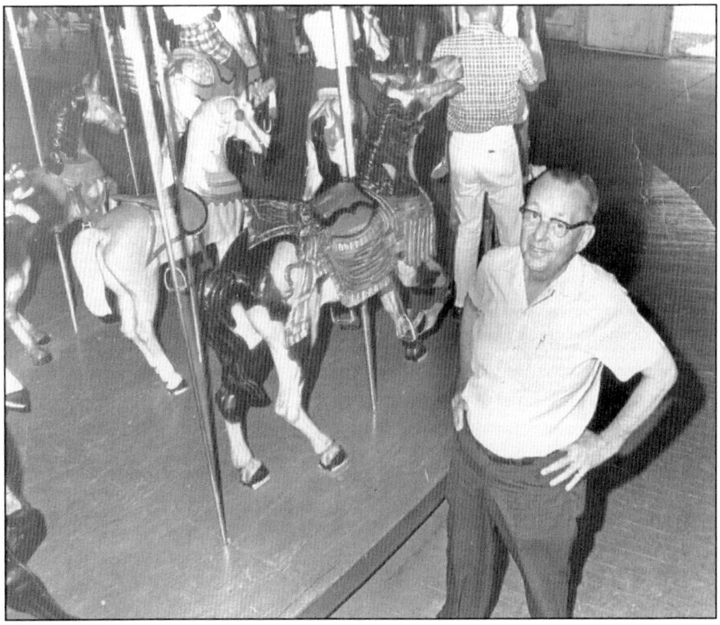

Bob Long (shown here around 1966) spent his boyhood summers working for his father at Eldridge Park during its peak years (1910–1916). The Long family were pioneers in the American carousel industry. When Bob and his wife, Ruth, took over operation of the park in 1924, he installed the park's third merry-go-round (his father had installed the second.) The Longs operated the park until 1981. (Courtesy of CCHS.)

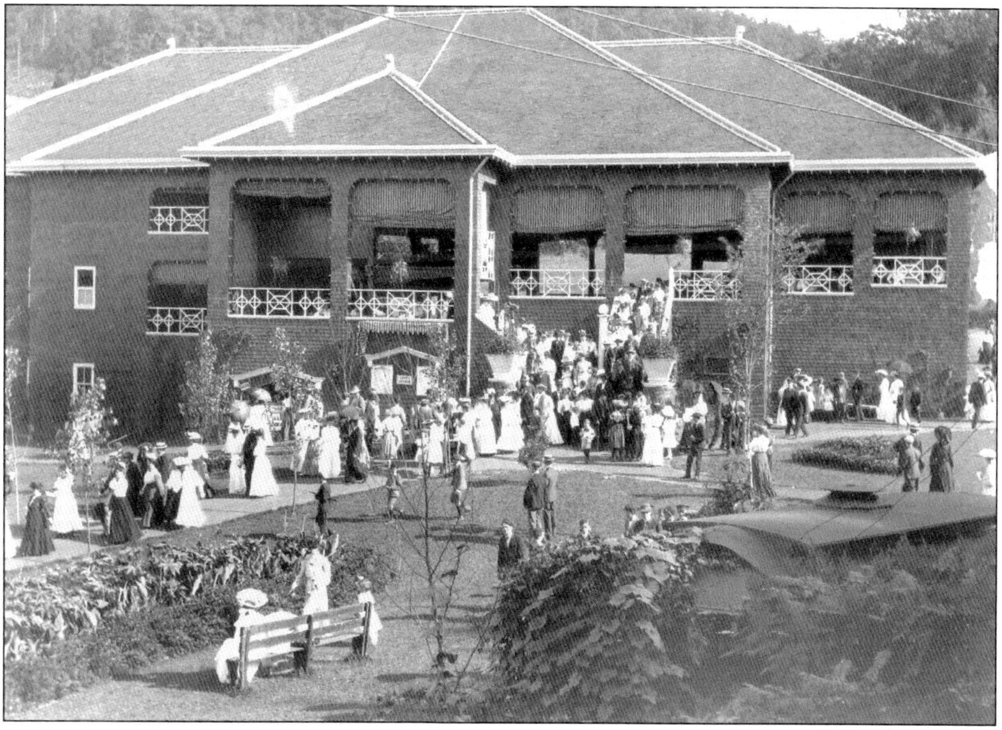

Rorick's Glen thrived from 1901 to 1917. Originally built on the west side of the city to stimulate streetcar business, it became a family-oriented open-air theater with considerable appeal for Broadway actors during the summer. It also had a miniature railroad, roller coaster, giant swing, restaurant, and dance hall. The automobile, movies, and World War I contributed to its decline. (Courtesy of CCHS.)

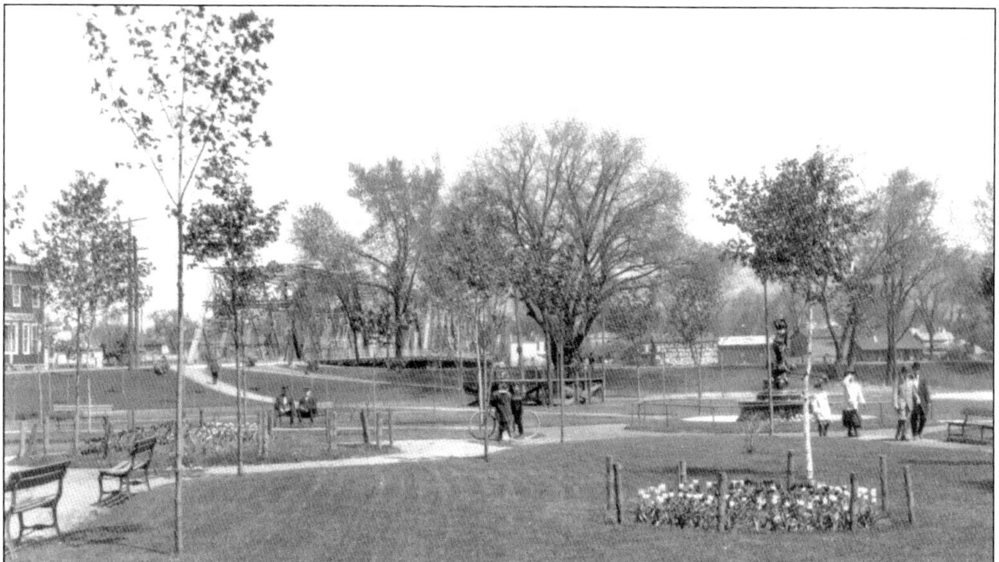

Riverside Park (now Brand Park) was purchased by the city in 1901. It was described as being east of Maple Avenue, near the Chemung River and south of Brand Park. One account said, "It is a favorite site for picnic parties and has a small pavilion." (Courtesy of CCHS.)

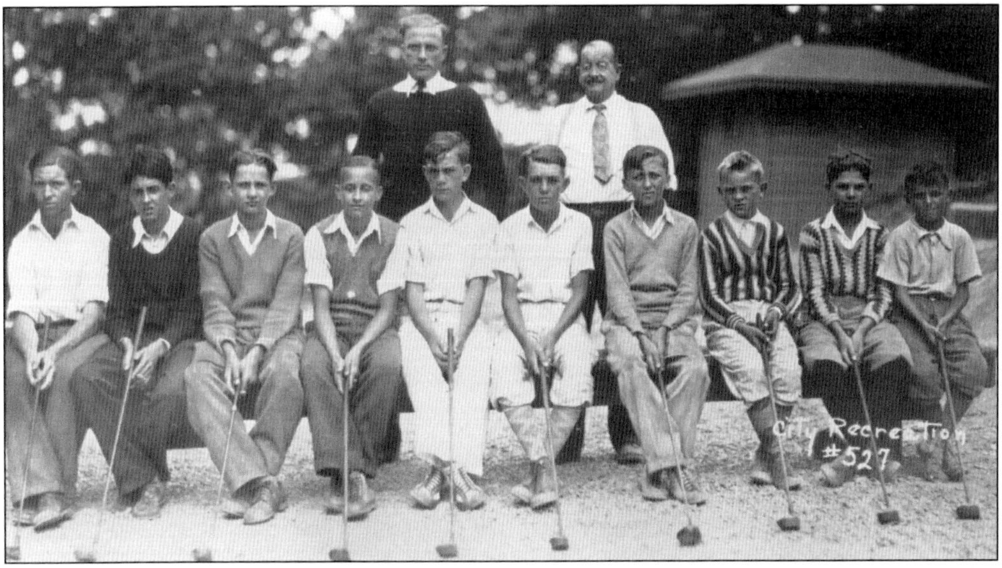

Elmira had a number of golf courses. Public links at Eldridge Park opened in 1923. The Eldridge course was abandoned in 1925 when a semi-private, nine-hole course was developed on Lower Maple Avenue (Riverside Golf Course). Mark Twain Park, which opened on East Hill in 1928, included a golf course, tennis court, and baseball diamond. The City Recreation League ran a golfing program at the East Hill course. Mike Rybak, future Mark Twain Golf Course superintendent, is shown here on the far right. (Courtesy of John Corsi.)

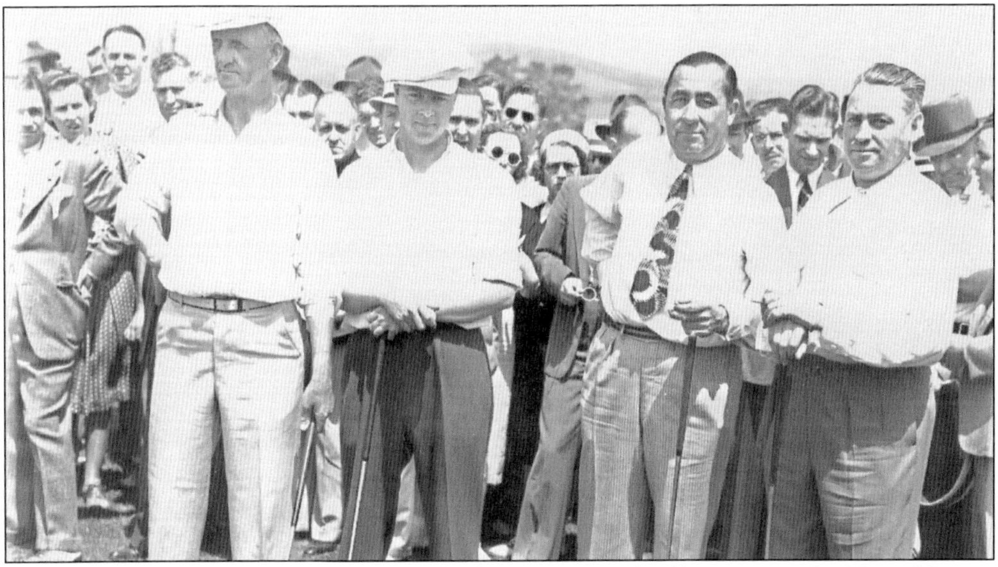

The city of Elmira is blessed with one of the finest municipal golf courses in the United States. In 1937, with WPA funds, the city council hired Donald Ross and Robert Trent Jones to design a course. The council acquired land, and construction started July 1 of that year. Workers were taken from city relief rolls. As high as 250 men were employed through December. The following spring, work resumed uninterrupted until nine holes were completed in May 1939. The golf course opened with an exhibition match featuring, from left to right, Elmira Country Club professional Tom Bonnar, Jim Hunter (an outstanding amateur player), Walter Hagen, and city judge Bill Phillips (president of the Mark Twain Advisory Board). (Courtesy of CCHS.)

Five

GOVERNMENT

When John Arnot Jr. was sworn in as the city of Elmira's first mayor on April 19, 1864, he and the new common council faced many challenges. The nation was in the midst of Civil War, and Elmira was intimately involved. The city became a state military depot in 1861, a federal draft rendezvous in 1863, and the site of the Elmira Prison Camp in July 1864. Some would eventually call Elmira the "Andersonville of the North." A majority of the survivors of the camp would remember it as "Helmira." Burials began at Woodlawn Cemetery in 1864 for those who had died in the prison camp. That portion of the cemetery would become the National Cemetery in 1877.

All of the military activity was complicated by a well-organized gang of thieves and counterfeiters who were operating over a wide territory. Elmira was one of their important centers of operation and, 40 years later, Elmirans were comparing this period to the Wild West. The eventual selection of John Stuart Knapp as police chief began the city's efforts to combat the crime wave.

Elmira was protected by six volunteer fire companies. Competition among them over territory, positions in parades, and other issues posed real challenges. In 1859, the state legislature granted a charter to the village to organize the Elmira Fire Department. It remained a volunteer organization until 1878, when the last volunteer company was disbanded.

The state legislature was busy in 1859. It not only created the fire department and the board of education, it also incorporated the Elmira Water Company for a cost of $50,000. In 1870, a million-gallon reservoir was built. By 1900, all utilities were merged into the Elmira Water, Light & Railroad Co. A public referendum in 1913 created the public entity known as the Elmira Water Board.

Not resting on its laurels, the legislature was busy in 1869, authorizing the establishment of an institution for male offenders between the ages of 16 and 30 who had never previously been convicted of a crime. Elmira was selected as the location. This facility would be called the New York State Reformatory. It opened in July 1876 with 30 inmates; by the following year, the population was 164.

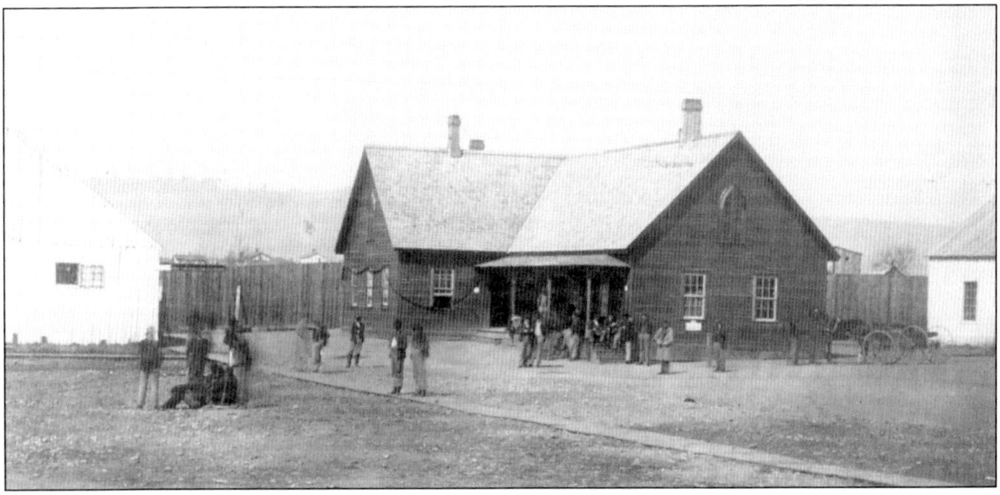

When Elmira was declared a military depot for western New York in 1861 and then a draft rendezvous in 1863, coordination was required. Four camps were built and, over the course of the Civil War, 20,796 soldiers were trained in Elmira's camps. Shown here is the administration building during the war years. (Courtesy of CCHS.)

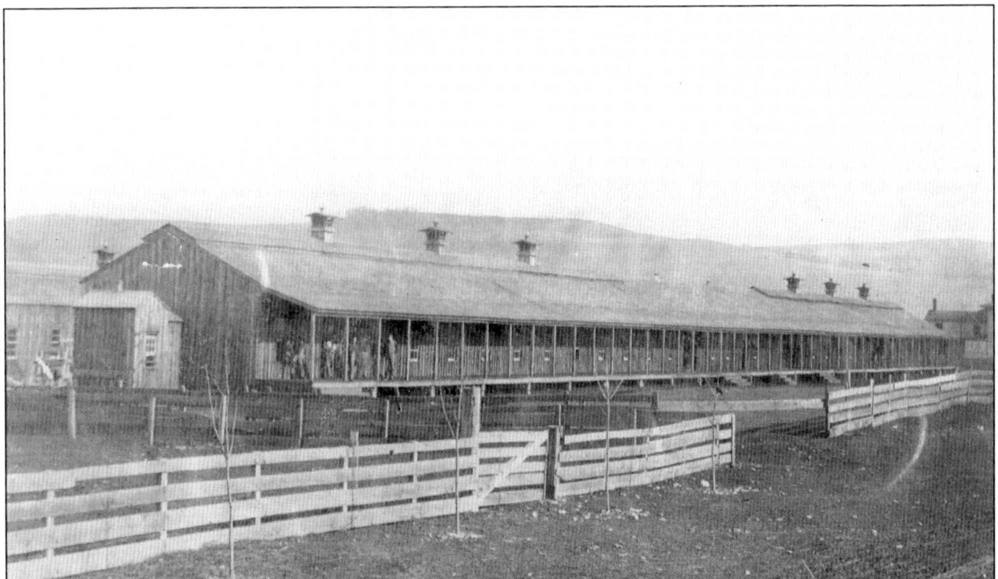

During the Civil War, death came more often from disease, infection, or unsanitary conditions than from bullets. With troops mustering in Elmira and the impending establishment of a prison camp, a hospital was needed. In 1864, a plan was made to build new 400-bed units within a mile of the barracks housing troops. This photograph is from around 1864. (Courtesy of CCHS.)

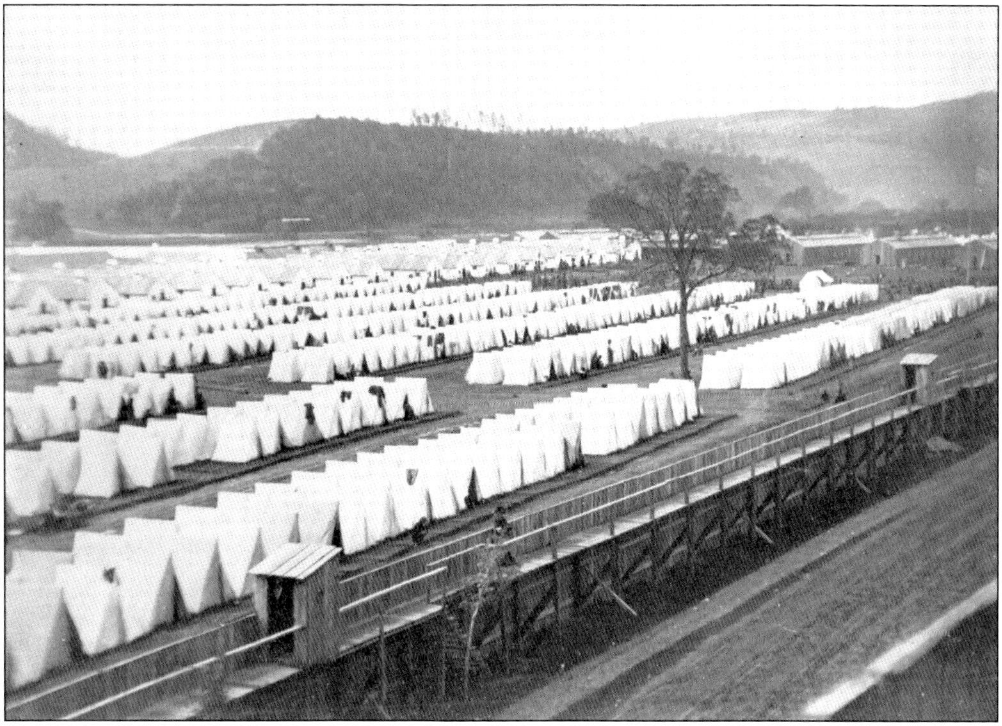

As Michael Horigan writes, tents were used to house over 5,000 Confederate prisoners in the late summer of 1864. Some prisoners slept in them until late December, when the last of the winter barracks were completed. (Courtesy of CCHS.)

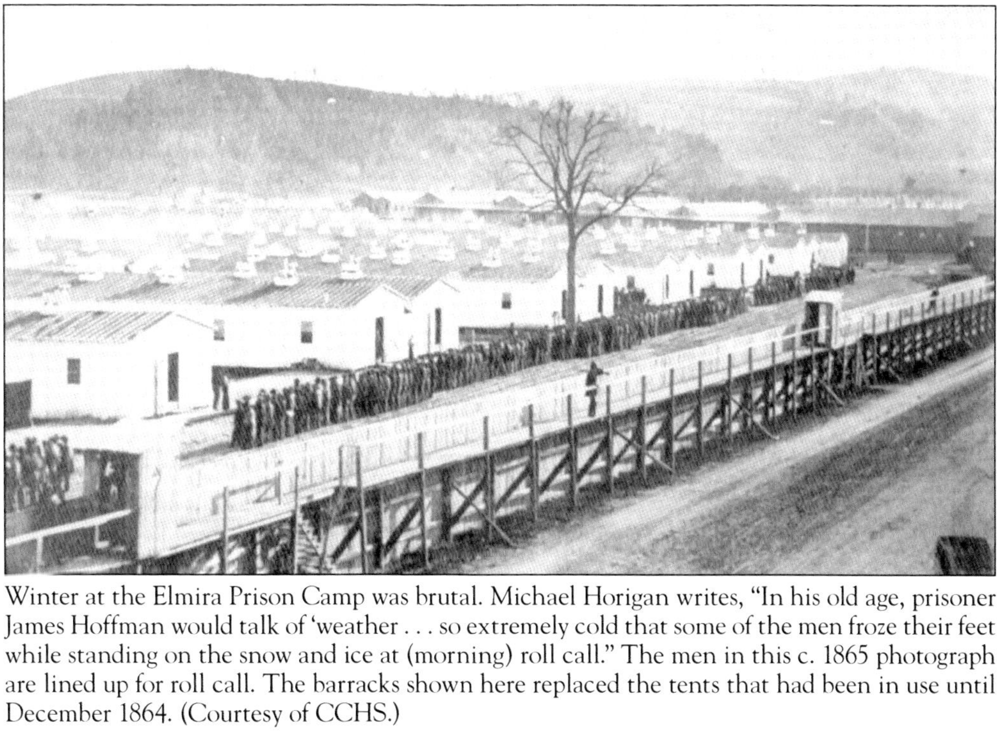

Winter at the Elmira Prison Camp was brutal. Michael Horigan writes, "In his old age, prisoner James Hoffman would talk of 'weather . . . so extremely cold that some of the men froze their feet while standing on the snow and ice at (morning) roll call." The men in this c. 1865 photograph are lined up for roll call. The barracks shown here replaced the tents that had been in use until December 1864. (Courtesy of CCHS.)

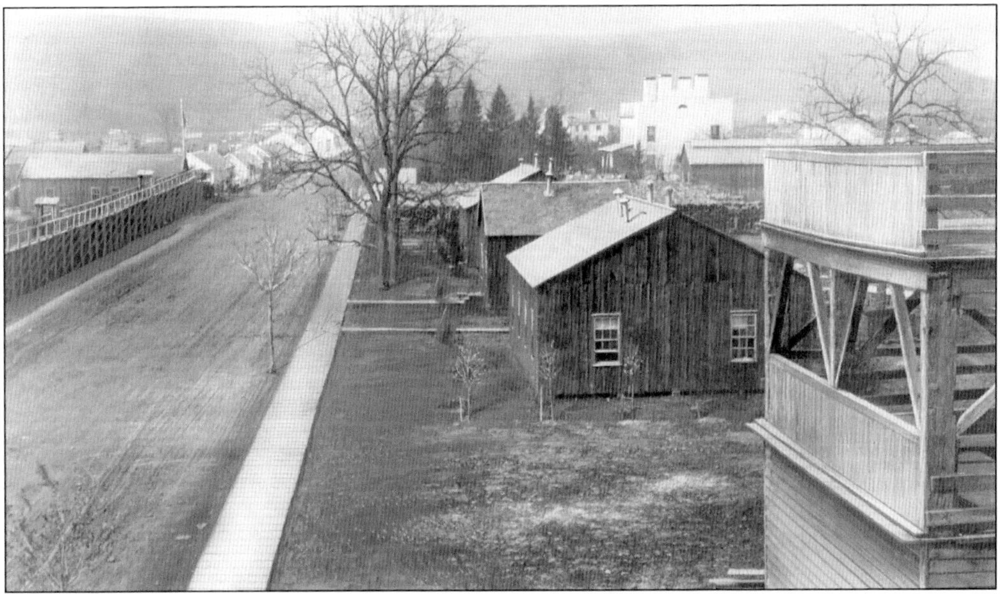

Looking west from the Mears brothers' observatory, customers could see the original observatory on the far right and, beyond that, three buildings that served as officer's quarters. The white brick Georgian-style structure in the background was the Foster home. As recounted by Horigan, the *Elmira Daily Gazette* noted the fine attraction of observatories and urged all strangers and citizens to visit them, because "the pictures taken from there will always be remembered." (Courtesy of CCHS.)

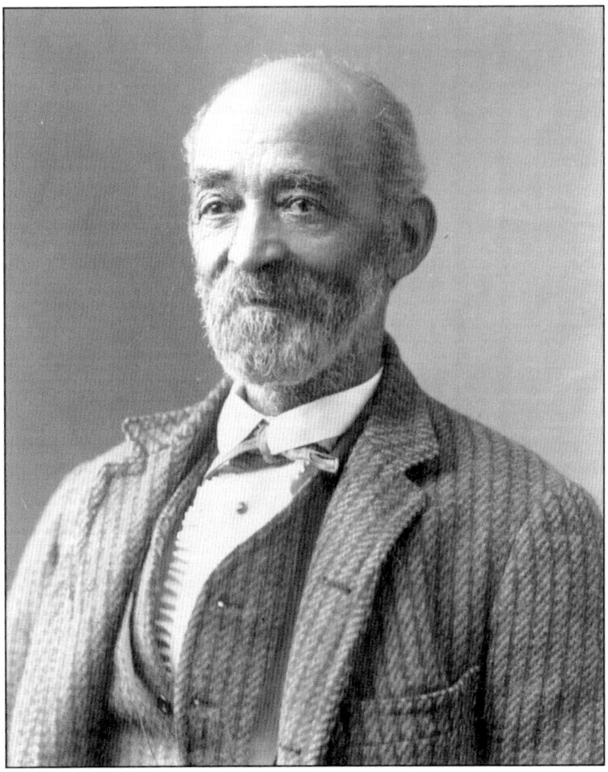

John W. Jones, a runaway slave from Virginia who came to Elmira in 1844, dug the graves and recorded the markers of the Confederate dead. Jones learned to read and write and served as sexton of the First Baptist Church until 1890. Before the war, Jones helped make Elmira a major link in the Underground Railroad, aiding slaves escaping to Canada. (Courtesy of CCHS.)

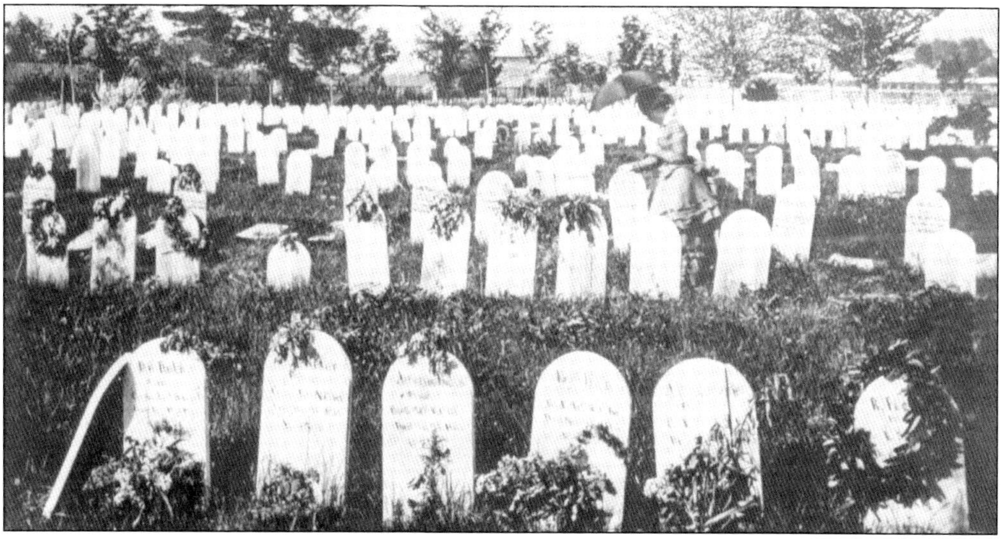

Approximately 12,000 prisoners were housed at Elmira. The remains of nearly 3,000 Confederate dead were laid out in what would become Woodlawn National Cemetery. In 1907, the original wooden markers were replaced with permanent stone markers put in place by the US government. The cemetery was cared for, under contract, by the city until 1946. This photograph is from around 1905. (Courtesy of CCHS.)

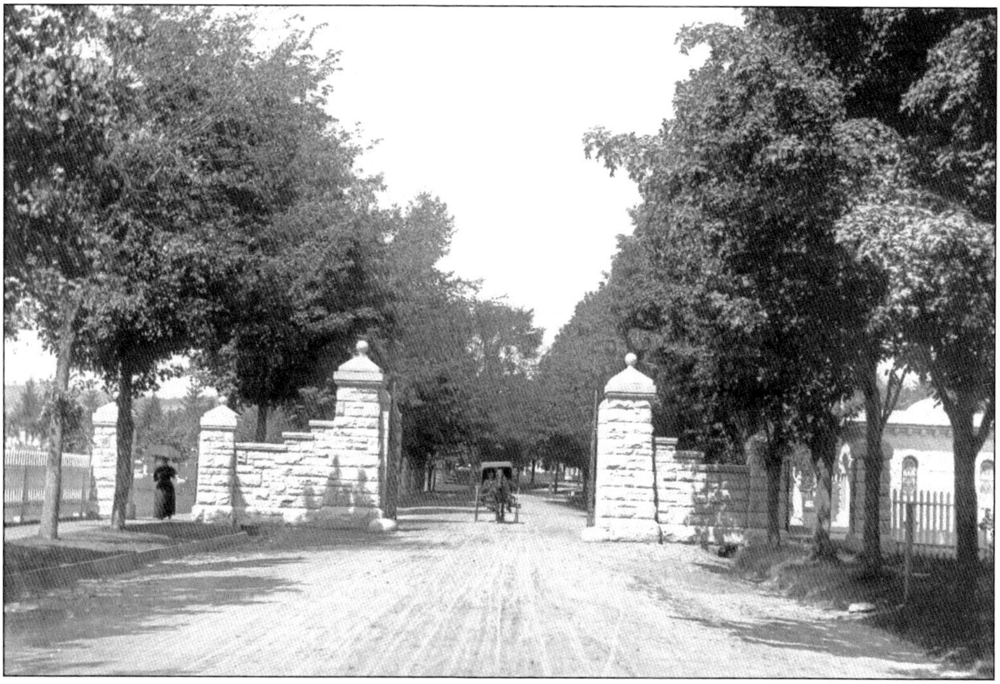

In 1858, local leaders saw the need to establish another cemetery for the city. This was an era when most burials were on church property or private grounds. Officials obtained a $10,000 loan from the state legislature on behalf of the village and purchased three 12-and-one-half-acre plots. The cemetery was expanded in 1874, 1892, 1899, and 1920 to approximately 184 acres. It became an example of the "park-like" cemeteries of the mid-1800s. The cemetery entrance is seen here around 1900. (Photograph by Elisha and Charles Van Aken, courtesy of CCHS.)

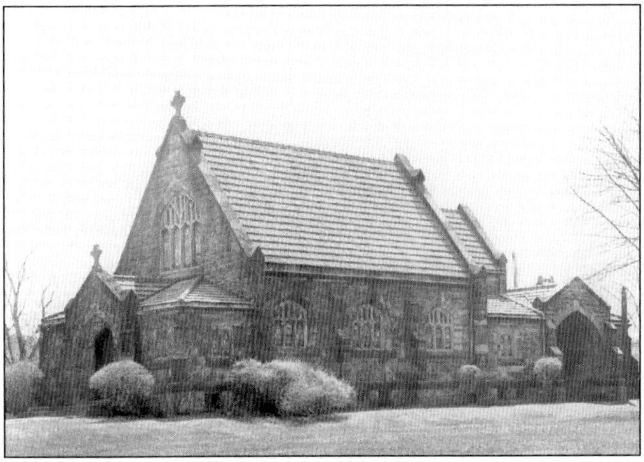

The headline in the *Telegram* of December 8, 1907, read, "A new mortuary chapel at Woodlawn. It may be a pleasure to die just to have a chance to have last rites observed in this artistic vestibule to the grave." In 1960, as funeral directors took over more of the burials, the decision was made to convert the chapel to office space. The cross was taken down, and the stained-glass windows were removed. (Courtesy of Woodlawn Cemetery.)

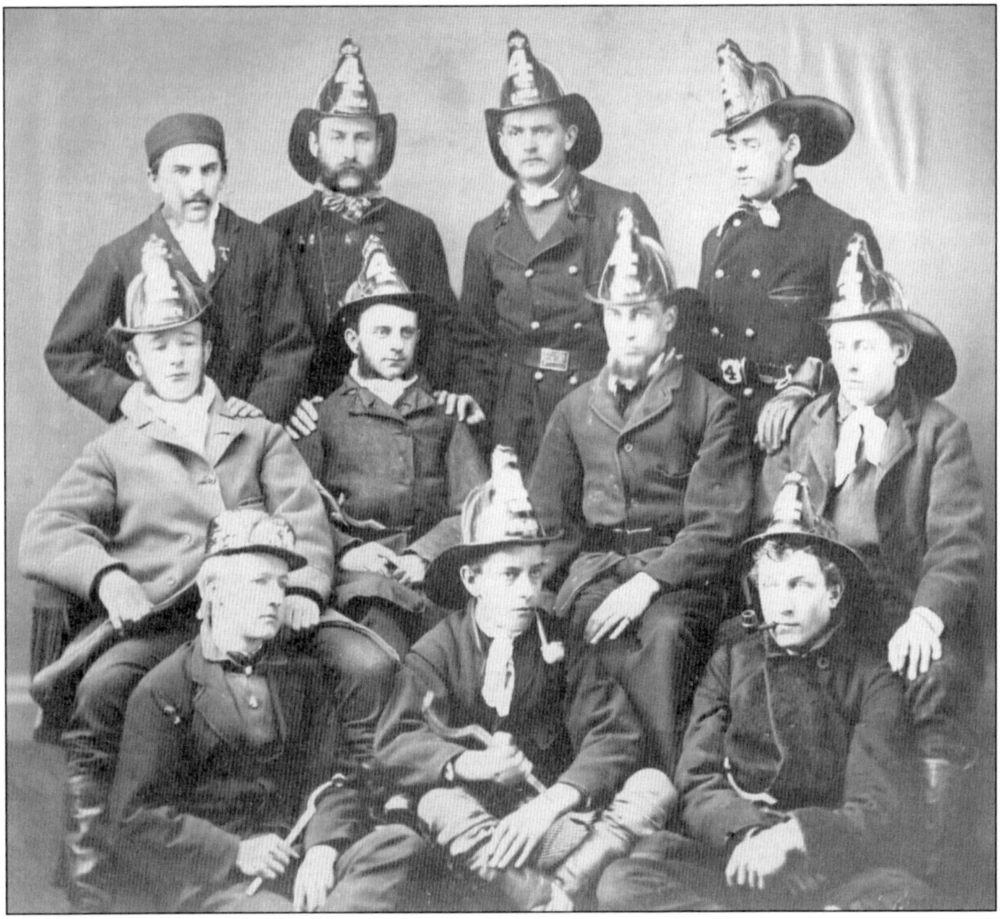

The Village of Elmira was incorporated in 1828. That same year, three fire wardens were selected. Over time, volunteer companies formed and were disbanded and new ones started. Competition between the organizations resulted in many fights. Sometimes, when more than one company responded to a fire, there was a race for the water supply, and in the scramble, fistfights often broke out and volunteers might step on each other's hoses. Often, the house burnt down. (Courtesy of CCHS.)

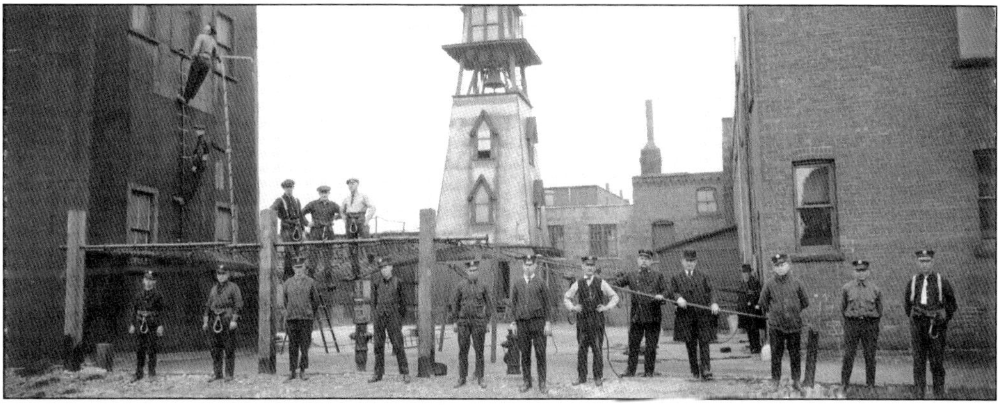

With professionalization of the Elmira Fire Department in 1878, training and organization became more prominent. Shown here are, from left to right: (on the ground) Pee Wee Miller, Dan Bermingham, Edward Ryan, Ben Prall, Henry Rorick, Leon Hazen, Chief John Espy, Commissioner George Romer, Bun Flynn, Dan O'Neil, Pete Gryska; (man against wall) unidentified; (on the net) unidentified, Butch Wheeland, and George Wick; (on ladder) John Hintz (above) and Ben Flynn. The training area was located behind the headquarters pictured below. (Courtesy of Fire Chief Patrick Bermingham.)

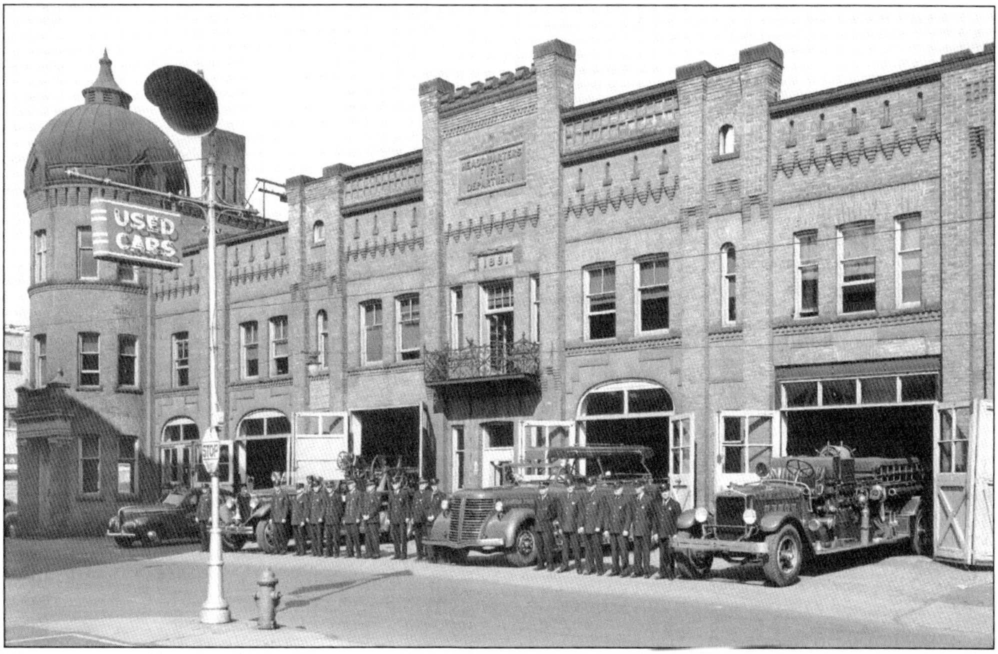

Elmira's second Central Fire Station and Headquarters was built in 1890. Shown here around 1947 are, from left to right, Charles Goldsmith, Glenn Peet, Frank Rhode, Earnest Naylor, mechanic Thomas Burke, Chief Louis J. Mosher, Capt. Benjamin Flynn Sr., Louis Allen, Capt. G. Marcus Walker, Robert Daly, Lt. William Volker, Roger Smith, John Kelly, Edward Sweeney, Patrick Reidy, and Charles DeSocio. This location was directly across Clemens Center Parkway from The Clemens Center. (Courtesy of Fire Chief Patrick Bermingham.)

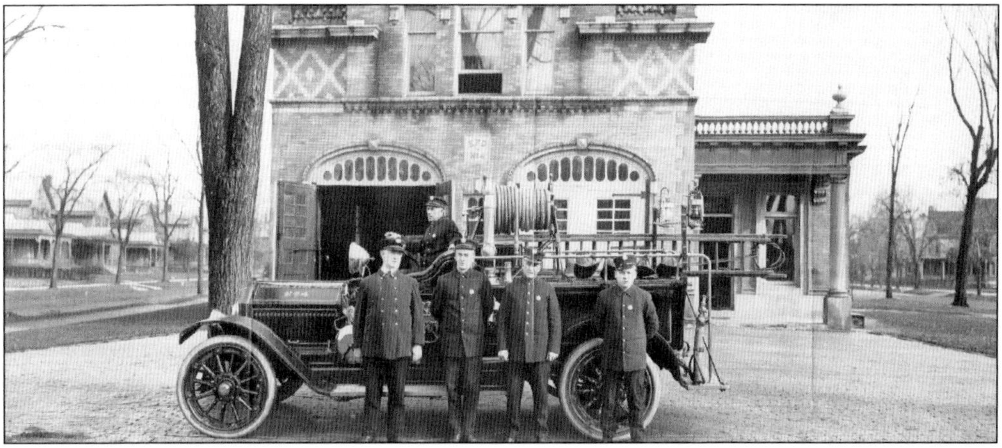

Standing in front of Station No. 4 on Maxwell Place around 1925 are, from left to right, Capt. John Holleran, Otto Leanser (in truck), John Crowley, Ceylon Miller, and Bunn Flynn. (Courtesy of Fire Chief Patrick Bermingham.)

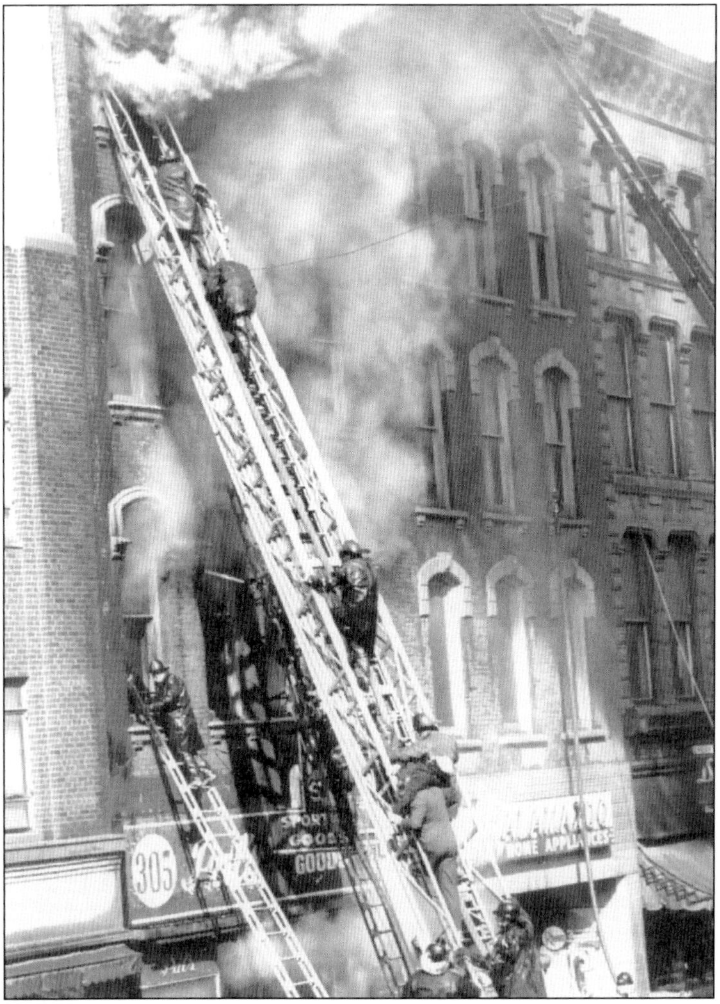

A fire took place at Pal's Sporting Goods Store on East Water Street on March 12, 1954. An unidentified firefighter maintains a hold on Fireman Lawrence E. Lilley Jr. (at top of ladder) after Lilley had been overcome by smoke. Two other firemen are rushing up the ladder to help, while another fireman and a civilian (about six rungs up) assist Fireman Felix J. Jankowski down the ladder after he had suffered a heart attack. Jankowski was pronounced dead at St. Joseph's Hospital. (Courtesy of Fire Chief Patrick Bermingham.)

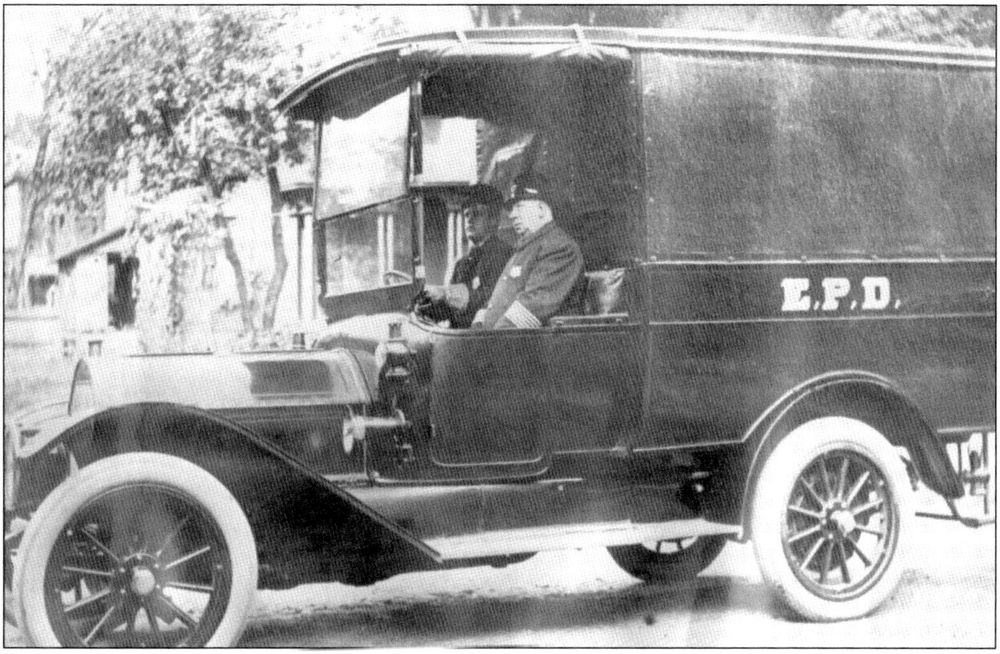

Elmira's police and fire departments became mechanized about the same time. In this c. 1913 photograph, Raymond Beardsly drives Officer John Twomey in the Elmira Police Department's first motorized patrol car. (Courtesy CCHS.)

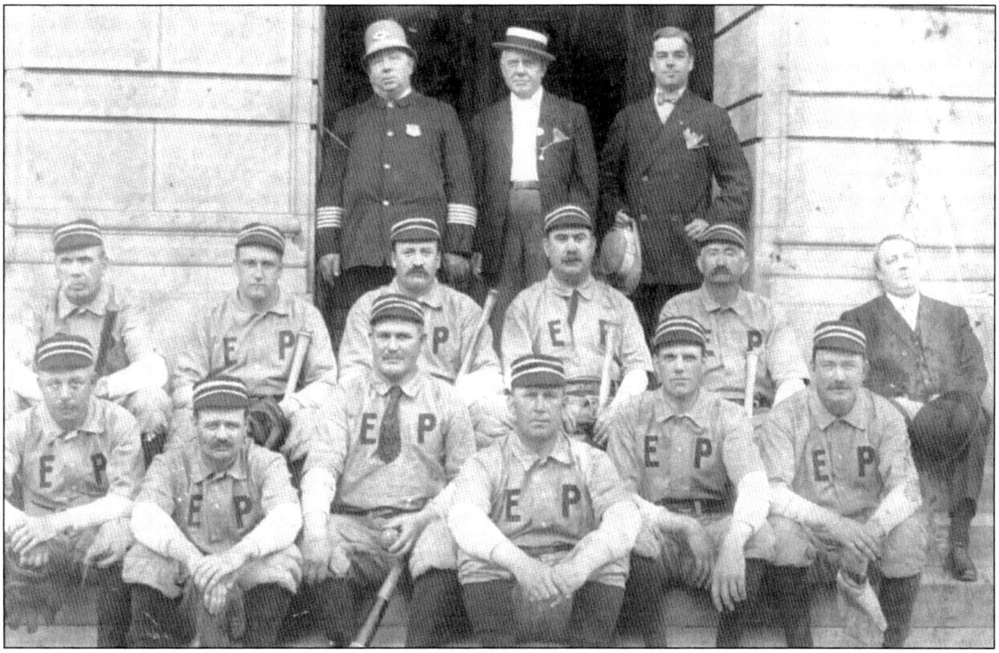

Baseball had great appeal in Elmira in the early 20th century, and the city's police department had its own team. Posing here around 1903 are, from left to right, (first row) Frank Bowen, Harry Laws, Patty Powell, Mike Lyons, Elvin Weaver, and Jack Flahive; (second row) Denny Dempsy, Charles Garbarino, Tom Mehan, Denny Crowley, Dan Curtin, and Harry Bogart; (third row) John Twomey, Jerry Bergan, and Roy Smith. (Courtesy of Elmira Police Department.)

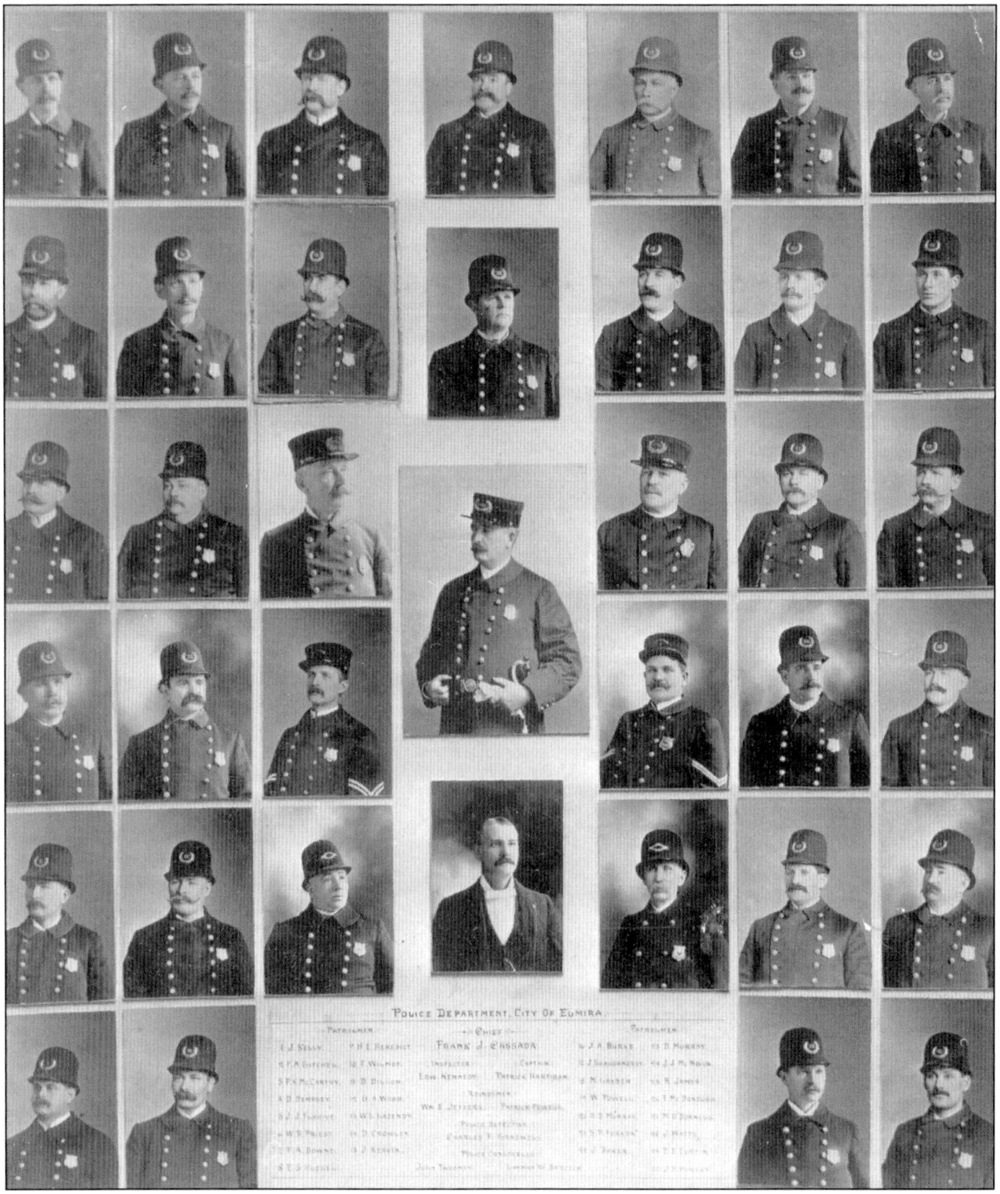

The Elmira police force had 38 men in 1901. From top to bottom, left to right, are (first column) J. Kelly, F.A. Gitchell, P.K. McCarthy, D. Dempsey, J.J. Flahive, and W.D. Priest; (second column) F.A. Bowne, E.G. Huegel, H.E. Benedict, T. Wilmot, D. Dillion, and G.A. Wood; (third column) W.L. Lasenby, D. Crowley, Inspector Edward Kennedy, Roundsman William E. Jeffers, and Constable John Twomey; (fourth column) J. Keavin, John Burke, Chief Frank J. Cassada, and Detective Charles G. Gradwell; (fifth column) J. Shaughnessy, M. Layden, Capt. Patrick Hartigan, Roundsman Patrick Powell, and Constable Layman W. Babcock; (sixth column) W. Powell, H.B. Murray, S.P. Korker, J. Baker, Dennis Murray, and J.J. McNevin; (seventh column) R. James, T. McDonough, M. O'Donnell, J. Watts, D.E. Curtin, and J. H. Hurley. Roundsmen walked the streets day and night to see that the patrolmen were at their posts. (Courtesy of CCHS.)

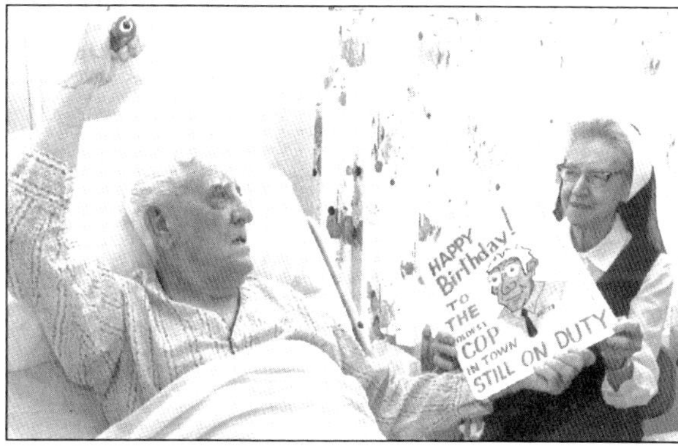

Lt. John "Sailor" Devlin, 89, the oldest active policeman still on duty, enjoys his birthday in the hospital after a fall near the police station. With Sailor around 1974 is Sister Vincent Joseph, who knew him in 1912 when he drove the Black Maria, a horse-and-buggy outfit. Devlin joined the Elmira Police Department in 1910 and retired in 1974. He was recognized by Ripley's Believe It Or Not! (Courtesy of CCHS.)

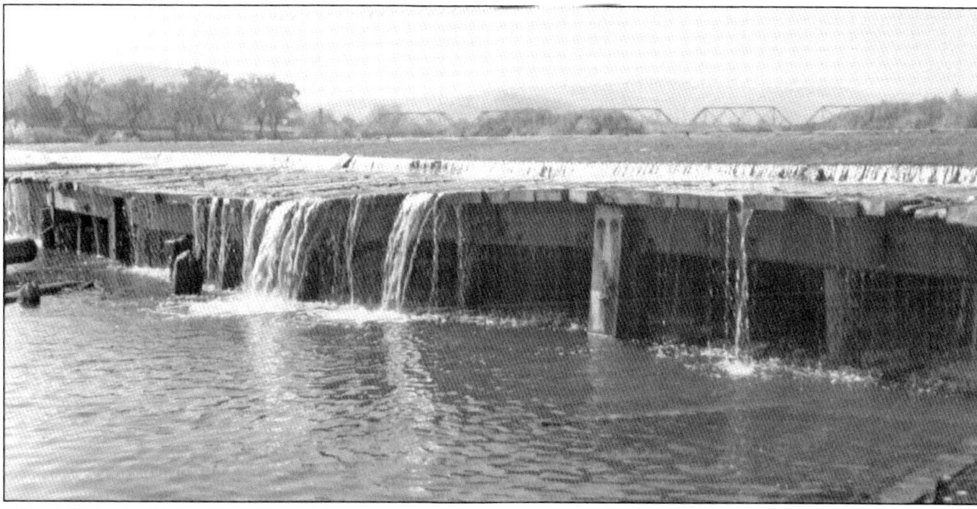

The Chase-Hibbard mill, on West Water Street between Columbia Street and College Avenue, was a landmark from 1885 to the 1930s. The dam across the river at that point had been built in 1828. It was constructed of a mass of stone and brush. Note in the background the original Walnut Street bridge, which was built in 1896. (Courtesy of Elmira Water Board.)

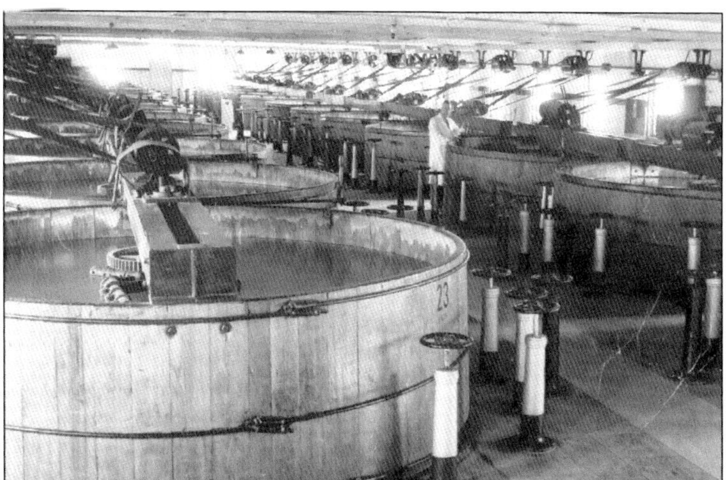

A severe typhoid epidemic swept the community in 1896, resulting in 46 deaths. The next year, a mechanical filtration plant was built on Reservoir Street west of Hoffman Street. The plant is shown here around 1900. (Courtesy of Elmira Water Board.)

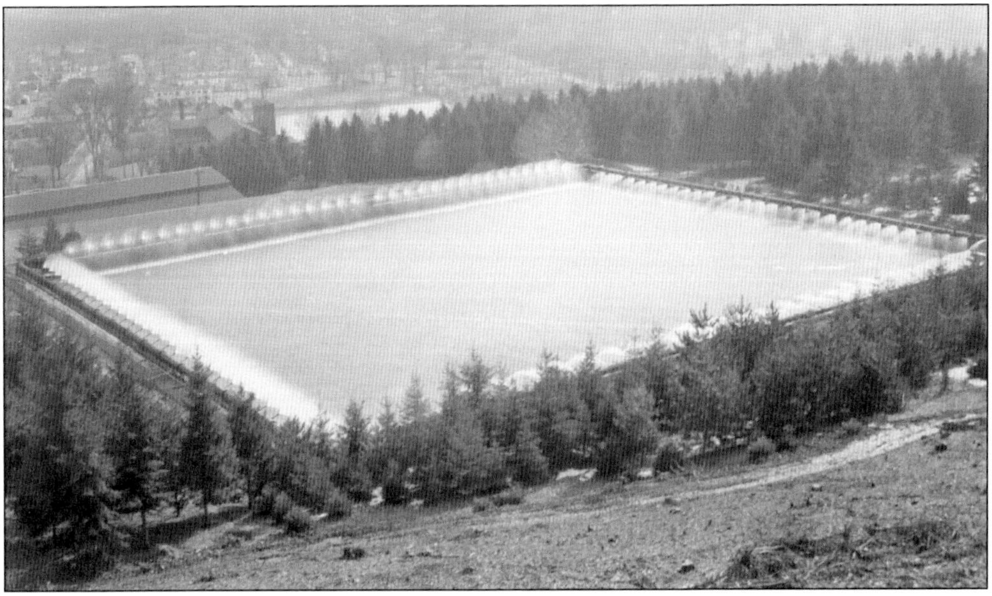

The Elmira Water Company was formed in 1859. Gen. Alexander S. Diven and two sons, along with others, formed the Elmira Water Works Company in 1869. Real progress came in 1870, when the 100-million-gallon reservoir was built on Upper Hoffman Street. (Courtesy of Elmira Water Board.)

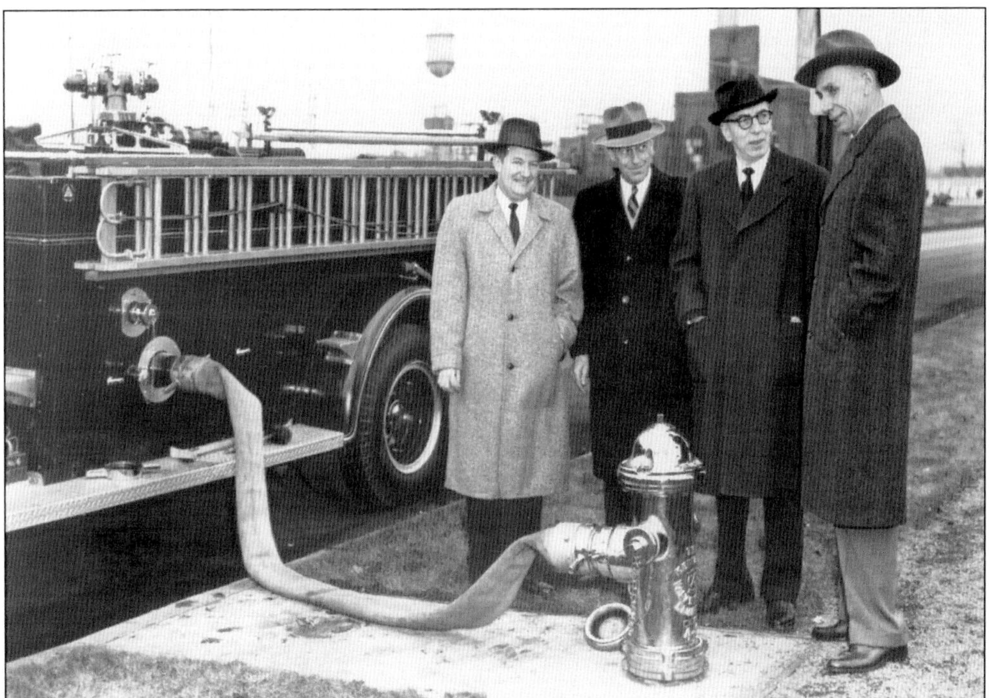

In this c. 1960 photograph, Mayor Edward Mooers (third from left), along with officials of the Elmira Water Board and the city, admire a new fire hydrant made by Kennedy Valve Mfg. Company. County historian Tom Byrne boasted that "Fire hydrants in use throughout the world proclaim their origin—Kennedy Valve Mfg. Co., Elmira, N.Y.'" (Courtesy of Elmira Water Board.)

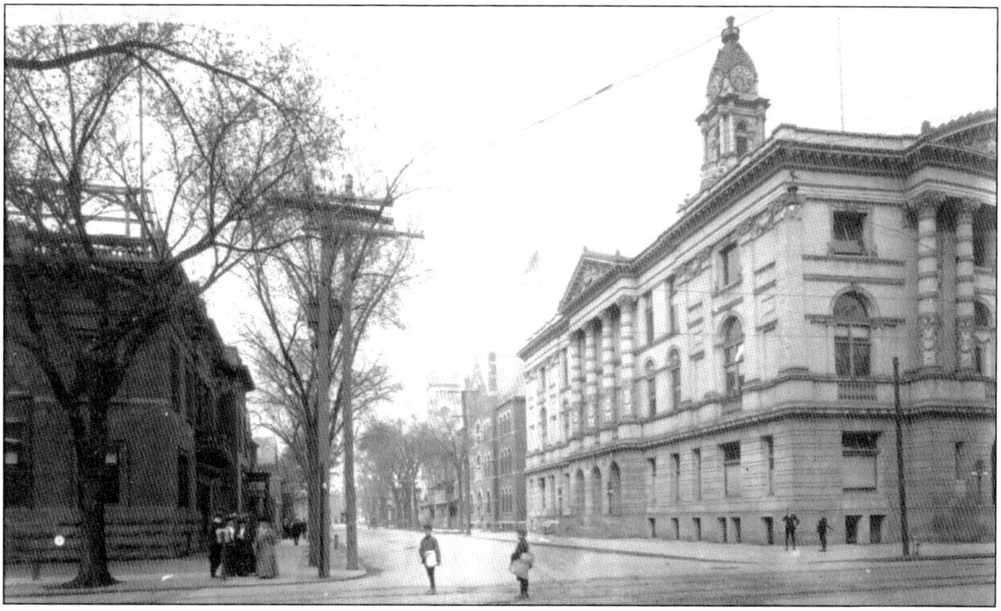

Elmira City Hall (shown here around 1900) was completed in 1896 for $118,000. Pierce and Bickford were the architects. The handsome pediments over the Church Street entrance depict the arts and sciences, and those over the Lake Street entrance depict Indian lore. Fire damaged the building in 1909, and taxpayers approved $30,000 for repairs. Note the Armory (now demolished) next to City Hall and the City Club on the left. (Courtesy of CCHS.)

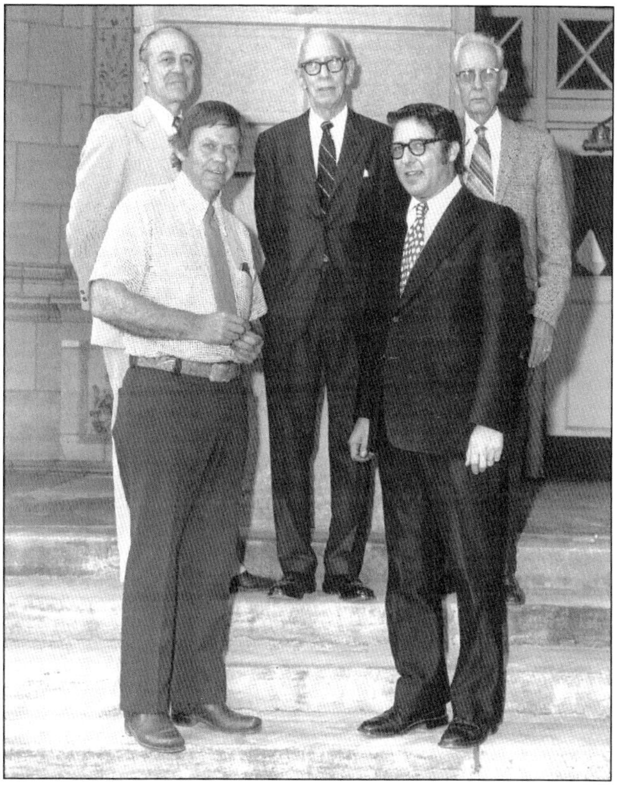

These five mayors of Elmira represent nearly three decades of city leadership. Beginning in World War II and ending with the Flood of 1972, they presided over challenging times for the city. The mayors are, from left to right, (first row) Howard H. Kimble (1966–1967) and Richard C. Loll (1972–1975); (second row) Edward T. Lagonegro (1962–1965, 1968–1971), Edward A. Mooers (1956–1961), and Emory Strachen (1942–1955). (Courtesy of CCHS.)

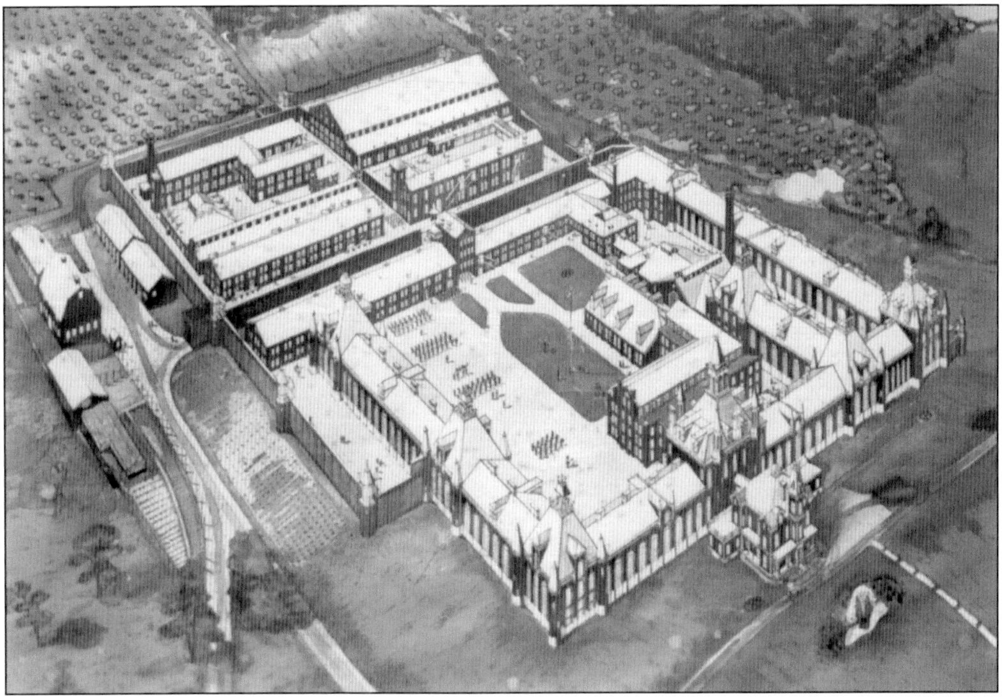

The New York State Reformatory opened in 1876, spanning 16 acres. Sitting on a hill, its Victorian towers and turrets made it seem "like a college or a hospital." In the original design, the superintendent's quarters were attached in the front of the building. This photograph was taken around 1913. (Courtesy of Don Blide.)

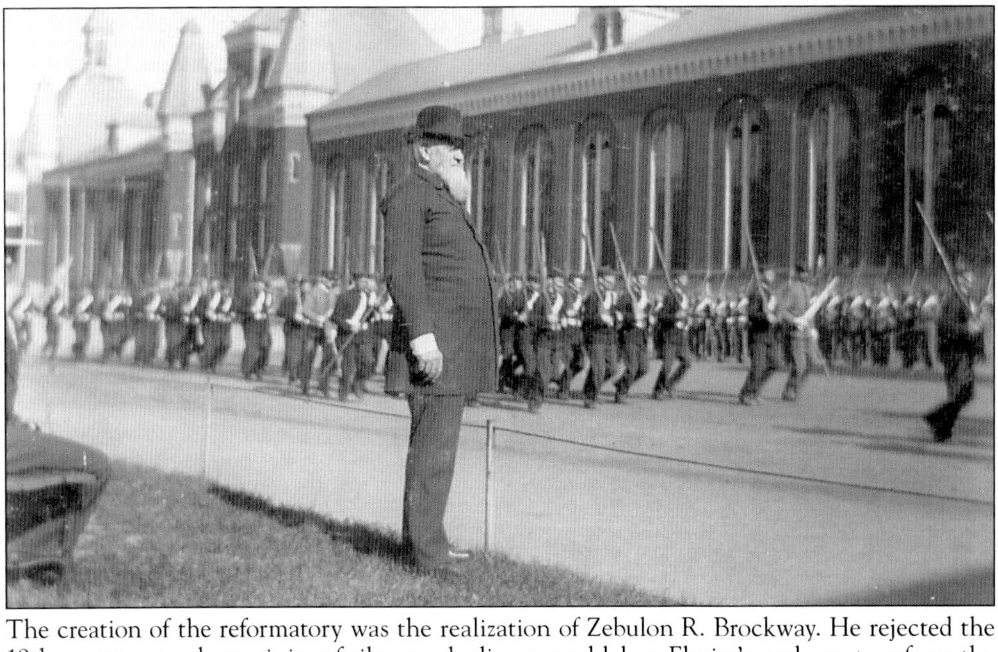

The creation of the reformatory was the realization of Zebulon R. Brockway. He rejected the 19th-century penology trinity of silence, obedience, and labor. Elmira's goal was to reform the convict. Brockway believed in proper education, recreation, and discipline for transgressors. He was superintendent from 1876 until 1900, when he retired at age 73. (Courtesy of CCHS.)

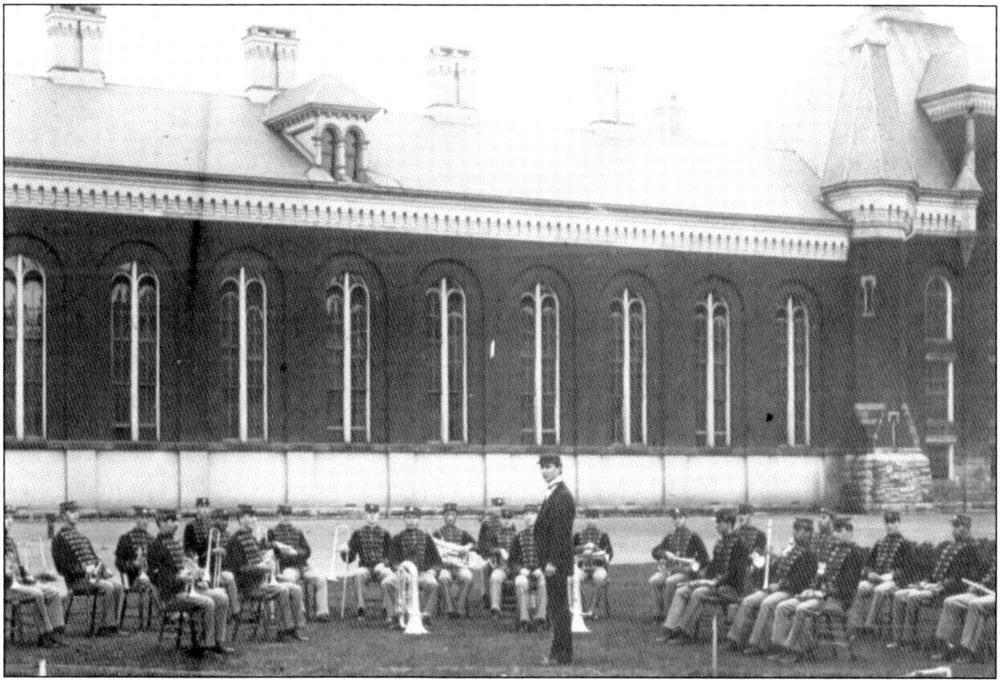

The reformatory had an inmate band (above) and a military organization that conducted dress parades (below). Inmates drilled for five to eight hours a day. The institution had a gymnasium for basketball, track, and boxing, a swimming pool, and a drill hall. (Courtesy of Don Blide.)

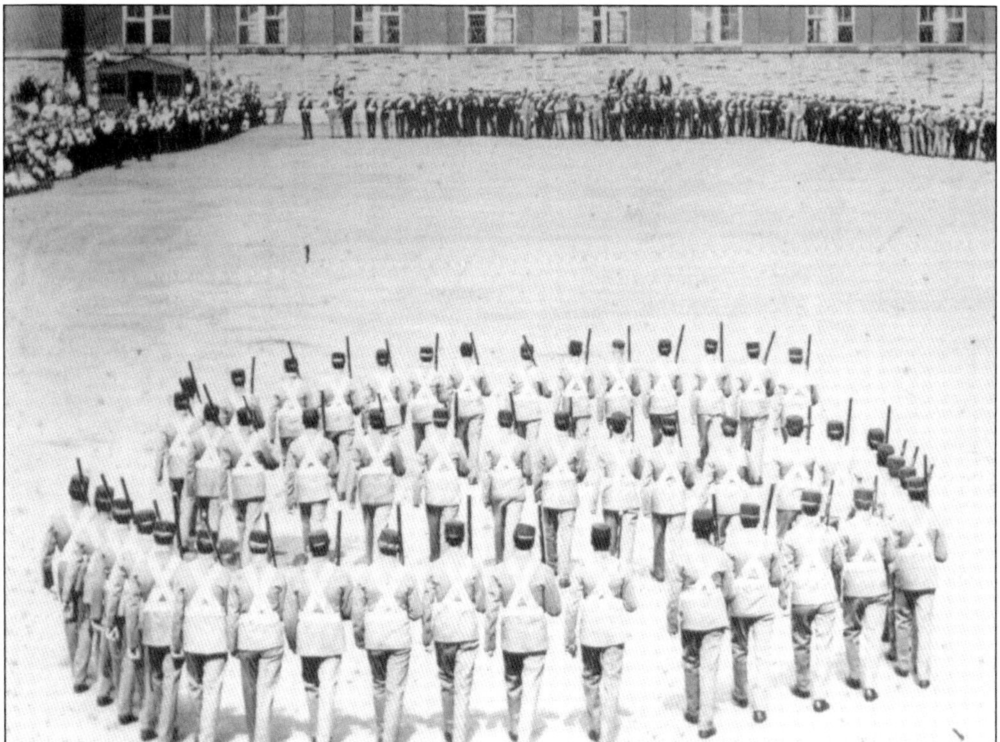

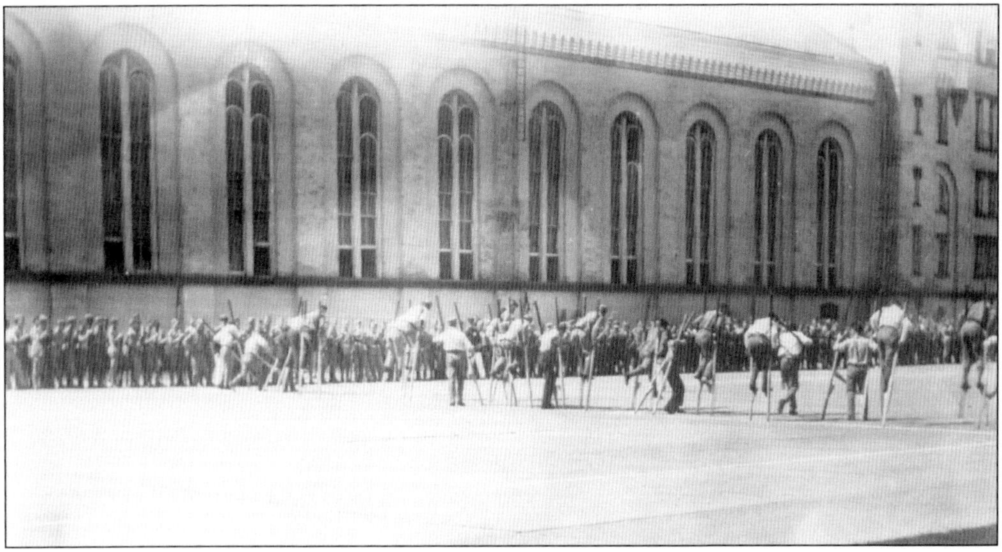

Superintendent Brockway was interested in the rehabilitation of prisoners. He felt that punishment alone was pointless. As a result, there were times when the prisoners just had fun, as seen in the above photograph. He also began a program known as "Sunday lecturers" for the inmates, at which prominent Elmirans would be invited to speak (below). The Reverend Thomas K. Beecher was a regular. (Above, courtesy of Don Blide; below, courtesy of CCHS.)

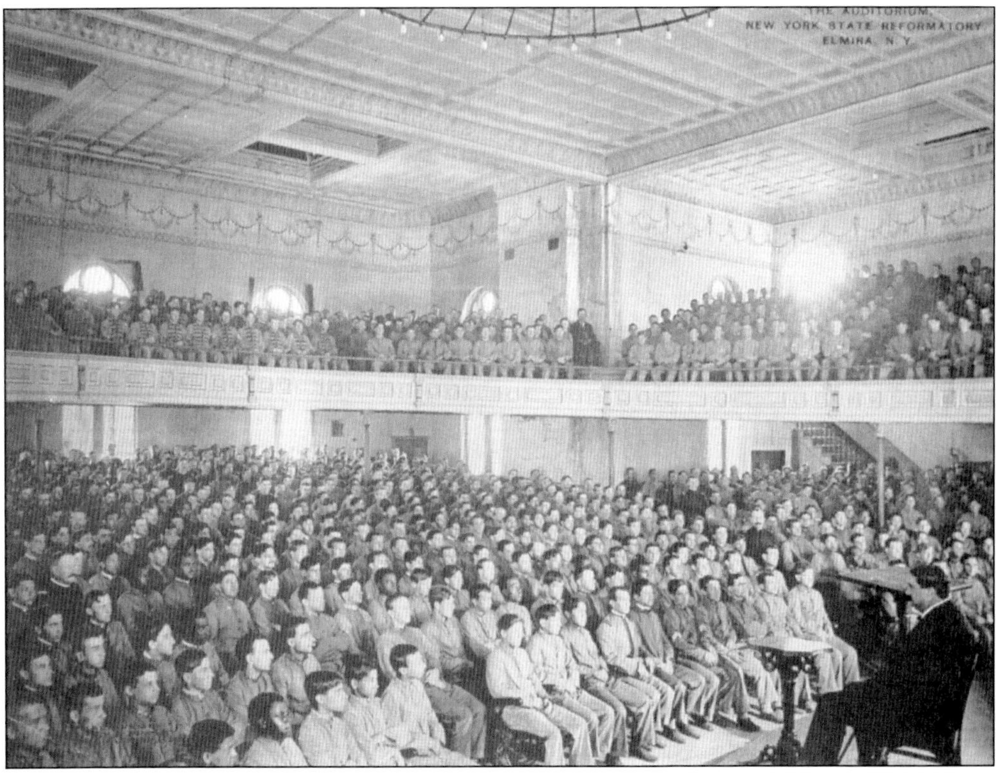

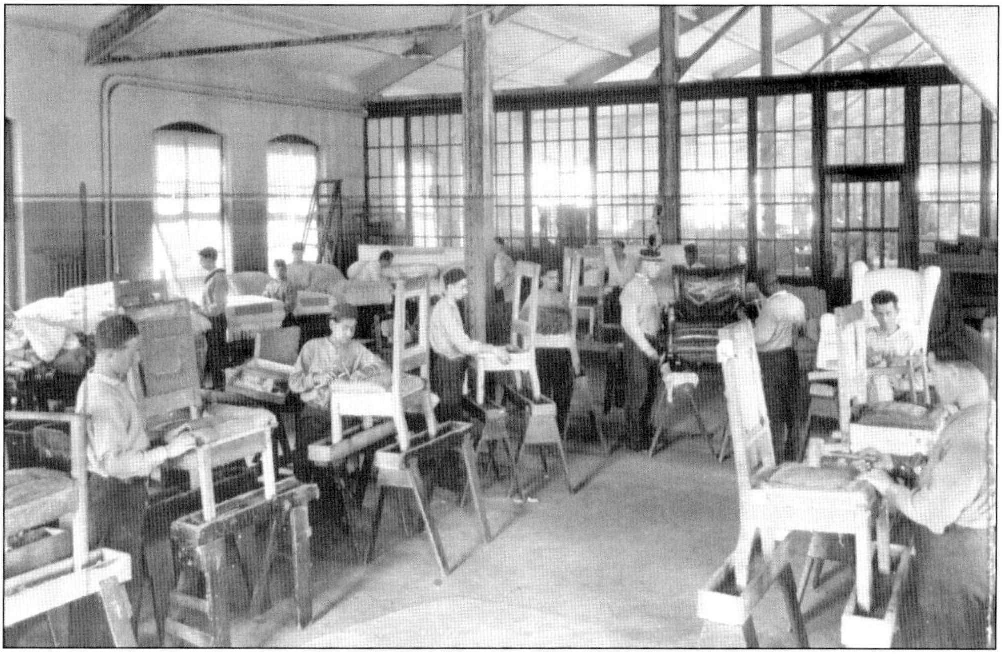

Under Zebulon Brockway's direction, factories and shops were built within the walls to manufacture articles for sale. In 1888, an entire building was set aside as a trade school. By 1894, instruction was provided in 34 trades, among them carpentry, cloth-cutting, plumbing, and telegraphy. (Courtesy of Don Blide.)

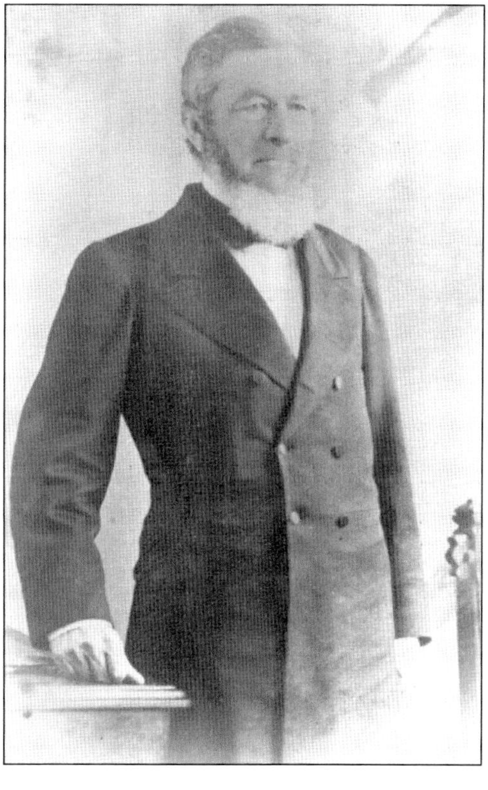

Lucius Robinson (1810–1891) was a successful New York City lawyer, editorial writer, and political figure. He came to Elmira in 1855 for reasons of health and settled in a home on Maple Avenue. Over the years, he was supported by both political parties. Elected as a Republican to the state assembly in 1859 and 1860 (one-year terms), he was elected state comptroller in 1861, 1863 (as a Republican), and 1875 (as a Democrat). In 1876, he was elected governor of New York as a Democrat. (Courtesy of CCHS.)

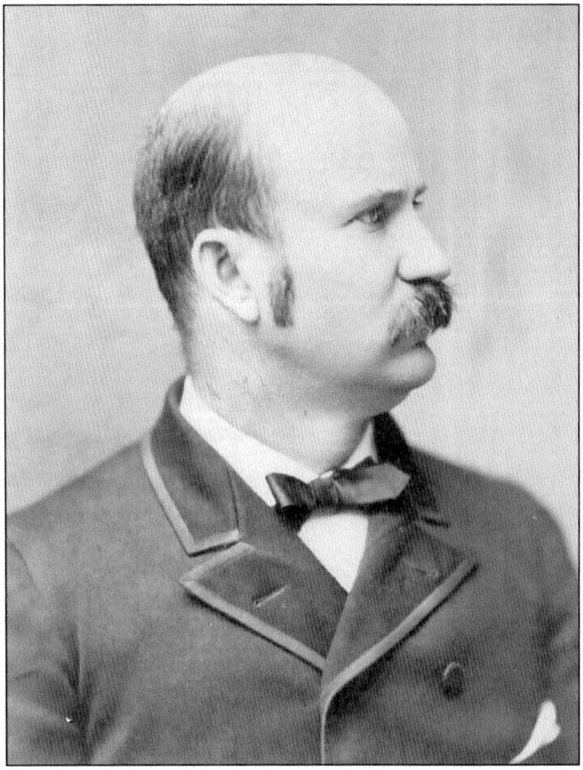

David Bennett Hill (1843–1910) was born in Havana, New York. He moved to Elmira at age 20 and was appointed counsel for the newly incorporated city. He was elected as a Democrat to the state assembly in 1869, as mayor of Elmira in 1882, and as lieutenant governor in 1882, moving up to governor when Grover Cleveland became president. He became a US senator in 1891, serving until 1897. In 1905, he retired from politics, selling his shares in the *Elmira Gazette* to a young journalist named Frank Gannett. (Courtesy of CCHS.)

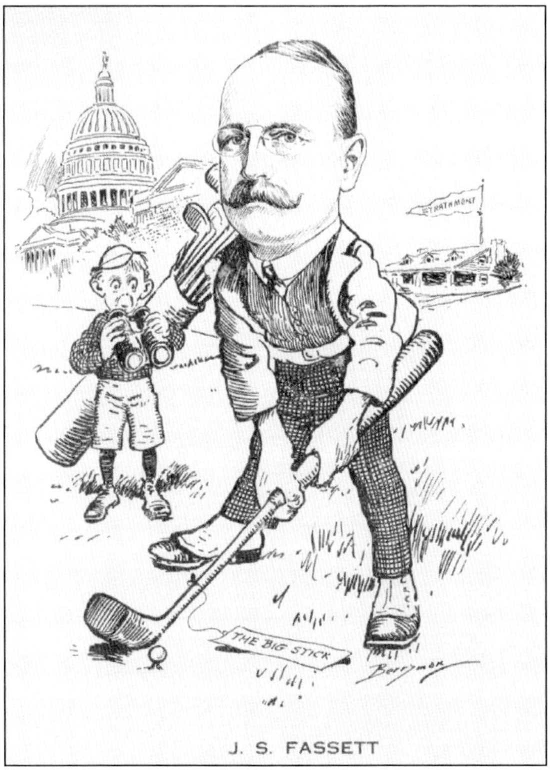

J. Sloat Fassett (1853–1924) and his family have played an important role in Elmira's story. His political career began as Chemung County district attorney. His daughter wrote that he was "26 years old and filled with crusading spirit." He would serve in the New York State Senate for nine years, was appointed Collector of the Port of New York by Pres. Benjamin Harrison in 1891, the same year he ran as a Republican candidate for governor. Fassett served in the House of Representatives from 1905 to 1911. He was a rival of Theodore Roosevelt. This caricature was done by Eugene Zimmerman. (Courtesy of CCHS.)

Six

City Life

In 1964, Elmira celebrated its centennial as a city. The first council meeting was recreated. There was a pageant, a parade, and a Centennial Grand Ball at the new Elmira Free Academy. That same year, Bobby Kennedy campaigned for United States senator outside the Mark Twain Hotel. Eight years before the Flood of 1972, Elmira still seemed to be the "Queen City." There were some signs that change was under way. The population in 1960 was 46,517, down from the 1950 peak of 49,716. In 1957, for the first time, the county budget exceeded the city budget. In 1964, urban renewal was undertaken.

During the first half of the 20th century, Elmira faced many challenges. There had been a flood in 1889, and then came the Flood of 1946, the worst in history. Elmira had to recover from both. During the Roaring Twenties, Elmira was called the "fun city." On the eve of Prohibition, the city hosted 49 saloons. While many closed, others became speakeasies. The town suffered during the Depression, with city workers not being paid for months at the end of 1931 and into 1932. Eventually these workers, along with schoolteachers, took a 10 percent pay reduction.

World War I and World War II brought the community together. In 1918, people gathered at the train station to cheer and sing "The Star-Spangled Banner" as draftees went to war. The citizens raised money through Liberty Bond parades and worked in the Red Cross and at canteens to assist soldiers. During World War II, the population boomed to over 50,000. Businesses converted to wartime production and residents saved scrap metal, lived with rationing, and, once again, bought bonds.

While all of this went on, life in Elmira continued. The public library was started, musical organizations were formed, and theaters were very popular. Community groups aimed to protect and improve the quality of life in the city. A new high school on the south side was constructed; eventually, many one-room schoolhouses would be sold as the Elmira School District consolidated. As 1960 approached and the baby boom's full impact was being felt, new schools were built.

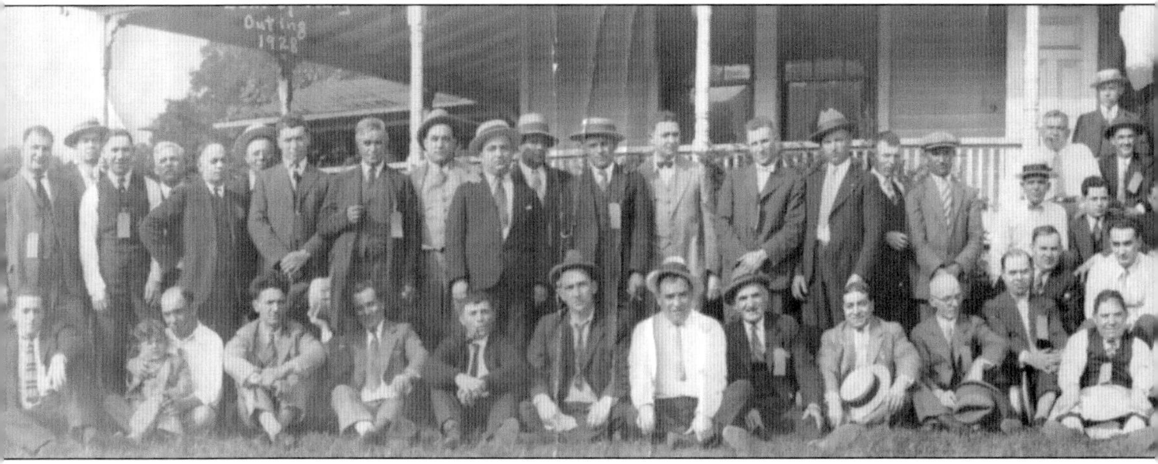

A headline in the July 7, 1914, *Elmira Advertiser* read, "Six Hundred Sons of Italy Gather and Condemn Actions of Theater in Alleged Discrimination." The Italian community was upset that the Colonial Theater would not allow Italians to sit on the first floor. The Christopher Columbus

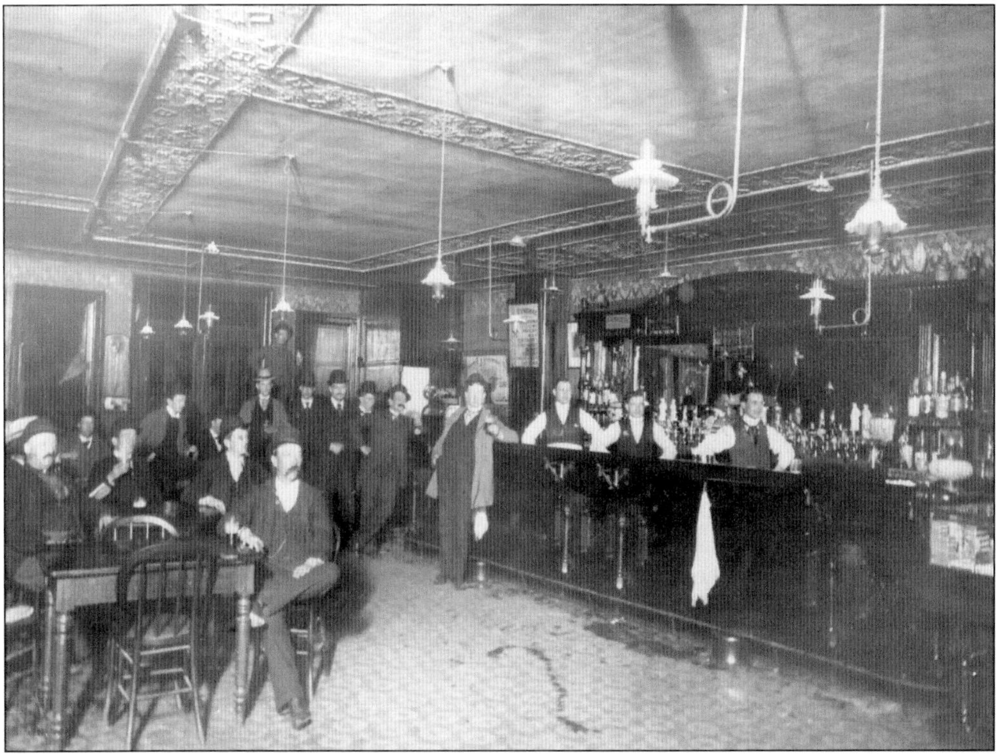

Lodges and fraternal organizations have been an important aspect of life in Elmira. The Benevolent and Protective Order of Elks Lodge No. 62 was chartered in 1887. With the completion of their lodge on Market Street in 1911, they had a permanent home until a devastating fire in 1989. County historian Tom Byrne noted that a feature of the new Elks Club was "a fully appointed rathskeller in the basement." The lodge is seen here around 1917. (Courtesy of B.P.O.E. Lodge No. 62.)

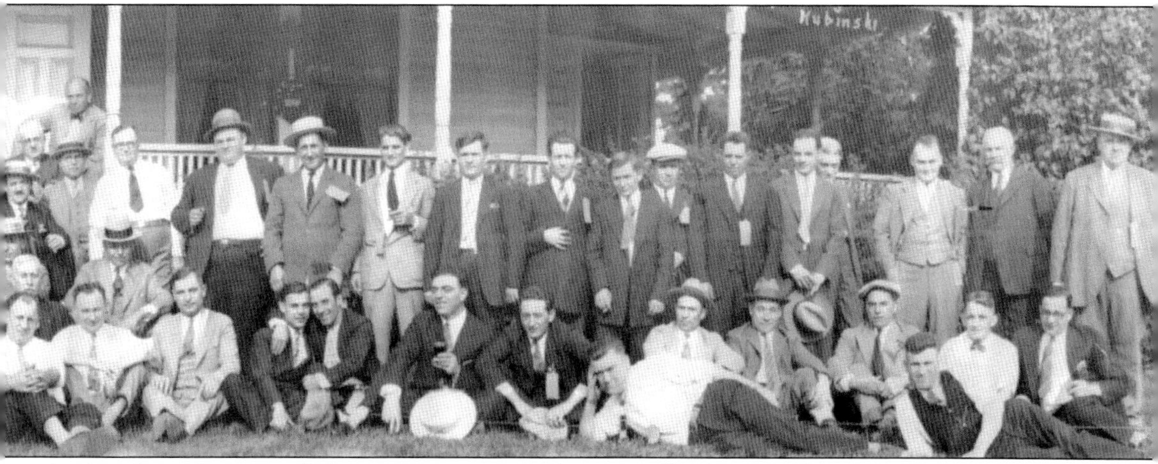

Lodge No. 155 organized the meeting at St. Anthony's Hall. The story demonstrates one of the roles of the Sons of Italy, which had been organized nationally in 1905. This photograph is from around 1928. (Courtesy of Ed Sophia.)

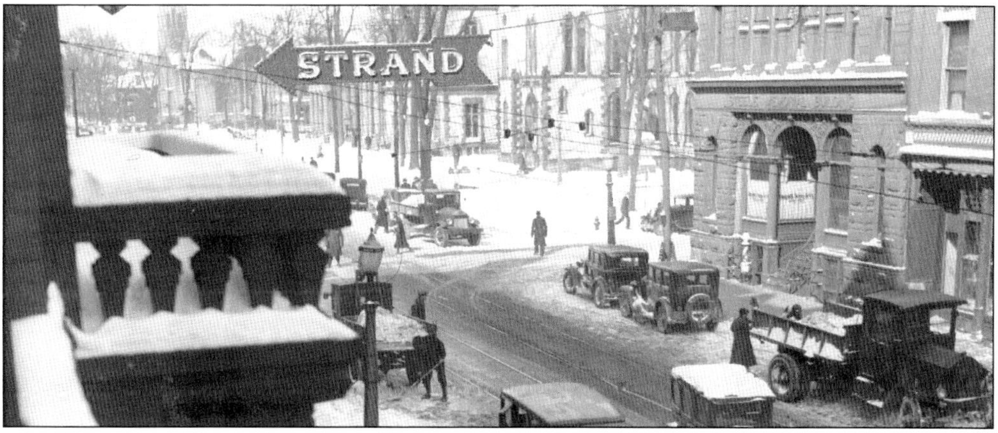

This 1930s winter day at the corner of Lake and Market Streets finds workers picking up snow the old-fashioned way: shoveling it into trucks. On the right is the original Steele Memorial Library building. Across Market Street are the county clerk's office and the courthouse. In the distance is the Lake St. Presbyterian Church. The Strand Theater was around the corner on Market Street. (Courtesy of the *Elmira Star Gazette*.)

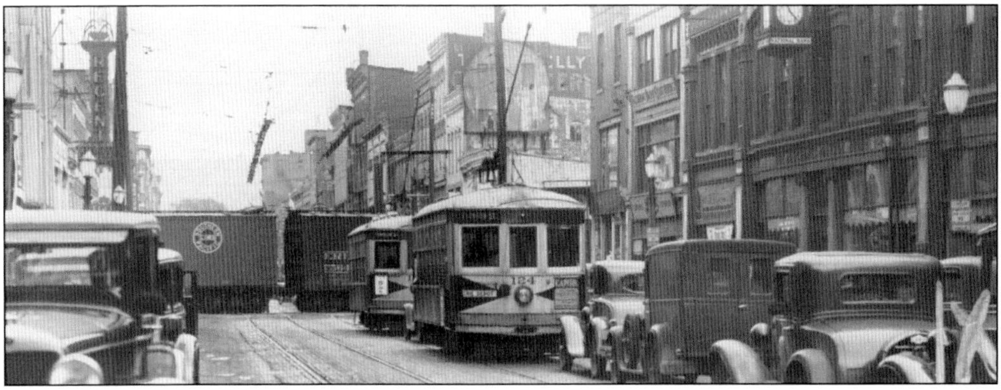

October 25, 1934, was "United Elmira Day," marking the official reopening of Water and Church Streets after the elevation of the railroad was completed. The event is described in Thomas Byrne's book *Chemung County: 1890–1975*. Governor Lehman joined the procession from the Mark Twain Hotel to the Water Street underpass. A *Star Gazette* editorial titled "The Great Reunion" pronounced it the end of the "old 'Chinese Wall' through the center of the city." This photograph is from some time before 1934. (Courtesy of the *Elmira Star Gazette*.)

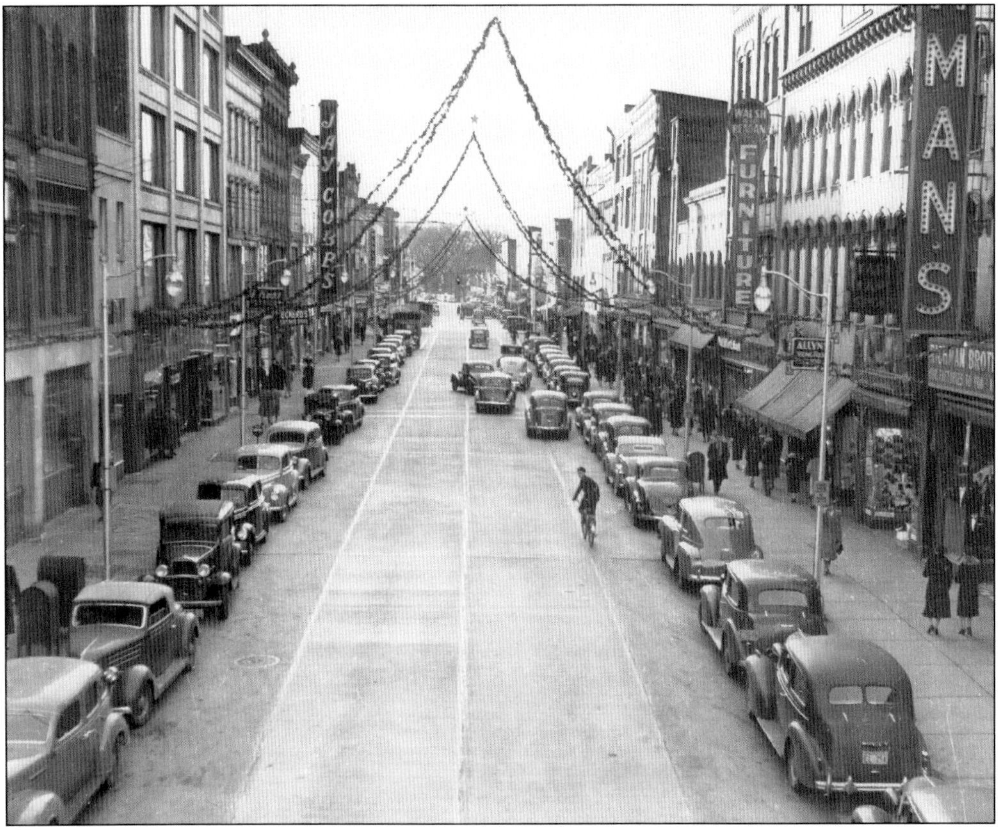

Water Street is busy before Christmas in the early 1940s in this west-facing photograph, taken from the railroad viaduct. On the left is Kobacker Furniture Co., Jay Cobbs Women's Store, and, farther down the street, Markson's Clothiers. On the right is Walsh and Regan Furniture Store. J.J. Newberry's is down the street. Elmira had a concentrated shopping district before the Flood of 1972. (Courtesy of the *Elmira Star Gazette*.)

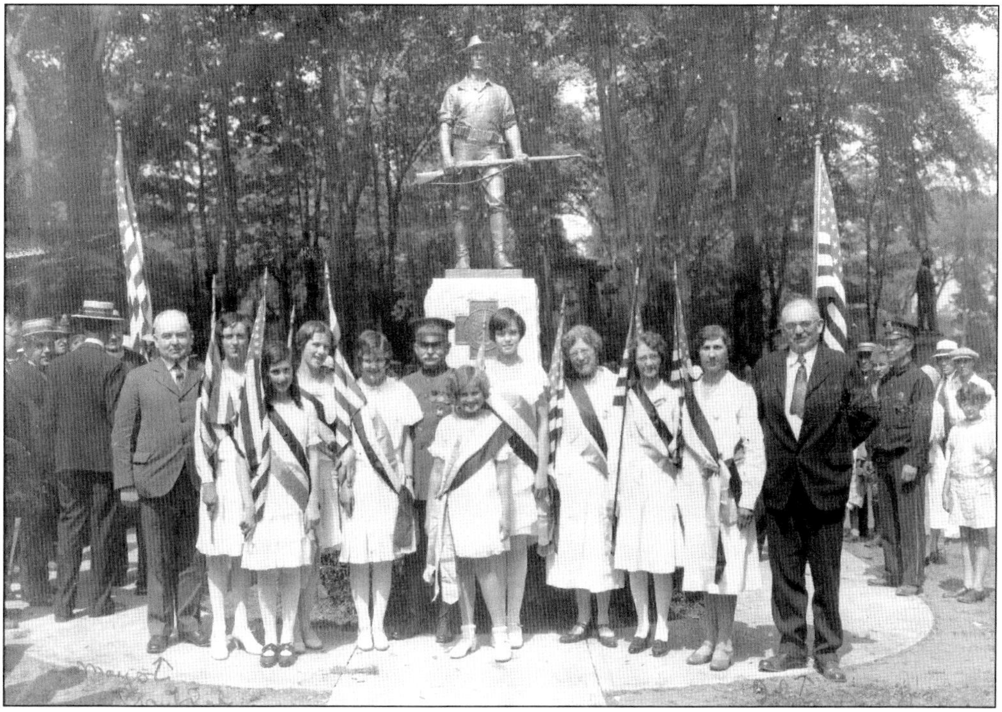

Citizens commemorate Spanish American War veterans in front of *The Hiker* monument in Wisner Park. According to *Outdoor Sculpture in Kalamazoo*, the statue's name evokes American soldiers' long hikes in the hot jungles in Cuba and the Philippines, and in relief during the Boxer Rebellion, all in the name of freedom, humanity, and patriotism. The popularity of the war resulted in many "Hiker" monuments around the country. Elmira mayor Frank Robinson stands at the right in this ceremony from around 1930. (Courtesy of CCHS.)

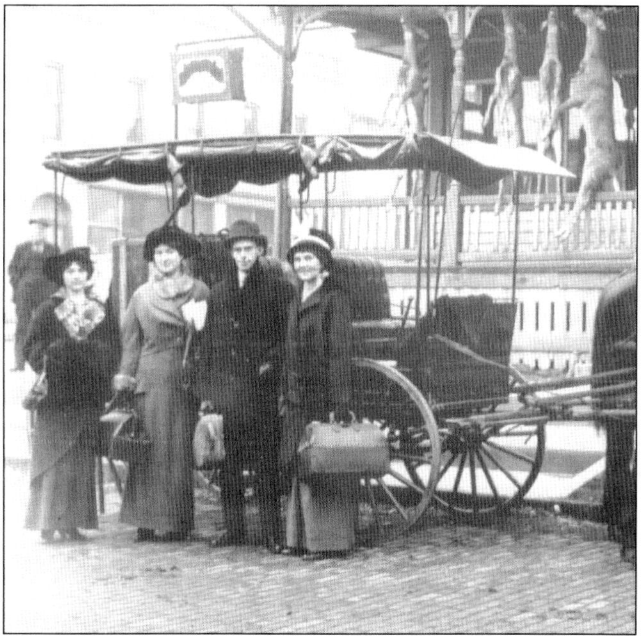

During the war years (1914–1918), The Kinyon Koncert Kompany was on extended tours throughout the Northeast, traveling by train, auto, buggy, and sleigh. The troupe performed in a different town each night, according to Walter MacPherson. His aunt, Elsie MacPherson Kinyon (at right), and her husband, Wilbur (second from right), formed the group. Elsie had been a soloist for the First Presbyterian and First Methodist Church choirs. They are pictured here around 1914 in Barnesboro, Pennsylvania, with Nellie Bowman (left) and Kathleen Bach (second from left). (Courtesy of Marge Macpherson.)

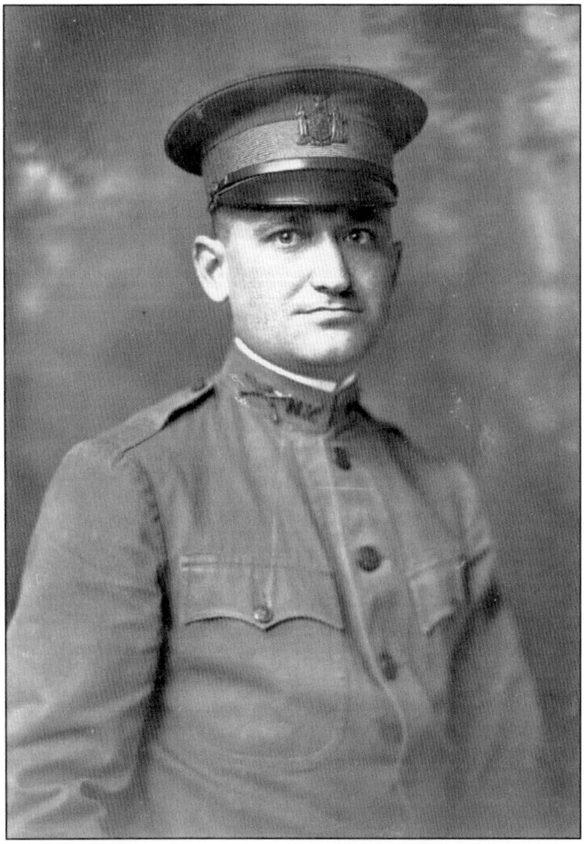

Lt. Harry B. Bentley of the 108th Infantry, Company L, was wounded on September 28, 1918, during an assault on the Hindenburg Line and died the following day. The Harry B. Bentley Post 443, American Legion of Elmira, was named in his honor. It was among the first American Legion posts to be granted a charter, on September 16, 1919. (Courtesy of CCHS.)

The bodies of Lieutenant Bentley and five others were returned to Elmira from France two-and-a-half years after the Armistice. This 1921 photograph shows the memorial service, held in the Armory. Thomas Byrne recounts the words of Mayor George Peck: "Their death and their burial is not alone a matter of private grief, but the whole city of Elmira is the mourner." Following the service, the caskets were taken to Woodlawn Cemetery. (Courtesy of CCHS.)

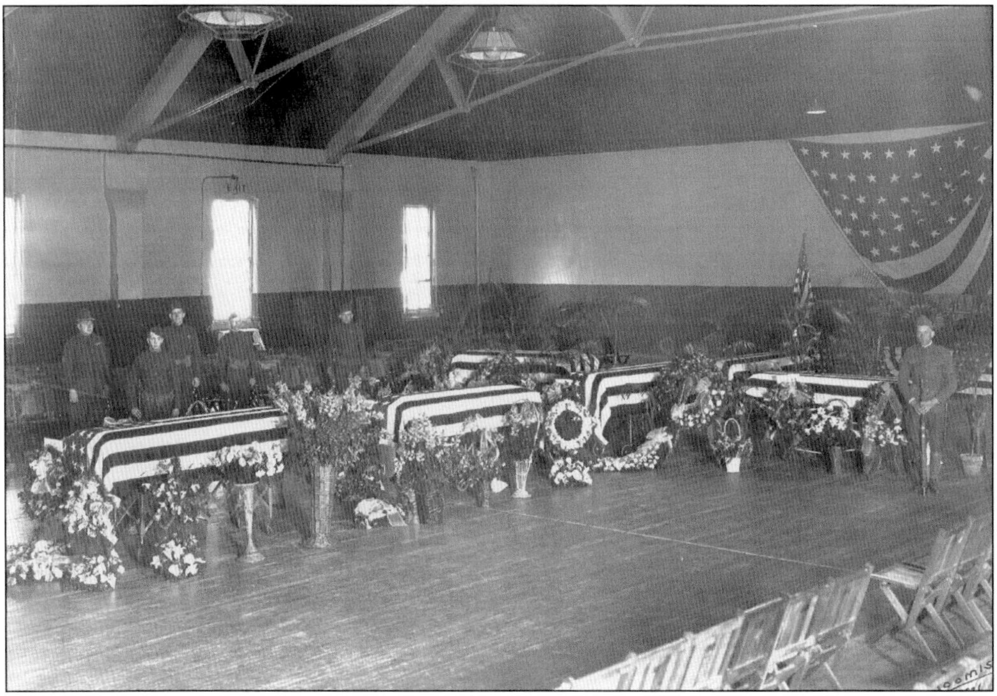

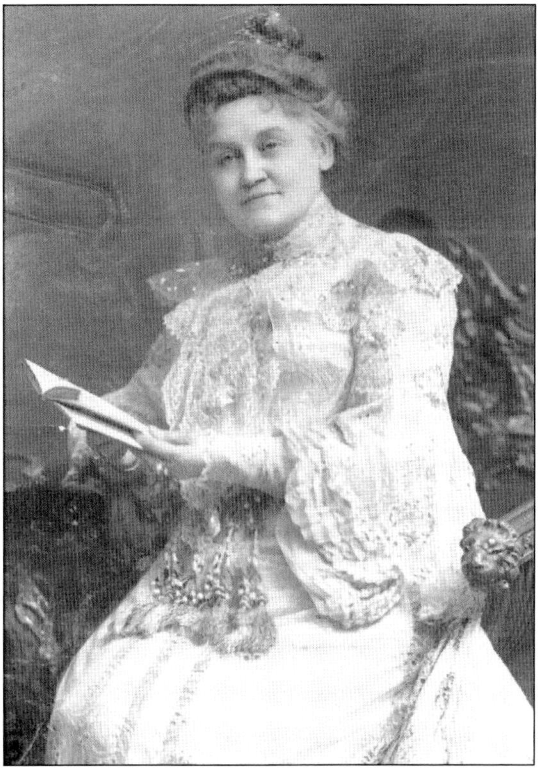

Esther Baker Steele and her husband, Dr. Joel Dorman Steele, produced textbooks in physics, astronomy, geology, zoology, physiology, and botany. They traveled and wrote histories of the United States, France, Greece, and Rome. Dr. Steele died in 1886, leaving a modest fortune to his wife. In a letter to her, he suggested providing a public library for the city. She put money aside annually until the building fund was adequate. The first library was located at the southeast corner of Lake and Market Streets. The cornerstone for the Steele Memorial Library was laid in 1895, and the doors opened on August 2, 1899. The library is at its third location today. Pictured below is a reading room in the original library. (Both, courtesy of CCHS.)

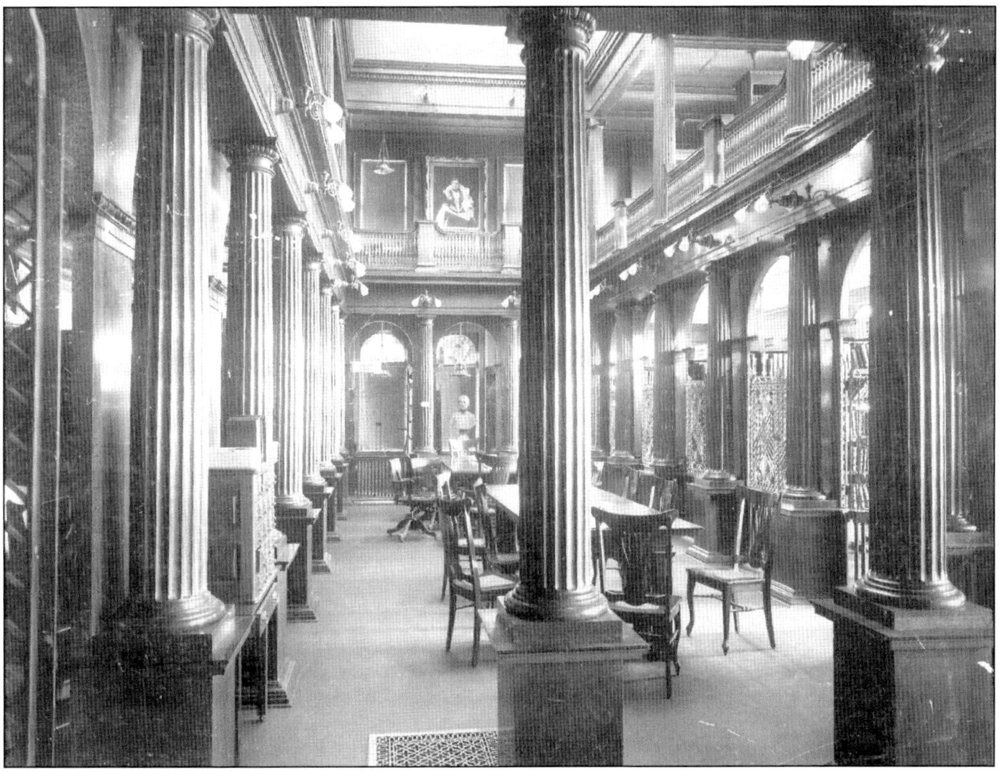

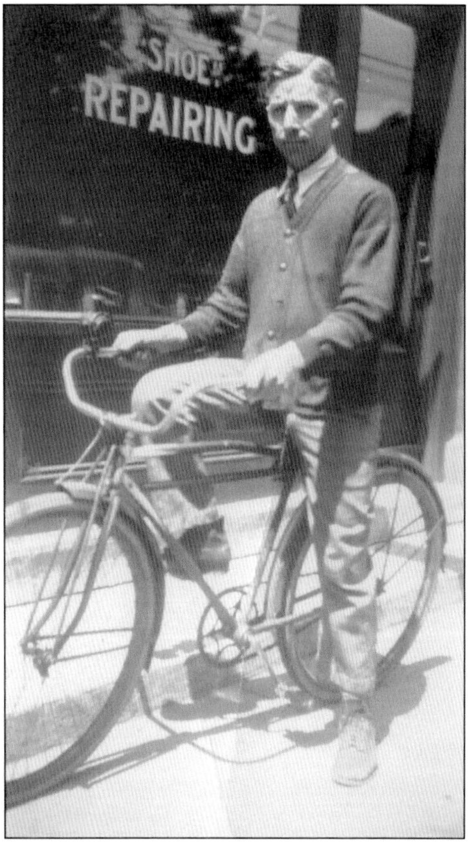

Avak Arikian, a poor Armenian shepherd fleeing the Turkish purge of his homeland, arrived in the United States in 1918 and came to Elmira in 1920. In 1921, he set up shop in partnership with Nazar Panosian. He started his own business in 1922, which became the Queen City Shoe Repair Service and a dry-cleaning establishment at the corner of South Main and Henry Streets. (Courtesy of John Arikian.)

Hal Roach (1892–1992) was born in Elmira and left for Hollywood at an early age. He became a comedy producer, working with Harold Lloyd, Will Rogers, and, most famously, Laurel and Hardy. He created the Our Gang kids. The City of Elmira honored Roach (center) in 1987 by naming the Grove Park Pavilion in his honor. City Councilman Jim Hare (coauthor), his wife, Alicia (left), and son Aaron visit with Roach at a picnic held in his honor at the home of Donna Kerr Nowlan on Winsor Avenue in 1987. (Courtesy of Jim Hare.)

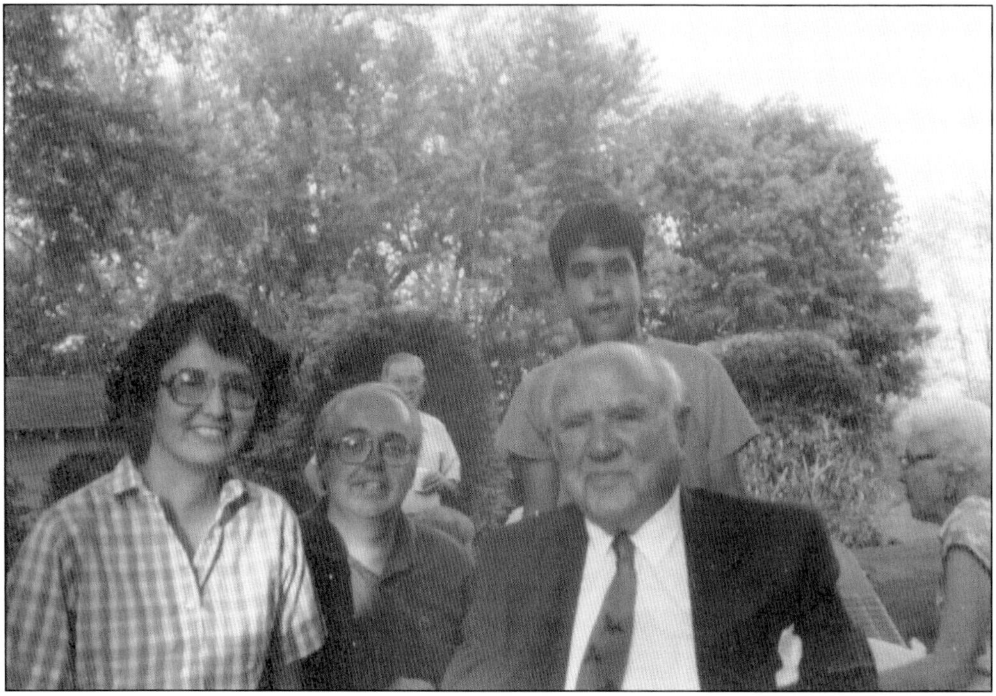

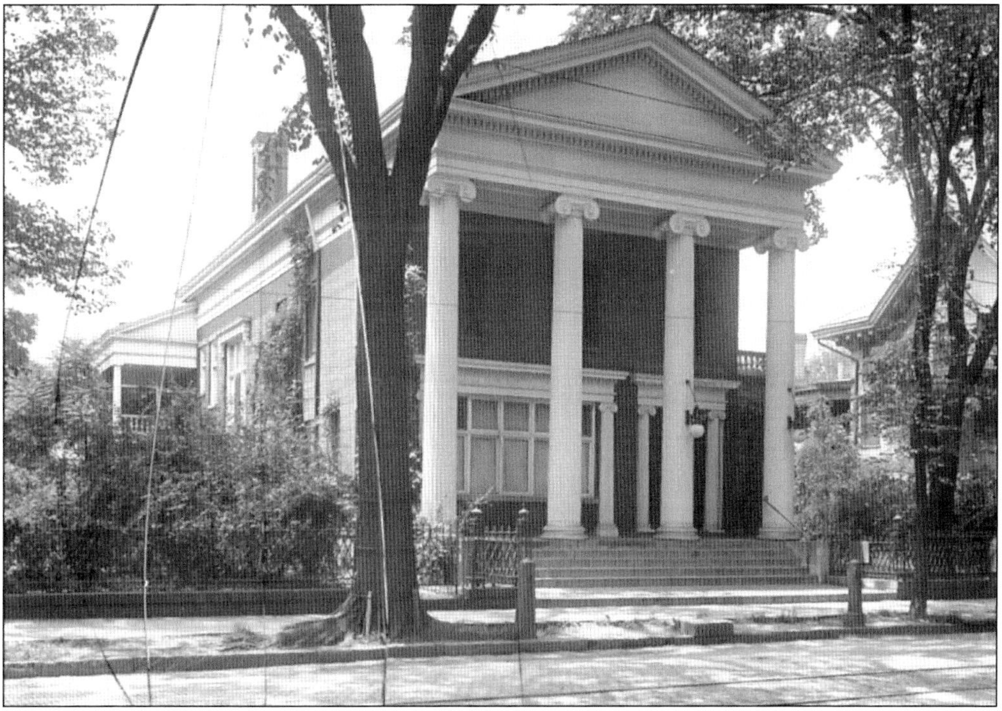

The Arnot Art Museum was built in the 1830s as a home by John Arnot. When his son Matthias H. Arnot died in 1910, he bequeathed his art treasures, the buildings, and the grounds to the public. He also left an endowment of $200,000, the income to be used for maintenance and additions to the collection. An additional $10,000 was to be used to convert the home into a public gallery. The museum is shown here around 1921. (Courtesy of The New York State Archives.)

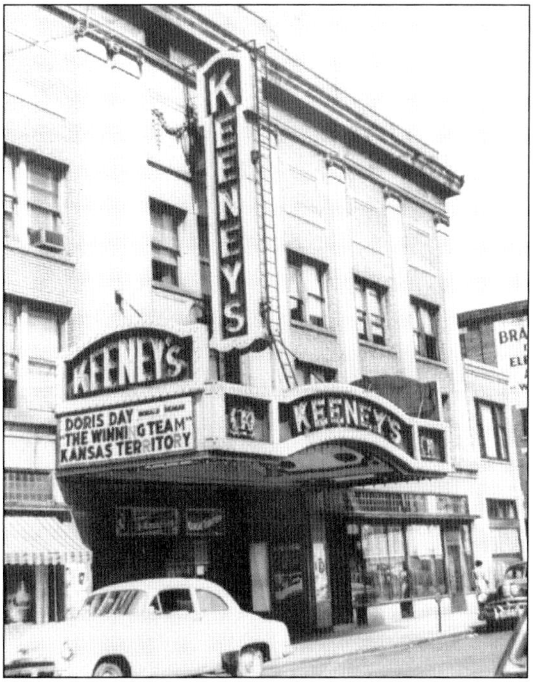

The Keeney Theater opened in December 1925. The idea of Sunday movies stirred controversy in the city. It was claimed that the "spiritual tone of the Lord's day" was in jeopardy and that the Sabbath was being "commercialized." In 1952, the theater was renamed the Elmira Theater, and it is shown here around that time. It is now the location for The Clemens Center. (Courtesy of Mike Kenna.)

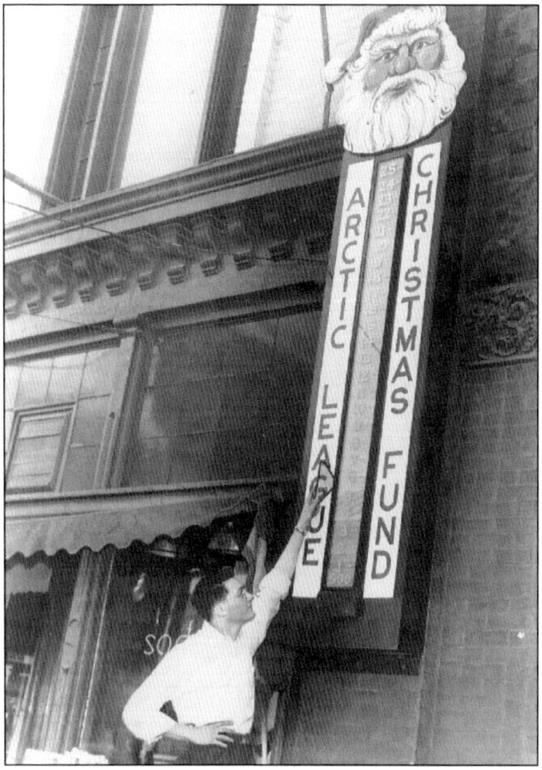

In 1912, a group of young Elmira businessmen created an organization, the Arctic League. Originally, it was a social group that gathered at Lagonegro's Cigar Store on Lake Street. On Christmas Day 1912, a ragged, cold, and hungry boy was found by Danny Sullivan. The league members took up a collection to feed and clothe him. They named the boy "Friday," after the day he was found. From this beginning, the Arctic League has grown in the last 100 years. With an annual fund drive and many volunteers, thousands of needy children in Chemung County have a joyful Christmas thanks to the Arctic League. (Courtesy of The Arctic League.)

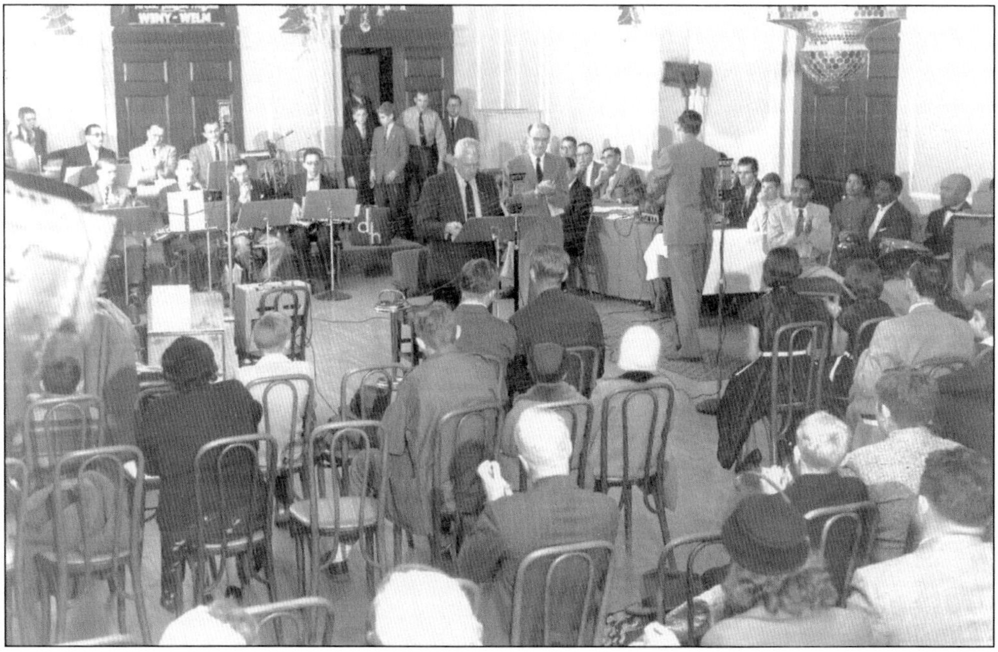

When radio came to Elmira in 1932, newspaper publisher Frank Tripp devised a radio program for the Arctic League. He was the master of ceremonies, and entertainment was provided by some of the area's talented citizens. The broadcasts originated from the Mark Twain Hotel. A program is shown here around 1950. (Courtesy of CCHS.)

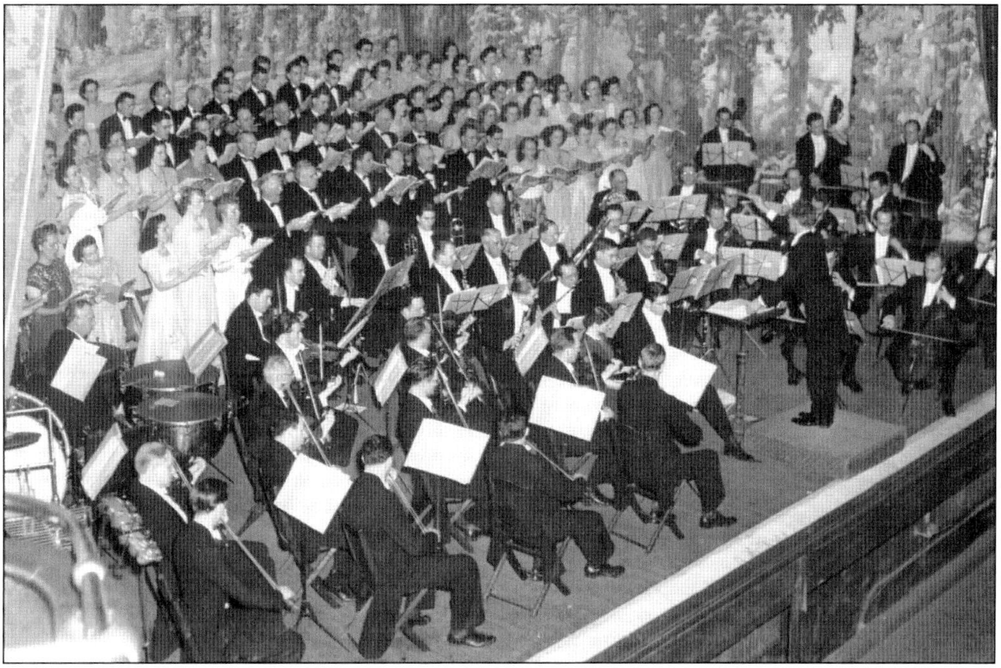

The Elmira Civic Chorus was the outcome of a Passion Play presented by the Elmira Lion's Club in the early 1930s. It had been directed by Jay Parker. The Elmira Symphony was revived in 1916, and in 1957 the two groups merged to form the Elmira Symphony and Choral Society. This photograph was taken around 1957. (Courtesy of the *Elmira Star Gazette*.)

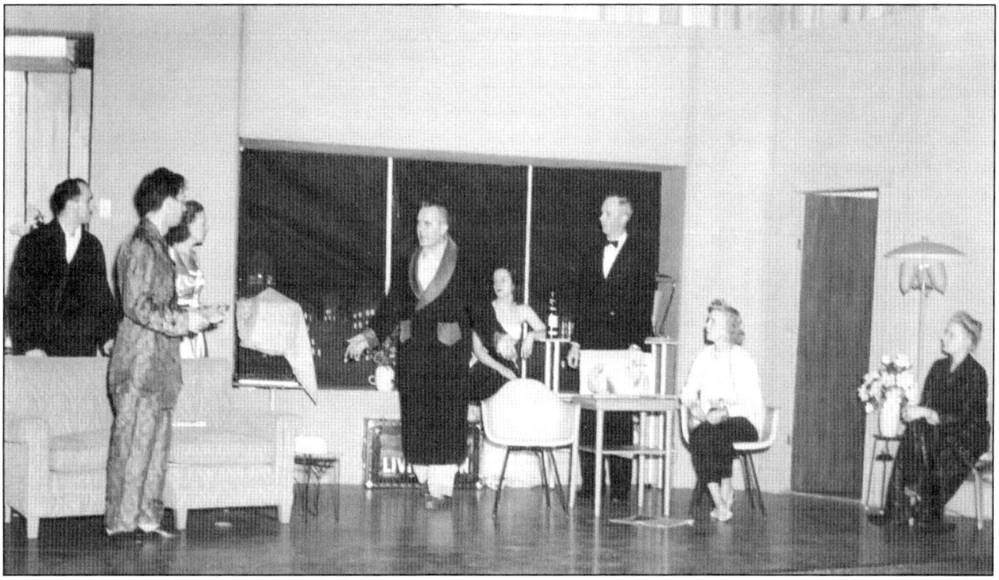

In 1944, Eleanor McKinnon Emery organized a meeting of about 30 people at the Steele Memorial Library to organize the Elmira Little Theater (ELT). To get ELT under way, each person contributed $1 toward the first budget. The first full-length production was the three-act play *The Man Who Came to Dinner*, performed at Cowles Hall. Since that time, community theater has thrived in Elmira. Shown here is the 1952 production of *Light up the Sky*, performed at Elmira Free Academy. (Courtesy of Elmira Little Theater.)

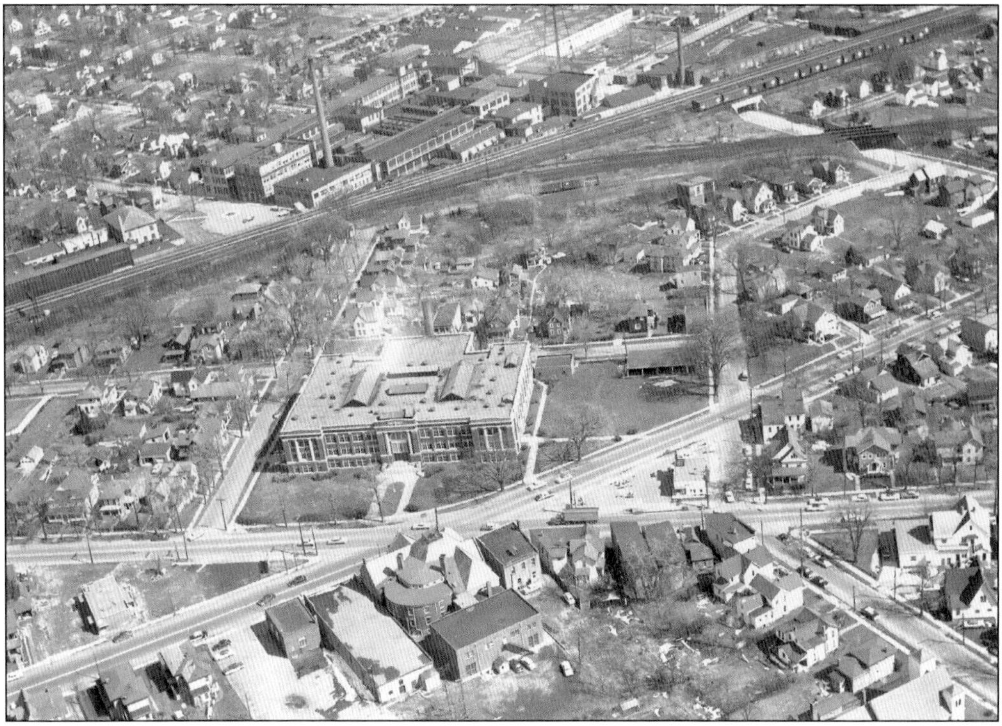

Elmira's south side had a much different look before 1960. Note the former American La France Plant at the top, since demolished. The houses around the high school were torn down after the Flood of 1972 to allow for the school's expansion, which in the end did not occur. At the bottom of the photograph is the former Centenary Church and Fire Station No. 3, both of which are now the site of a Walgreens. (Courtesy of CCHS.)

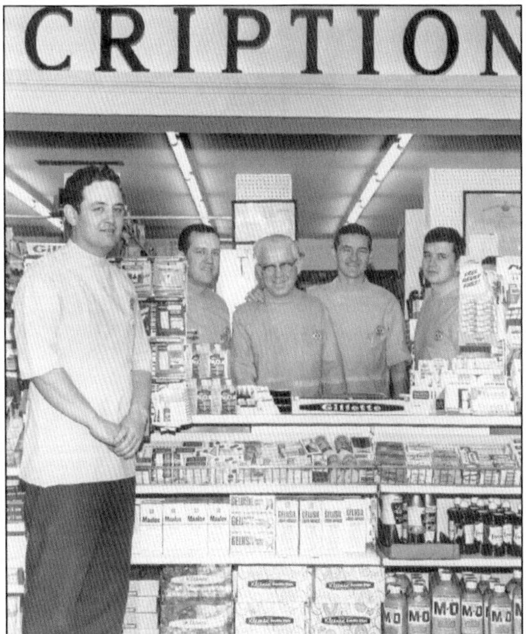

Families have played a major role in building Elmira. Francis Thomas Steed (center) started the family business in 1938 in Nichols, New York. He purchased Gerould's Pharmacy in Elmira in 1945. Now in their third generation of operation, Gerould's has become a household name. Shown here around 1968 with their father are, from left to right, Francis, Jerry, Bill, and Pat. (Courtesy of Bill Steed.)

BIBLIOGRAPHY

A Century of Public Education in Elmira, 1845–1945. Compiled by a Committee of Elmira Women Classroom Teachers of NYST Association, Elmira, NY: 1945.

Barber, W. Charles. *Elmira College: The First Hundred Years*. New York: McGraw-Hill Book Company, Inc. 1955.

Byrne, Thomas, *Chemung County: 1890–1975*. Elmira, NY: Chemung Co. Historical Society, 1976.

Elmira Christian Center, Pentecostal Tabernacle, Its History: 1944–2009. Elmira, NY: Elmira Christian Center, 2009.

Hoffman, Edward B. *First Presbyterian Church of Elmira, The First 200 Years*. Elmira, NY: Donation of Fred Petrie, 1995.

Horigan, Michael, *Elmira: Death Camp of the North*. Mechanicsburg, PA: Stackpole Books, 2002.

Jerome, Robert D. and Herbert A. Wisbey Jr. *Mark Twain in Elmira*. Elmira, NY: Mark Twain Society, Inc. 1977.

Peirce, H.B. and R. Hamilton Hurd. *History of Tioga, Chemung, Tompkins and Schuyler Counties*. Philadelphia: Everts and Ensign, 1879.

The New Book of Grace Church. Elmira, NY: Grace Church, 1993.

Towner, Ausburn. *Our County and Its People: A History of the Valley and County of Chemung*. Syracuse, NY: D. Mason & Co. Publishers, 1892.

Trinity Church 1833–1983. Elmira, NY: Trinity Church, 1983.

Walshak, Hank. *Elmira College Still Ahead of Its Time*. Elmira, NY: Elmira College Press, 2005.

Willis, Resa. *Mark and Livy: The Love Story of Mark Twain and the Woman Who Almost Tamed Him*. New York: Atheneum Publishers, 1992.